"'Mexico' Mike Nelson is a gringo who knows more about Mexico than most Mexicans."

—*Contenido*

"Those considering moving to Mexico would do well to order this book."

—*New Orleans Times-Picayune*

"This book is for downsizing victims, someone in search of discovery, retirees, lovers of Mexico. ... Insider scoop and costs on real estate, employment, medical care, the Internet, and daily living."

—*Book Reader*

LIVE BETTER
South of the Border
IN MEXICO

EDITION
4

LIVE BETTER
South of the Border
IN MEXICO

PRACTICAL ADVICE FOR LIVING AND WORKING

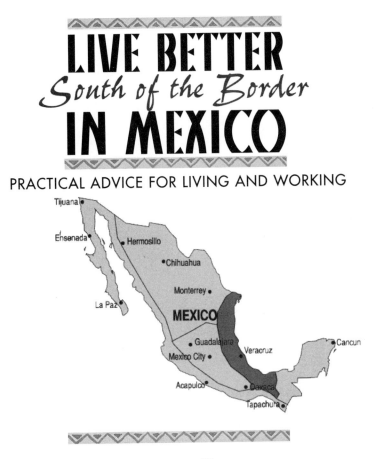

"Mexico" Mike™ *Nelson*

FULCRUM

Fulcrum Publishing
Golden, Colorado

ABOUT THE AUTHOR
"Mexico" Mike™ Nelson

"Mexico" Mike Nelson was born in 1950 in Las Cruces, New Mexico. He's lived in both Peru and Mexico. The Mexican magazine *Contenido* said of him, "Mexico Mike is a gringo who knows Mexico better than most Mexicans." In 1977, after a stint as a staff writer on *The South American Explorer Magazine* (Lima, Peru), he paddled a dugout canoe alone up part of the Amazon River. This adventure ended when he got heatstroke and was saved by a kindly native. He gave up jungle exploring in 1979 in Honduras. In 1999, his brief, ill-fated attempt at bullfighting lasted for two bulls and he was nearly gored. Since then, he has concentrated on less-dangerous pursuits, such as writing.

A rolling stone, he has called several cities and states home: Los Angeles, San Diego, and San Francisco, California; New Orleans, Louisiana; Memphis, Tennessee; Austin, Edinburg, Galveston, and McAllen, Texas; and Seattle, Washington.

"Mexico" Mike has published fifteen books, mostly about Mexico, ranging from social observations to travel. He was an internationally syndicated newspaper columnist, with his work appearing in *The McAllen Monitor* (Texas), *The News* (Mexico City), *Attención* (San Miguel de Allende, Mexico), and *The Coastal Current* (South Padre Island, Texas). Because of his extensive knowledge of Mexico, he has been profiled in dozens of newspapers and magazines, including *The Wall Street Journal, The New York Times, Texas Monthly, The Guardian* (Manchester, England), *The News* (Mexico City), *Attención* (San Miguel de Allende, Mexico), the American Airlines in-flight magazine, and more.

He was the official media spokesperson for Mexico's Ministry of Tourism and has been interviewed on many dozens of radio and TV stations in the United States, Canada, and Mexico.

In recent years, he has devoted much time to the founding and operation of a nonprofit support group for people with the emotional challenge of getting rid of stuff, Clutterless Recovery Groups. He is the executive director of this organization.

He currently lives with his dog, Fluffy, near McAllen, Texas.

The information in *Live Better South of the Border in Mexico* is accurate as of May 2005. Prices, hours of operation, addresses, phone numbers, Web sites, and other items change rapidly. If something in the book is incorrect, please write to the author in care of Fulcrum Publishing, 16100 Table Mountain Parkway, Suite 300, Golden, Colorado, 80403.

Library of Congress Cataloging-in-Publication Data
Nelson, Mexico Mike, 1950–
Live better south of the border in Mexico : practical advice for living and working / Mike Nelson. — 4th ed.
p. cm.
Includes bibliographical references and index.
ISBN 1-55591-546-9
1. Mexico—Guidebooks. I. Title.
F1209.N444 2005
972—dc22
2004024354

Printed in the United States of America
0 9 8 7 6 5 4 3 2 1
Editorial: Katie L. Raymond, Faith Marcovecchio
Design: Ann W. Douden
Cover illustration: Mathew McFarren
Maps: Chris Yelland

Fulcrum Publishing
16100 Table Mountain Parkway, Suite 300
Golden, Colorado 80403
(800) 992-2908 • (303) 277-1623
www.fulcrum-books.com

Contents

Preface

Here is an example of how living in Mexico is different from living in the United States or Canada, contributed by a longtime friend, Sherry McFarlane, now living in San Miguel de Allende, Guanajuato. She gives folk art tours of Mexico that are head and shoulders above anyone else's. Contact her at mexfolkart@hotmail.com.

"Great news! We are now operational, we have a coffeepot."

In the States or Canada: You break the glass pot and you go to Wal-Mart and get a replacement.

In Mexico: You break the glass pot. You try to find out where you can get an electric coffeepot, since they do not even sell glass pots by themselves. You find out that it is in Querétaro, which is more than one hour away on roads you won't drive. You find a friend going to Querétaro. You give her 300 pesos for a new coffeepot of her choice (U.S. $30). She goes and gets one and brings it back to you. She tells you that it was Mex $380. You come up with exactly 80 pesos and take them to her at a party that night. She says she will bring the coffeepot to Garden Club on Tuesday. You are thrilled because there is no parking anywhere near her house. You take a plastic shopping bag to Garden Club and get the coffeepot, which is a very nice Mr. Coffee one. You take it home and look at it.

It takes basket filters. You have more than 100 cone filters. You go to the grocery store to buy the filters; they only carry cone filters. You mention it to your friend Linda. She has basket filters and her new coffeepot takes cone filters. You give her all of your cone filters, and she will have basket filters for you tomorrow.

The next day you look at your nice new coffeepot again. You realize that the coffeepot plug's prongs have one big side and one smaller side. Your kitchen socket is for two small prongs. (It is common in older houses in Mexico to have pre-polarized electric plugs.) You go to your toolbox to get some sandpaper. Sandpaper does not file down metal, you discover. You go to the hardware store and buy a metal file (but first you had to look up "file" in the dictionary so you could ask for it). You accomplish that. You take it home and file the plug down on the big side. It fits. Meanwhile, you have run into Alfredo, Linda's driver, on the street and he has the filters for you. At last you have an operational coffeepot!

And people always ask, "What do you do all day in Mexico?"

If you can look at the sometimes-convoluted process of buying a coffeepot as an adventure, not a chore, then you'll enjoy living in Mexico.

This edition has been expanded to include information about working in Mexico and being transferred there by your company. I've also included some cities that most people would not necessarily choose as retirement havens.

In the more than thirty years that I have traveled, done business in, and lived in Mexico, I've gotten a reputation for honesty and insight. Part of my writing career was spent as a journalist, so I tend to try to give a balanced view of the facts. I have my prejudices, or preferences, as I prefer to call them, and, occasionally, I will give you outright opinions. Some of you may disagree with them due to your own prejudices or preferences. That's fine. What you read here is written with the intent of educating and entertaining, while avoiding travel-writer hyperbole.

Ever since I "discovered" Mexico, I have heard about how too many gringos have "ruined" idyllic locations. In Sedona, Arizona, I was accused of being one of the ruiners myself because I was writing a piece about it. People have told me for thirty-five years that there was a boom going on in Mexican real estate (with a few exceptions, such as during the economic troubles). There will always be a boom in real estate until you buy some. Then your own real estate seems to bottom out while everyone else's goes up. Prices of real estate and the cost of living have gone up since the last edition of this book. But, tell me, has real estate gotten cheaper for you to live in Canada or the United States?

I sincerely hope that those of you who read this book will not be the kind of people who "ruin" a place by their attitude. When you have finished, I expect that you will be more likely to appreciate the Mexican culture and wish to understand it and contribute to it rather than just squatting in what you consider a third-world (and Mexico is not third world) country because it is cheap. If that describes you, throw this book away and consider it an investment in international relations.

I have many Mexican friends, including professionals and common folks. Since I respect Mexico and her people, I am concerned about preparing foreigners who might want to move there for the realities, without any hype. The biggest bit of advice you should take from this book, as I frequently say, is that not everyone who wants to move to Mexico should move to Mexico.

Introduction

Today there are many books on the market about living in Mexico. Some of them are written by friends of mine. Some of them are good. So why should you buy this one? We buy books that speak to us, that speak our language. Mine is not the only good one. What I offer you, the reader, is a very personal and yet very objective overview of what living in Mexico is like and why it may or may not be for you.

Hundreds of thousands of loyal readers have bought my Mexico books throughout the more than twenty years I've been writing about this perplexing and fascinating country. I'd like to think that, as you read, you feel as if you are my friend, my brother, or my sister. I will never knowingly steer you wrong.

FOLLOW YOUR DREAMS

What I believe I bring to the table, your table, is honesty, humor, and insight. I no longer do "travel" writing. I try to bring the discipline of a journalist to whatever I do. Sure, I do accentuate the positive, since that is my nature, but I believe you should also be aware of the negative. Instead of hyperbole, I give you objectivity.

Buying this book doesn't preclude you from buying someone else's as well. You are considering a major change in your life. Invest in yourself. Take what you need from my books and leave the rest. In the final tally you are the real expert, you know what is right for you. I am only a guide. Follow your heart and your dreams and you can't go wrong.

Since the last edition of this book was published, much has changed and much has remained the same. New cities have been added to better assist those of you who will be transferred by your companies, and, more importantly, information about working and doing business in Mexico is a major addition to this edition. I have also included a cost-of-living calculator for most cities and towns gringos consider, as well as a chart of estimated living costs.

Mexico will always be Mexico. It will always be unique. People's reasons for moving there ebb and flow with the times. When I wrote the first edition, the United States was in the midst of terrible downsizing by corporate America. Many people moved to Mexico to find a new way of life. Meanwhile, the American economy (and Mexico's) then went through a period of expansion. And yet today we're back to hearing "downsizing" in the daily news. People are again searching for another way to live. For many, Mexico answers that call.

Mexico isn't for everyone, but it's perfect for many. Much of the advice I wrote in previous editions remains the same. By all means, if Mexico is for you, move! But some people won't like it.

What I've endeavored to do—and what sets my writing apart from many others—is to give you both the good and the hard-to-adjust-

to facets of living in Mexico. Living there is not for everyone, and you deserve to have the facts in order to make an intelligent decision. If Mexico is indeed for you, you'll find tools here to know what to expect and what adaptations you'll want to make to be happy.

COST IS ONLY ONE FACTOR

Cost has always been a factor in people's decisions to move to Mexico. It still makes economic sense to live there if your income is limited or you have retired. However, living there may be more expensive than you think.

There are a variety of lifestyles in Mexico for the cost conscious. The Mexican government has decided that a foreigner needs to have a monthly income of $1,000, single, or $1,500, couple, to officially live in Mexico. That is right in the middle of the truth. You can be comfortable on those amounts. If you are frugal, you can live on $600 to $800, single, or $800 to $1,200, couple, a month, but not like a king or queen, as some would have you believe—it will be a challenge. If you have a monthly income of around $2,500, single, or $3,500, couple, you can definitely live like a prince or princess.

Costs have risen since the last edition. But please, don't just think in terms of money when considering moving. Money is always important, but what is more important is your lifestyle and general standard of living. You will find that the pace of life and the warmth of the people are the real attractions to living in Mexico.

> *As many expats have said, "It's not that I live so much more cheaply in Mexico, it's that I live so much better."*

Can you live on $600 a month? I know people who do, but it takes a frugal mind-set. Can you live on $1,000 a month? Yes, but you would have to choose your place to live and your lifestyle with care. Can you live on $1,500 a month? Absolutely! A couple could get by on that amount, but more likely couples should expect to spend about $2,000 a month to live a happy life.

Burst your bubble? That's not my intention. Two thousand dollars a month is $24,000 a year. You have to take things in perspective. Rather than pick an amount to spend, why not take a careful inventory of what you're living on now? Then deduct about 20 percent. That is how much less expensively you can live in Mexico by making a few adjustments to your lifestyle.

Housing is always the biggest cost of living. Depending on the location, you can buy a two-bedroom house for anywhere from $60,000 to $250,000. That's quite a spread. But think about it. If someone asked you how much a house costs in the United States, the first thing you would ask is, "In what state?" California is much more expensive than Nebraska. So it is in Mexico. Cancún, Cozumel, Mexico City, and Monterrey are expensive. Most of Baja is priced similarly to California, San Miguel de Allende is in the middle, and

Chapala is a little bit less expensive. Beachfront property will always be high. Smaller towns, such as Mérida or those in Colonial Mexico, Oaxaca, and others along the Gulf Coast, are at the bottom end of the price spectrum.

Okay, Mike, what will rents cost?

As I say in the book, there are people who swear they can rent an apartment for $250 to $300 a month almost anywhere in Mexico, but it's unrealistic for most. Generally, for a decent place rents will vary from $400 a month (which is rare in gringo settlements where the bottom line is more likely to be $600) to $1,500 a month (for a middle-class, one-bedroom apartment or condo on the lower end to a middle-class two-bedroom house on the higher end), depending on where you live. In out-of-the-way locales, it is still possible to rent a house (a one-bedroom comfortable house or condolike apartment) for as little as $400, with a little luck and connections.

BUYING A HOUSE

Buying a house, to my way of thinking, is not cheap. Most people pay about $90,000 to $140,000 for a home in a gringo town. However, property taxes are a huge savings. If you pay more than $500 a year, you are living in a mansion.

What will be considerably less expensive for you is anything that requires labor. Maids, gardeners, repairmen, etc., will always cost less in Mexico than in the United States. This could be a big improvement to your style of living that's unattainable at home.

FOOD

Food, in general (excluding imported items), could cost a bit less, but unless you eat more fresh vegetables, will probably be close to what you're paying now. Dining out isn't expensive. You can find good, filling meals in most locations for $6 to $12 per person. You probably spend that much at a fast-food place here. Speaking of fast-food, most of the well-known chains are in Mexico, though they are more expensive than Mexican family–owned restaurants.

SAFETY

Safety is another concern, at least in the minds of Americans who are inundated by stories of kidnappings and such taking place in Mexico. Your chances of getting kidnapped are so slim they are not worth worrying about. Megarich Mexicans and Americans are kidnappers' targets; you and I are not.

I really get a bee in my bonnet when someone rants about terrorists and their connections to Mexico. Sure, some enter the United States *via* Mexico, but the likelihood of a terrorist act *in* Mexico is much slimmer than in the States. (By the way, Mexico took a neutral stance on the war in Iraq.)

CHILDREN

Children are safer in Mexico than in the United States. Mexicans don't have to have the paranoia that we have about molesters, kidnappers, or other bad people. It is still common in smaller towns, and to an extent in cities, for children to play happily in the zócalo, or town square (you'll learn a little Spanish in these pages), unsupervised. They still walk home from school.

If you move with your children, you'll find public schools for them to attend that are safe, and except in large cities such as Mexico City, Guadalajara, and Monterrey, nearly completely free of gang influences. Any town with a population of Americans working there will offer Montessori schools and other private schools that teach in English. The cost to attend these schools in Mexico will be considerably less than you'd have to pay at home.

MEDICAL CARE

Medical care is a major reason why many people move to Mexico, especially for those without insurance. Even health insurance is cheaper in Mexico. Many advances have been made in Mexican medical care, and there are more resources for you to check out before you go. There are hospitals that are just as good, and in some ways better, than hospitals in the United States and Canada. If your major expense at home is medical care, by all means, figure that in Mexico you can pay at least half of what you are paying in the United States.

INTERNET AND TELEPHONE CONNECTIONS

Internet and telephone connections have changed dramatically, for the better. In many cases it is now possible to conduct an online business from Mexico, though I'd still be wary of living via stock market trading (which I have done many times). With all the advances in phone services, your Internet connection (usually via digital subcriber line, or DSL) will still not be as dependable as it is in Canada or the States. But now you can also get a new telephone line for a new house in a matter of days or weeks instead of spending months in frustration.

Yes, there is a lot that has changed in this edition. What has not changed is my personal style of writing. I talk to you as if we were talking in my living room, peppering the chapters with personal stories about what it's really like to live and travel in Mexico.

If you need more guidance about driving through, moving to, or working in Mexico, you can call me at 888-234-3452 or e-mail mexicomikenelson23@mexico mike.com. I make a living from services such as this, so only call if you are serious and are willing to pay me for my time. Thank you for taking the journey to a new life with me.

—"Mexico" Mike

Part One

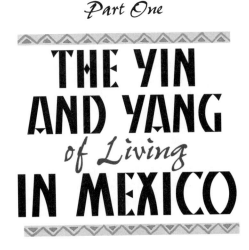

THE YIN AND YANG *of Living* IN MEXICO

HOW MEXICANS FEEL ABOUT AMERICANS

Listen to what one woman, Margot Lindsay-Valdes, an American who married a Mexican physician and has lived in Chihuahua for many years, has to say about moving here and staying here:

> Mexicans love Americans, and I have been treated as a queen since I moved here. People will go out of their way to be hospitable and try to communicate with you.
>
> I was very isolated for a time and frustrated when I could not speak Spanish. When I learned the language, a whole new world opened up to me. I use my Spanish a lot in the United States too. People are shocked that a redheaded woman is fluent in Spanish. It is great! The more you make an effort, the more you will be rewarded.
>
> When I first moved here, I had a hard time. I was constantly comparing things to what I knew in the United States. I also labeled everything as either Mexican or American. I created my own frustration. I think, as Americans, we tend to do this. People are good and bad everywhere, but we blame large groups instead of specific individuals or ourselves.
>
> In Mexico, there are less rules than up North. I saw this as a bad thing. I felt I could not control my situation. Now I see the lack of rules as a type of freedom, a thing that makes Mexico unique. If you want to paint your house purple, you can do that. Not everything looks the same, as it does in the United States. It makes me rethink the word "freedom" when you are told your house has to look exactly the same as your

neighbors. Hmm, sure, everything looks orderly and perfect up North, but I am beginning to find that very boring.

When I finally accepted the fact that things weren't better or worse in one place or another, just different, I started to calm down. Differences can be good; not everyone has to think your way to be right. I still get frustrated at times, but find I am frustrated with myself, not the place I live in. I sometimes miss things from the United States, things that I used to take for granted, such as libraries, other conveniences.

Because I am surrounded by fewer choices, I am a lot more appreciative of what I have. If I had continued to live in the United States, I would never have changed my attitude or perspective as much as I have since living here. Mexico has made me a better person because I have rediscovered values that I feel Americans have lost. Mexico, to me, is the United States I grew up in, the way things were in the sixties. Unfortunately, [many cities in Mexico are] turning into anytown, USA. I plan on enjoying it until it does.

There is a big difference between the north and south of Mexico. The work ethic in the north is more similar to the States, and the pace is faster than in the south. If I were to retire, I would pick a beach or an area with a milder climate, but I would not hesitate to stay in Mexico. I think now is a good time to get your digs in since the country is changing so quickly.

COST-OF-LIVING CITY COMPARISON CHARTS

COST-OF-LIVING CITY COMPARISON CHART

Percentages are based on a combination of housing costs (an average of buying and renting) and the variations in the cost of living in each town. For instance, sometimes the housing will be cheaper in a city, but you will pay more for electricity or use more because of the climate. There is also a variation in the costs of entertainment and foodstuffs. There is an element of subjectivity, based on my experience and feedback from expats. You could find a $250 apartment in San Miguel de Allende when the average rent is much higher. You could buy a $60,000 home somewhere when the average is more than $100,000.

With those caveats, I believe this to be an evergreen comparison. The cost of living will go up, most likely, but the comparison to other areas will be consistent. However, any one area could go through a real estate boom and become much higher. Frankly, I believe that $15,000 may be an impossible amount of money to live on in Mexico in the near future. I've used it as a bottom line because I could live there for that and know people who do. For most people, $20,000 is a more realistic figure. But I wanted to show that if you have the will, there will always be a way. Whether you can enjoy yourself on a frugal budget is something only you can answer. You'll only know after you have tried it. At $600 a month, rent will be nearly half your living expenses.

The average American spends 31 percent of his income on housing, according to Department of Census statistics. How valid is that? How many people are "house poor" in high-cost areas of the country, spending 50 percent or more on housing? One advantage Mexico has over the United States and Canada is that, housing aside, you can always live more frugally. The average middle-class Mexican earns about $18,000 a year and supports a family.

Note: You will not see a correlation between these figures and the U.S. State Department per diem rates. Living in a town has a completely different cost basis than staying in hotels and eating out all the time.

Please see chart on following page.

Income (based on U.S. dollars) City	State	% of base	**$15,000** Cost to live in the following cities	**$20,000**
Acapulco	Qro.	90	$13,500	$18,000
Alamos	Son.	115	$17,250	$23,000
Any small town		60	$9,000	$12,000
Cabo San Lucas	BCS.	170	$25,500	$34,000
Cancún	QR.	140	$21,000	$28,000
Chihuahua	Chih.	85	$12,750	$17,000
Cozumel	QR.	160	$24,000	$32,000
Cuernavaca	Mor.	115	$17,250	$23,000
Ensenada	BCN.	155	$23,250	$31,000
Guadalajara	Jal.	90	$13,500	$18,000
Guanajuato	Qto.	80	$12,000	$16,000
Guaymas	Son.	85	$12,750	$17,000
Huatulco	Oax.	145	$21,750	$29,000
Ixtapa/Zihuatnejo	Gro.	155	$23,250	$31,000
Jalapa	Ver.	85	$12,750	$17,000
Kino Bay	Son.	110	$16,500	$22,000
La Paz	BCS.	145	$21,750	$29,000
Lake Chapala	Jal.	95	$14,250	$19,000
Loreto	BCS.	135	$20,250	$27,000
Mazatlán	Sin.	75	$11,250	$15,000
Mérida	Yuc.	70	$10,500	$14,000
Mexico City	DF.	155	$23,250	$31,000
Monterrey	NL.	130	$19,500	$26,000
Morelia	Mich.	75	$11,250	$15,000
Oaxaca	Oax.	85	$12,750	$17,000
Pátzcuaro	Mor.	75	$11,250	$15,000
Playa del Carmen	QR.	150	$22,500	$30,000
Pto. Penasco	Son.	160	$24,000	$32,000
Pto. Escondido	Oax.	90	$13,500	$18,000
Pto. Vallarta	Jal.	125	$18,750	$25,000
Rosarito	BCN.	150	$22,500	$30,000
Saltillo	Coah.	70	$10,500	$14,000

$25,000	$30,000	$35,000
$22,500	$27,000	$31,500
$28,750	$34,500	$40,250
$15,000	$18,000	$21,000
$42,500	$51,000	$59,500
$35,000	$42,000	$49,000
$21,250	$25,500	$29,750
$40,000	$48,000	$56,000
$28,750	$34,500	$40,250
$38,750	$46,500	$54,250
$22,500	$27,000	$31,500
$20,000	$24,000	$28,000
$21,250	$25,500	$29,750
$36,250	$43,500	$50,750
$38,750	$46,500	$54,250
$21,250	$25,500	$29,750
$27,500	$33,000	$38,500
$36,250	$43,500	$50,750
$23,750	$28,500	$33,250
$33,750	$40,500	$47,250
$18,750	$22,500	$26,250
$17,500	$21,000	$24,500
$38,750	$46,500	$54,250
$32,500	$39,000	$45,500
$18,750	$22,500	$26,250
$21,250	$25,500	$29,750
$18,750	$22,500	$26,250
$37,500	$45,000	$52,500
$40,000	$48,000	$56,000
$22,500	$27,000	$31,500
$31,250	$37,500	$43,750
$37,500	$45,000	$52,500
$17,500	$21,000	$24,500

Income (based on U.S. dollars)

City	State	% of base	$15,000 Cost to live in the following cities	$20,000
San Carlos	Son.	130	$19,500	$26,000
San Felipe	BCN.	120	$18,000	$24,000
San Jose del Cabo	BCS.	165	$24,750	$33,000
San Miguel de Allende	Qto.	100	$15,000	$20,000
San Quintin	BCN.	130	$19,500	$26,000
Veracruz	Ver.	90	$13,500	$18,000
Any small town		65	$9,750	$13,000

FIGURE YOUR TRUE COST OF LIVING

These are average prices over the entire Republic based on expat surveys. If you pay more or less rent/mortgage or spend more/less on entertainment and travel, your costs will vary. These costs are meant to represent an "average" (not frugal), comfortable lifestyle for one person or a couple. You can live on these amounts if you are reasonable with your money, and

Category	Annual or Monthly Range	Single Monthly Average	Couple Monthly Average	Single Monthly Average	Couple Monthly Average
HOUSING Rent (monthly)	**Monthly Range** $400–$900	$400	$400	$650	$650
	$500–$1,500				
Mortgage	$0–$1,000 month				
Property Taxes	**Annual Range** $100–$800	$25	$25	$25	$25
UTILITIES Electric	**Annual Range** $600–$1,200	$55	$65	$55	$65

LIVE BETTER *South of the Border* IN MEXICO

$25,000	$30,000	$35,000
$32,500	$39,000	$45,500
$30,000	$36,000	$42,000
$41,250	$49,500	$57,750
$25,000	$30,000	$35,000
$32,500	$39,000	$45,500
$22,500	$27,000	$31,500
$16,250	$19,500	$22,750

have as comfortable a lifestyle as you have at home, or better. These approximations are nationwide averages. Obviously, Baja, Cozumel, Mexico City, or any city with more than a 100 rating on the cost-of-living scale, will be more expensive. But this is a fair approximation of average, overall, countrywide living costs.

Single Monthly Average	Couple Monthly Average	Explanation
$1,000	$1,000	Decent place, nothing fancy. 1 BR house, apartment, condo
		2 BR house, condo
		Most people buy outright. However, financing is now available with 50 percent down. You'll pay more than renters, but you'll put so much down, your mortgage + fiedocomiso fees will be less than you're paying at home. Prices vary so much, there's no average to figure.
$25	$25	Always less than in the United States or Canada.
$55	$65	Generally less. Though higher per kilowatt hour, less energy is used, except in beach areas in the summer.

Category	Annual or Monthly Range	Single Monthly Average	Couple Monthly Average	Single Monthly Average	Couple Monthly Average
	MonthlyRange				
Gas (Propane)	$150–$300	$20	$30	$20	$30
Water (Tap)	$300–$500	$25	$35	$25	$35
Bottled Water	$300–$400	$25	$50	$25	$50
Cable or Satellite TV	$40–$100	$55	$55	$55	$55
Phone	$40–$55	$50	$50	$50	$50
Internet (High Speed)	$50–$65	$50	$50	$50	$50
Long-Distance Phone	$25–$100	$60	$75	$60	$75
Cell Phone	$40–$80	$50	$70	$50	$70
SERVICES	**Annual Range**				
Maid	$1,000–$1,500	$20	$20	$20	$20
Gardener	$2,000–$2,500	$50	$50	$50	$50
Benefits for Above	$250–$300	$23	$23	$23	$23
FOOD	**Annual Range**				
Groceries (Annual)	$3,000	$225	$350	$225	$350
EATING OUT	**Annual Range** $1,200–$3,600	$150	$300	$150	$300
ENTERTAINMENT					
Enjoy Yourself!	**Annual Range** $600–$1,200	$60	$120	$60	$120

Single Monthly Average	Couple Monthly Average	Explanation
$20	$30	Always less. Many houses use propane.
$25	$35	Generally less, though you may have to add in cost of bottled water.
$25	$50	
$55	$55	
$50	$50	
$50	$50	
$60	$75	Assumes you have a calling plan.
$50	$70	
$20	$20	Usually a couple of times a week. On the high side.
$50	$50	Usually several times a week or full-time. On the high side.
$23	$23	You must pay annual bonus of one month's salary. (Based on figures given.)
$225	$350	Not much cheaper overall than in the United States, perhaps 10–15 percent. Includes fresh seafood, fresh vegetables, and a reasonable amount of chicken and beef (which are are more expensive than in the United States or Canada).
$150	$300	Two people can eat out for $6 at breakfast, $8 at lunch, $20 at dinner. You can spend more (or less). This is based on middle-class family restaurants.
$60	$120	You'll go to art events, concerts, clubs, hot springs. That's why you're here—to have a better, not just cheaper, life.

Category	Annual or Monthly Range	Single Monthly Average	Couple Monthly Average	Single Monthly Average	Couple Monthly Average
AUTO INSURANCE					
(Annual)	$600	$50	$50	$50	$50
Gasoline	$1,225	$102	$123	$102	$123
HEALTH CARE	**Annual Range**				
Doctors/Dentists	$1,000–$3,000	$85	$170	$85	$170
Health Insurance	$400–$600	$42	$83	$42	$83
Medicine	$500	$42	$83	$42	$80
TRAVEL					
Travel (Mexico)	$2,000	$167	$250	$167	$250
Travel (U.S. or Canada)	$3,000	$250	$375	$250	$375
Mexican Tax: 15 percent on most everything	$200–$600	$248	$497	$248	$497
MISC.	**Annual Range**				
Art or language lessons, handicrafts, fun stuff. Don't forget having fun!	$1,000–$2,000	$100	$150	$100	$150
TOTALS					
Monthly, with health insurance		$2,428	$3,549	$2,678	$3,795
Yearly of above		$29,140	$42,584	$32,140	$45,544
Monthly, excluding maid, gardener		$2,335	$3,456	$2,585	$3,702
Yearly, excluding domestics		$28,024	$41,468	$31,024	$44,428
Monthly, excluding health insurance, domestics		$2,167	$3,119	$2,417	$3,369
Yearly of above		$26,004	$37,428	$29,004	$40,428

Single Monthly Average	Couple Monthly Average	Explanation
$50	$50	
$102	$123	Figured at 8,000 miles a year, 18 MPG., $2.75 a gallon (Mexico). Assume continued price hikes. You will probably drive fewer miles in Mexico, and most activites are accessible by walking or public transport. An additional 20 percent is added for two people.
$85	$170	Assumes regular doctor visits, tests.
$42	$83	Assumes getting a Mexican carrier or expat insurance, not IMSS.
$40	$80	The same drugs often cost from 40–70 percent less than in the United States.
$167	$250	Exploring Mexico.
$250	$375	You will return at least once a year.
$248	$497	This is probably low. But it's based on the other on costs except rent, labor, gas, and where included in price.
$100	$150	
$3,027	$4,145	
$36,320	$49,744	
$2,934	$4,052	
$35,204	$48,628	
$2,767	$3,719	
$33,204	$44,628	

WHAT THINGS COST IN MEXICO

Updated prices for darn near anything in Mexico are available at the PROFECO site: www.profeco.gob.mx/html/inicio/inicio.htm. It's in Spanish, so go to the left-side menu, click "*Consumo informado,*" then "*Quién is quién en.*" Then "*los precios*" from the side menu, then "*precios Minimos y Maximos,*" then "*Seleccione Ciudad.*" Then pick a city. You'll get a drop-down menu of major items. These prices are what you'd pay at large grocery store chains like Soriana, Gigante, Comercial Mexicano, etc., and the government-run ISSTE stores. Smaller, locally run stores will be higher, but offer more of a social experience in addition to providing foodstuffs. They will vary slightly, according to your area. Obviously, these prices will fluctuate, but they could be a handy guide to compare your second-highest cost of living, after rent or mortgage payments.

SPANISH NAME	ENGLISH NAME
Frutas y Verduras *Precios en los mercados estaré la mitad*	**Fruits and Vegetables** *Market prices will be about half*
Manzana (1 kg)	Apple (1 kg)
Platanos (1 kg)	Bananas (1 kg)
Cebolla (1 kg)	Onion (1 kg)
Naranja (1 kg)	Orange (1 kg)
Papa (1 kg)	Potato (1 kg)
Tomate (1 kg)	Tomato (1 kg)
Lacteos	**Dairy Products**
Mantequilla (225 gr)	Butter (225 gr)
Queso Cheddar (10 revanadas)	Cheddar Cheese (10 slices)
Queso Gouda (1 kg)	Gouda Cheese (1 kg)
Leche (1 lt)	Milk (1 lt)
Bebidas	**Drinks**
Coca Cola (6 pack)	(Duh!) Coca Cola
Cerveza Bohemia (6 pack)	Bohemia Beer (dark, excellent)
Cerveza Corona Extra	Corona Beer
Vino Tinto (750 ml)	Red Wine (750 ml)
Agua (1 lt)	Bottled Water (1 lt)
Jugo de Fruta (Jumex) (1 lt)	Fruit Juice (Jumex brand) (1 lt)
Carnes y Aves	**Meats, Birds**
Pollo (Entero)	Chicken (whole)
Huevos (1 Docena)	Eggs (1 dozen)

Prices of fresh fruit and vegetables are so low, they don't even rate. Fresh mangoes, bananas, papayas, tomatoes, etc., will be cheaper in markets than in the stores. Pistachios are very inexpensive and sold all along the roads, at crossroads by vendors. They're also sold in stores and markets. I used a rounded figure for the currency conversions. Frankly, it's easier to do in your head and it doesn't really make that much difference if your dollar is 11.4 or 8.9 to the peso. Don't be one of those aggravating people who calculates to the centavo, except for large purchases. Once you're living in Mexico, learn to think in pesos. Life will be so much easier. Foods are sold in grams, kilos or kilograms, or liters. Don't mistake a kilo for a pound. It's about 2.2 pounds and is a lot. If you were a hippie in the sixties, you'd know what a kilo was.

| | MINIMUM | | | MAXIMUM | |
Peso	USD (11:1)	CDND (9:1)	Peso	USD (11:1)	CDND (9:1)
$15.00	$1.36	$1.67	$25.00	$2.27	$2.78
$6.50	$0.59	$0.72	$6.90	$0.63	$0.77
$15.90	$1.45	$1.77	$15.90	$1.45	$1.77
$8.00	$0.73	$0.89	$8.20	$0.75	$0.91
$15.50	$1.41	$1.72	$15.90	$1.45	$1.77
$19.90	$1.81	$2.21	$22.90	$2.08	$2.54
$7.80	$0.71	$0.87	$14.00	$1.27	$1.56
$9.00	$0.82	$1.00	$15.30	$1.39	$1.70
$41.00	$3.73	$4.56	$94.00	$8.55	$10.44
$7.00	$0.64	$0.78	$7.50	$0.68	$0.83
$26.96	$2.45	$3.00	$26.96	$2.45	$3.00
$44.32	$4.03	$4.92	$44.32	$4.03	$4.92
$25.20	$2.29	$2.80	$31.00	$2.82	$3.44
$40.00	$3.64	$4.44	$95.00	$8.64	$10.56
$5.45	$0.50	$0.61	$12.50	$1.14	$1.39
$10.80	$0.98	$1.20	$15.30	$1.39	$1.70
$18.00	$1.64	$2.00	$18.75	$1.70	$2.08
$8.50	$0.77	$0.94	$16.90	$1.54	$1.88

SPANISH NAME	ENGLISH NAME
Trucha (1 kg)	Trout (1 kg)
Carne Molida de Res (1 kg)	Ground Beef (1 kg)
Jamon de Puerco (1 kg)	Ham (1 kg)
Chuletas de Puerco (1 kg)	Pork Chops (1 kg)
Cereales, Dulces, Tortillas	**Cereals-Grains, Cookies, Tortillas**
Pan Blanco (1 Barra)	White Bread (1 loaf)
Korn Flakes (350 gr)	Corn Flakes (350 gr)
Harina de Trigo (1 kg)	Wheat Flour (1 kg)
Arroz (1 kg)	Rice (1 kg)
Galetas Dulces (Gamesa)	Cookies (Gamesa brand, coconut)
Tortilla de maiz (1 kg)	Corn Tortillas (1 kg)
Azucar, Café, Miel	**Sugar, Coffee, Honey**
Azucar, Morena (2 kg)	Dark Sugar (Unrefined—Brown) (2 kg)
Azucar Refinada (2 kg)	Refined Sugar (White) (2 kg)
Café Soluble, Nescafé Clasico (200 gr)	Instant Coffee, Nescafé (200 gr)
Café Soluble, Nescafé Clasico Descafienado (200 gr)	Instant Coffee, Nescafé Decaffeinated (200 gr)
Café Tostado y Molido Mexicano Original (500 gr)	Toasted and Ground Coffee, Mexicano Original brand (500 gr)
Café Tostado y Molido Mexicano Original Descafienado (500 gr)	Toasted and Ground Coffee, Mexicano Original brand Decaffeinated (500 gr)
Miel de abeja (500 gr)	Honey (literally, "syrup of bee") (500 gr)
Diversos	**Miscellaneous**
Alka-Seltzer (12 pack)	Alka-Seltzer
Aspirina (40 pack)	Aspirin
Head & Shoulders (400 ml)	Head & Shoulders Shampoo (400 ml)
Barra de Jabon	Bar of Soap
Detergente (1 kg)	Detergent (1kg)
Pañal Pampers (18 pack)	Diapers

LIVE BETTER *South of the Border* IN MEXICO

Peso	MINIMUM USD (11:1)	CDND (9:1)	Peso	MAXIMUM USD (11:1)	CDND (9:1)
$55.00	$5.00	$6.11	$61.90	$5.63	$6.88
$39.00	$3.55	$4.33	$46.90	$4.26	$5.21
$95.00	$8.64	$10.56	$144.50	$13.14	$16.06
$40.00	$3.64	$4.44	$44.90	$4.08	$4.99
$13.00	$1.18	$1.44	$14.00	$1.27	$1.56
$16.00	$1.45	$1.78	$18.60	$1.69	$2.07
$4.30	$0.39	$0.48	$6.50	$0.59	$0.72
$7.30	$0.66	$0.81	$8.30	$0.75	$0.92
$13.75	$1.25	$1.53	$18.95	$1.72	$2.11
$4.40	$0.40	$0.49	$4.60	$0.42	$0.51
$15.90	$1.45	$1.77	$18.40	$1.67	$2.04
$18.60	$1.69	$2.07	$19.90	$1.81	$2.21
$33.00	$3.00	$3.67	$36.50	$3.32	$4.06
$28.70	$2.61	$3.19	$41.90	$3.81	$4.66
$28.80	$2.62	$3.20	$34.15	$3.10	$3.79
$34.15	$3.10	$3.79	$34.15	$3.10	$3.79
$34.95	$3.18	$3.88	$39.30	$3.57	$4.37
$10.00	$0.91	$1.11	$10.90	$0.99	$1.21
$11.50	$1.05	$1.28	$12.40	$1.13	$1.38
$42.00	$3.82	$4.67	$46.70	$4.25	$5.19
$6.00	$0.55	$0.67	$6.35	$0.58	$0.71
$15.80	$1.44	$1.76	$17.60	$1.60	$1.96
$38.50	$3.50	$4.28	$42.30	$3.85	$4.70

Chapter 1
WHAT TO EXPECT
LIVING IN GENERAL

The first question people put to me is, "Can I live in Mexico on my retirement income?" Read three books on living in Mexico and you'll get three answers. My answer is, "Probably." It depends on how big your check is. I know many people who live on $1,200 to $1,500 a month, single, or $1,500 to $2,000 a month, couple. I also know people who live on less than $1,000 a month. I could. If you can live in the United States or Canada on whatever you make, you can live a better life in Mexico on the same amount.

The "average" gringo who's not on a tight budget spends about $2,500, single, or $3,400, couple, a month to live a comfortable lifestyle, including medical care, health insurance, and trips to explore Mexico. It also budgets for one trip a year back home to the States or Canada. That means renting a one- or two-bedroom apartment, eating out a couple of times a week, having a phone (with high-speed Internet service), a maid, a gardener, and entertainment. This is based on interviews with several dozen expats and Mexicans in the "gringo" business.

Could you do this in Cabo San Lucas or Cozumel? It's possible, but you'd have to be frugal. San Miguel de Allende, Lake Chapala, and most cities in Mexico are livable within this range. But it means you will have to be careful about where you rent. You won't be able to live in the choice (high-end) parts of town unless you sacrifice elsewhere. Some medical care is included in your lifestyle, but a catastrophe or lingering illness will wipe you out. But if you were living in the States or Canada, even with Medicare or Health Canada, there would always be additional costs. At least in Mexico medicines and doctors' care are considerably cheaper.

The Mexican government thinks you need a $1,000 monthly income (this amount will probably go up, not down) in order to get an FM-3 permit (see chapter two for more information on these and other visas). At that income level you should be able to live a somewhat better life than you can live in your home country, but you're going to have to be frugal.

Can you live on less? I know people who do. They swear they can find a $250 apartment in Mexico almost anywhere. They cook at home. They eat at family restaurants and taco stands. They use Internet cafes instead of having the service with their phone. In fact, they don't have phones.

What's a comfortable figure to live a lifestyle that would seem luxurious to you? Except for Cabo and Cozumel, if you have $2,000 to $2,500 a month in income, you can live very well, including a house payment or renting a pretty nice house. If you have enough to buy a house outright and have that much or more, you would have no worries.

BENEFITS

Although many people will say that cost is the reason they want to move to Mexico, that's only the superficial aspect. There's a sense of freedom and of rediscovering yourself that motivates many of us to live away from the comfort and security of our own country. We're looking for a better way of life. We may be sick of the harsh winters of our homeland, of the crime and constant living in fear, or merely of the constant sameness that deadens our souls. No matter what our reason for wanting to try life in another country, we must first be motivated to leave. After we have passed that hurdle, we must then begin to think of the practicalities, of the cost of living.

Of course, if you have a very limited income and are barely making it in the United States, then you want to be sure that you are not jumping out of the frying pan into the fire. Frankly, there are some parts of the United States where you can live as cheaply as in Mexico.

MEXICO CAN UNLEASH THE ARTIST WITHIN YOU

If you are artistic, or have always wanted to develop your gifts, are someone who wants to get away to write your book, compose great music, or paint your pictures, I can think of no better place to do so than in Mexico. Artistic people are honored. When you say you are a writer, musician, painter, or sculptor, etc., people will look at you differently. (Well, in my case, they usually give me the same look they give children and lunatics, but there are probably other reasons for that.)

You won't even have to put up with the question that every writer (well, this one, anyway) hates, "Have I read anything you've published?" Someday I'm going to blurt out what's on my mind: "How the heck do I know what you've read?" The underlying question is, of course, "Are you famous?" Now that I've published at least seventeen books, I still hate the question. How about you? When I lived in Puerto Escondido, I decided that I'd put an end to that and made up a book title. I hadn't published a single thing then, but even the made-up title didn't help. People responded with, "I never heard of it," which made me feel even worse.

It's these little cultural differences that make living in Mexico more attractive. In Mexico, it doesn't matter if you're "famous." Unless you've been translated into Spanish, a Mexican wouldn't have read you. They do not care as much about fame. (Of course, music stars, movie stars, etc., are still treated as royalty, but Mexicans know how to draw the line.) They don't expect us to be well known. They care more about knowing the person inside. Mexicans respect the artistic gift. Period. In the United States, we're more interested in celebrity.

What if you just want to get away from the rat race?

ESCAPING THE RAT RACE

You may be someone who's had it with the rat race and you just want to get away. You've saved a certain amount of money and think you can survive for a year if you watch your pennies. You want to know exact costs. I was in that boat the first time I moved to Mexico. I lived on $2,000 for a year, many years ago, because that was how much money I had. Don't try to stretch out your money for a specific length of time. Living costs what it costs. Live as long as you can and don't skimp on what you need. Look at this as an adventure and realize that you can't predict costs to the penny. You'll find yourself setting a budget and finding a way to live on it. Keep your real goal in mind: to rejuvenate yourself. That will take as long as it takes.

HOUSING COSTS

Throughout the book I have included a range of housing costs. They are not gospel. These will, no doubt, change, probably going higher in most areas, but they will give you a general idea of what to expect. They provide a comparison of relative costs for cities and towns you are considering. The properties at the lower end of the scale are less plentiful than the ones at the higher end. I've excluded incredible bargains, as these are fleeting. I've also thrown out the multimillion-dollar luxury homes and condos.

While the range is rather broad, it does give you an average high and low to look for when shopping. Some expats may disagree with my low-end prices. Not every gringo has the same lifestyle. I could live in the low-end apartments and houses I include. I have. I have friends who have. Others could not. It's a matter of whether *where* you live (a particular house) matters more than *how* you live. A bargain is only a bargain if it makes sense to you.

Old-time expats will tell you that you can't find a decent house for less than $100,000 or an apartment for less than $800 in their community, when I've listed houses in the $40,000 range and apartments in the $400 to $500 range. They couldn't find them, but you can. These are not shacks, but simple concrete structures that Mexicans would find perfectly suitable. Look at them and see if they appeal to you.

Most things are cheaper in Mexico.

PROPERTY TAXES

Property taxes (known as *predial*), for instance, are ridiculously low. Depending on the community, they are sometimes as low as $60 a year for a $150,000 house ($300 on a $300,000 house). While taxes vary from city to city, they run from about .04 to .1 percent. That's *point* 1 percent, not 1 percent, of the appraised value at the time of sale (in most communities—there may be exceptions), versus a U.S. average of 1.25 percent (and much higher in many cities). There are no estate taxes in Mexico, and you can give your property to an immediate family member (spouse or children) without a tax penalty. There is a capital gains tax when you sell property, however, and it is complicated, based on the value, inflation, number of years you lived there (to figure out the inflation-adjusted value), the assessed value by the municipality (not necessarily the sales price), and probably continental drift adjusted by the phases of the moon. Consult with a *notario publico* before you sell. When you buy property, there is about a 2 percent sales tax.

Another thing is that if you live there only part-time, you have to pay a tax to Hacienda (the Mexican tax agency), but it is miniscule. However, not paying it can cause you a lot of grief.

Financing is now available for real estate purchases, but beware of ghosts.

REAL ESTATE OPTIONS

Real estate titles can now be guaranteed by Stewart Title, First American Title Company, and others. This is a big change since the last edition of this book. You can now finance property throughout all of Mexico through an American collateral mortgage company, both for residential and commercial property. While there are a few companies offering this service, as a developer for a large housing project who called me for advice said, "I've talked to several people who claim they can finance property in Mexico. As they say in Mexico, they were *fantasmas.*"

Literally, *fantasma* means "a ghost," but it is commonly used to describe ideas or people whose promises are insubstantial or who promise more than they can deliver. I learned this word from the owner of the spa Ixtapan de la Sal, who was leery of my reservation service representing them because so many people claimed to have such businesses and few did. There's a lesson here for those of you who want to start a business: Gringo businesses come and go in Mexico, so expect a little hesitancy from other Mexican businesses. It took me three years to get a contract with Ixtapan.

As we go to press, there are a few companies now financing property for foreigners in Mexico. There is updated information available on my Web site. (See www.mexicomike.com/Real%20Estate/collateral_mortgage.htm, or just click on the menu for "Living/Travel" from the home page.) Generally speaking, what I hear from potential lenders is that you'll need about 50 percent as a down payment, the interest rate will vary, and will be about two to three points higher than if you were purchasing property in the United States or Canada, but it will always be less than you'd pay with a Mexican company.

Mexican banks can now finance real estate for a fairly reasonable interest rate. It used to be that interest rates could run as high as 27 percent for large purchases in Mexico, but now, although they are higher than U.S. or Canadian banks, they are no longer exorbitant. But, they generally only finance for five years.

Buying and Renting

Unadvertised bargains exist that will lower your housing costs considerably, but you have to be there to find them. Under no circumstances should you rent or buy a place solely from an Internet ad. It is not that the companies on the Internet are unreliable or dishonest; they are the same companies you will deal with once you get there. However, it is always a good idea to actually see places before renting, and certainly before buying. Check out the neighborhood.

Safety isn't the only concern. Are there barking dogs that will keep you awake? (This is a big deal in my world, and I own a very well-behaved cocker spaniel, named Fluffy. Mexicans get a big kick out the name. In fact, they look at pet ownership quite differently than we do. For many Mexicans, a dog's main value is that of a watchdog, so chaining him to a tree outside is not considered cruel.)

Mexicans love their music. Drive by at different times of the day to see how much your neighbor's musical selections will affect you. A charming downtown apartment near the zócalo may seem as though it's a dream come true, but see how well you dream when the church bells start ringing at a very early hour, later in the day, and at inexplicable times throughout the day.

Traffic noise seems to be worse at night, when the roads are full of buses and trucks whose drivers think a muffler is a sign of weakness. (When driving, you'll see signs at the entrances to cities saying *"Cierre su escape."* This doesn't mean to close your escape. It means that trucks and buses should close their baffles. Similar to most Mexican road signs, it is routinely ignored.)

How close to a bus route is your abode? Does the gas man come at seven in the morning, or even earlier if you are first on his route? How far are you from a neighborhood cantina? While you may want to frequent cantinas or nightclubs, they make lousy neighbors. What about parking? These are all things you can only know when you are there.

Rental Housing Bargains

Now for the bargains. After you have been around for a while, you'll get to know other gringos who may go back home for an extended period, especially in the summer. Some of them would love to have a responsible house sitter. You may even be able to house sit without paying rent. After all, you are doing them a favor. Sometimes local gringos who own rental property would rather rent to another gringo and will give you a better deal on rents than the asking price. This works both ways. (However, some gringos have inflated ideas about the value of their worth and that of their house and will gouge you.) Some RVers own spaces that have a permanent trailer or small house on the lot; they also need trailer sitters.

Look around for roommates, as there are plenty of people who are living in a house or apartment who either can't afford it on their own or just want some company.

And if you really want to get to know the Mexican culture, and are not too concerned about your privacy, sublet a room or two from a Mexican family. Some would love to have the income, and you'll be a source of entertainment for their family, as we gringos have strange ways. You can negotiate for a room with or without meals. You should be able to rent a room for between $70 and $120 a month.

QUALITY OF LIFE

The real reason to move to Mexico.

The *numero uno* reason for moving to Mexico is that your quality of life will be better. If you come from the Frozen North (as I call everywhere north of Texas), you'll be getting away from the biting cold that demoralizes you and makes your joints ache. You'll be getting away from a siege mentality that affects so many of us who live in cities. You'll be getting away from your boring neighbors who are afraid to take any chances in life. You'll be going to a place where you can find yourself and enjoy life again. Most importantly, you'll be putting yourself into an environment where people still care about each other and courtesy is a way of life (okay, except on the roadways—traffic is traffic, but at least there are no snipers or road rage).

Children and Schools

Mexico is child friendly. If you have children, you will be able to relax more here. I can't think of anything better than being a kid in Mexico. They have more freedom. Except in large cities, you don't have to worry about weirdos and depraved creeps who will kidnap or molest your kids. It is not unusual to see Mexican kids in the town square at ten o'clock at night. It would be irresponsible of me to say that nothing bad ever happens in Mexico. It does, but not with the frequency that it does in the United States.

Even in the big cities, gang activity is not anywhere near the scale it is in the United States. Drug use is not as prevalent (though it certainly does exist) and weapons in schools are pretty darn rare. If there are weapons, they are much more likely to be knives than guns. It's just a better environment for children in all respects.

Speaking of respect, Mexicans honor teachers. Mexican kids (and yours) do not get away with the abuse that American kids give their instructors. A lot of my friends are teachers, and while most are dedicated, they agree that in the United States a sizeable number of educators are burned out and just marking time toward retirement. Mexican teachers' salaries are pitiful. Yet the Mexican teachers I know are happier to be doing what they do than many teachers in the United States. It is true that Mexican teachers sometimes strike to get better pay, but wouldn't you? If you can hire a teacher as a tutor, your kid will get great help and you'll be doing something good.

There are private bilingual schools in many cities in Mexico. Every city with a sizeable population of foreigners will have at least one, and all the larger cities have two or three. If there are foreign workers at the international companies with offices in a city, you can bet there is an English-language school. There are also Montessori schools that teach in both languages. Your children won't be going to school with only other gringo kids. There will be Mexican children whose families can afford the tuition and want more challenging courses than those offered in public schools (gee, does that sound familiar?). These families also want their kids to learn the international language, English. (One cultural note: Mexican kids from rich families generally don't mix with the foreign students, but middle-class kids seem to mix better.)

What if you decide on a smaller town that doesn't have an English-language school? Your kids will be welcome at regular public schools. I have known several Americans and Canadians who have chosen to send their kids to Mexican schools. Unlike here, the kids won't be put into special classes that attempt to teach them in both languages: They will have to learn Spanish. Is this a bad thing? Absolutely not! What better opportunity for them to truly become international citizens? Admittedly, you will have to do some extra tutoring to help them along, and you might even learn Spanish yourself. The classes might not be as demanding as those in many U.S. and Canadian schools, but you can bridge that gap yourself. Moving to Mexico will give you more freedom to be able to do things with your kids.

Mothers often employ chauffeurs to drive their kids to various activities. This can be a great service, and as your kids get older, it doesn't hurt to have a person who is with them at all times, keeping an eye on their activities.

Regardless of whether your kids go to a private or public school, your involvement will be welcomed. By getting involved with your kids' schooling, you can get to know your kids better. By getting involved with your children's schools, you can get to know other Mexican families and truly become part of the community.

Maids

You will most likely have a maid (sixty pesos a day) and a gardener (2,500 to 3,000 pesos full-time), both of which you probably didn't have at home. You may have your maid come twice a week or live with you. If she lives there, you are expected to provide (at no charge) living quarters and meals.

One thing to remember about hiring a maid: Should you let her go, you'll have to pay her one month's salary for each year worked, plus holiday pay, but you don't have to pay her social security. For other employees, you have to pay social security and the severance pay mentioned above.

Don't brag about your maid!

A great thing about living in Mexico is the fact that you can pay very little for services. A maid for a week will probably run you around $40. When you have a good person to help you in your house, you usually will want to pay more to keep her. Many people have gardeners or handymen who will do most of the work around the house. You usually find these people by word of mouth, through a sister of a maid next door, etc.

People with young children sometimes have live-in maids. Almost every house in Mexico has a maid's room (it is standard) even if you don't have a maid. It is a good idea to be around during the first stages of having help in your house. Sometimes you have to go through many people to find someone who is right for you. (A little joke here is to never tell anyone how good your maid—or your husband—is or someone will steal her or him from you!)

Home Delivery!
In some cities, it is possible to have everyone come to you. You see many motorbikes around bringing food, medicines, etc., to people's houses at no extra charge. This is great if it's in the middle of the night and you have a sick child in need of medicine. It's also nice to be able to have all types of food delivered to your house.

PLUSSES AND MINUSES

I give you the plusses and minuses of living in Mexico so that you can make up your own mind. Mexico is not the cheapest country in the world to live. Yes, it costs less to live there with a better standard of living than it does in the United States or Canada. But if money is your only motivator, there are other countries that cost less. Mexico is not paradise. It is as close to a perfect place to live for many people as there will ever be, but it is not perfect. While there are many reasons to live there, there are also many why it may not be for you.

Mexico is right for many. The U.S. embassy in Mexico City estimated that in 2001 there were more than 600,000 Americans living in Mexico. An estimated 300,000 Canadians live in Mexico, at least part-time.

You can live comfortably in Mexico for about $25,000 to $30,000, single, or $35,000 to $45,000, couple, a year in most places. It is still possible to live on $12,000 to $15,000, single, or $15,000 to $20,000, couple, or less in some locations, if you are really frugal. That's about what I live on in the States.

DON'T GO IF ...
If you are moving to Mexico only because it is cheaper than the United States or Canada, you are moving for the wrong reason. My advice then: Don't go. If you are moving only because of the weather, you are moving for the wrong reason. If you are the sort of person who has to have things your own way, the way everything "should" work out according to you, you will be very unhappy living in Mexico. Many retired military officers live in Mexico and have adjusted very well. They were ready to leave their old ways of doing things behind and have embraced new ones, where there is always an element of surprise to planned events.

If you have only been to the beach resorts or to the interior tourist destinations, you do not have an accurate picture of Mexico. If you have only vacationed there, you do not have an accurate picture of living there.

DO GO IF ...

If the lower cost and the wonderful climate are factors, but your main reason for choosing Mexico is that you love the people, are flexible, and want some adventure in your life, you are moving for the right reasons and will probably be happy there.

Much Has Changed

While much has changed in the years since I first wrote this book, and much has improved, Mexico is still Mexico. That means it is unique. It has a culture that changes slowly, no matter how technocratic the government is. Overall, it is easier to live there today than it was ten years ago, and much easier than it was twenty years ago. By easier, I mean that Mexican banking is now more similar to American banking and less like a labyrinth; you no longer need to be a devotee of Kafka to cash a check. Internet service has also improved. You can now get DSL (common) or cable Internet service (not as common) in your home.

Goods you are used to are available from Sam's, Wal-Mart, Costco, Home Mart (owned by Home Depot), and other international chains. Costs of imported goods have gone down. For instance, I recently purchased stockings for a girlfriend ("not for me," he said hastily) that were a name brand sold in the United States for less in Acapulco than at home. Getting back through customs with twenty pairs of lace stockings took some explaining, but I figure a bargain is worth stocking up on.

You can now get a new phone line without waiting for Hades to freeze over. You can, thanks to a variety of calling plans, call back to the States, Canada, and Europe without taking out a second mortgage on your house. You can now operate an Internet business or be a stock trader in Mexico.

Overall, life is just easier in Mexico today than it was even five years ago.

NOT ALL IS SWEETNESS AND LIGHT

I am not going to give you a glowing, hyperbolic report on living in Mexico that sounds as if it was written by a public relations agent. I have lived for extended periods in Mexico, in and out of Central America for thirty years, and once operated importing businesses selling goods from Mexico, Guatemala, and Honduras. Mexico is different from Central America. Frankly, I believe that for most people Mexico is a better choice.

I love Mexico and believe that most of you will too. However, similar to a lover who has been in a relationship for many years, I have gone beyond the romance stage and see her for what she is. You are entering a relationship. Any successful relationship requires compromises (which could be why I have two exes and no wives). Do your part and Mexico will do hers.

Mexico is still a beauty, but there are the inevitable flaws. Some parts of her are sagging, and some of the promises she made to an impressionable youth have not come true. I, of course, am not perfect either, but that is the subject of a much longer book. I will give you as honest an impression of the joys and headaches of living in Mexico as I can. You will have to make up your own mind. To do so, you will have to visit and see for yourself.

WHEN THINGS GO WRONG

Just as in our home countries, things don't always work out right. A business may overcharge us, perform shoddy work, or not do what it promised when it promised, or a government official may have dragged his feet in helping you. In the States, we have offices such as the Consumer Protection Agency. In Mexico, there is a national agency called Procuraduría Federal del Consumidor (PROFECO). It's in Spanish, but if you want to make a complaint against a business, gas station, cop, government official, etc., call their toll-free number (800-468-87-22, which could change, however, finding it is not hard) and choose "*Presenta tus quejas o denuncias,*" or go to their Web site (www.profeco.gob.mx).

You may want to allow the company or person that has wronged you seventy-two hours to fix the problem, as by law this is how much time they have. But don't let yourself be taken advantage of. Sometimes just letting a company that has mistreated you know that you know your rights will get them moving. Once you start the ball rolling, it will take a week or two for you to get an appointment to get their balls rolling. I'm not promising that they'll be more responsive than their U.S. or Canadian counterparts, but sometimes you'll be pleasantly surprised.

SPEAKING SPANISH

Sopa *isn't soap.*

One thing I'm often asked about is, "Do you have to speak Spanish to live in Mexico?" The answer is no, but one of the most arrogant things gringos do is move, live permanently in the country, and never learn a lick of Spanish. I've included listings of Spanish language schools for many cities, and you should attend one. It wouldn't hurt to get a start before you leave by buying the books mentioned below.

If you really want to learn Spanish, get the U.S. State Department's *Foreign Service Institute Language Course*, sold in bookstores. There are a couple of companies that package it, but Multilingua is the least expensive. A great book for those who already know a little Spanish is *Breaking Out of Beginner's Spanish* by Joseph J. Keenan (University of Texas Press).

If you just want to learn enough Spanish to communicate and enough slang to sound as if you understand the culture, get my e-book, "*Mexico" Mike's Bastante Español, Modismos Y Slang (with enough slang to make you sound cool).* (It's available online at www.mexicomike.com, just click "Books.") I'm not a linguist, cunning or otherwise. I've taken the most common mistakes (mostly learned the hard way) and given you easy ways to avoid them. There's a lot of humor in this little book. For instance, don't confuse *sopa*, soup, with *jabón*, soap, just because they sound similar in English. I did and it was hilarious.

Instead of boring you with a lot of grammar rules and phrases, such as "The red vase is on the table," or "Your mother makes good tortillas," I'll give you the common questions you'll get, such as "Where are you going?" from the drug police. I've found that confusing "Where are you going?", "*¿A donde va?*", with "Where are you coming from?", "*¿De donde viene?*", seems to upset them. If you're heading south and you say you're going north, they either think you are crazy, lost, or lying. Cops being cops, they usually opt for the latter. The best answer to "*¿De donde viene?*" is *Estados Unidos* (or *Canadá*). If they tack an "*anoche*" on the end, it means "Where were you last night?" Try not to smile lustily and look at your traveling companion.

Knowing what others are saying is more important to foreigners than what they're going to say. Naturally, in my e-book I cover every driving situation you'll run into (or hopefully won't run into). I will keep you out of trouble. (For instance, instead of asking a butcher if he has *huevos*, you'd better ask him for *blanquillas*, if you don't want to offend his manhood. I found this out the hard way, since all my Spanish books had only *huevos* for eggs. *Chichis* is an impolite way to refer to a woman's breasts (among others). Use *senos*, which is rather clinical, or, more commonly, *pechos* instead. (The polite way to say "penis" is *pene*.)

ATTITUDE IS EVERYTHING

My love affair with Mexico started in 1957, thanks to my father. He thought he wanted to move to Mexico that year. He was a forceful man, but a highly impractical one. My dear mother always went along with his flights of fancy and was always there to bail the family out when his flights crash-landed.

Don't be an Ugly American/Canadian.

I've included this very personal story about my father because it's a universal story. My father was an Everyman who want to move to foreign lands. He wanted to go, but for the wrong reasons. I loved my father, but today I recognize his flaws. If he had read a book such as mine before going to Mexico, he might have had a better chance at making it, or he might have chosen not to have gone at all. I feel that I have done a worthwhile service if I discourage some people from moving to Mexico, just as much as when my writing encourages others to move.

As it was, the available literature at the time only talked about how cheap it was to live there. Even today, some magazine articles and some books concentrate on that aspect. I would like to give you a much richer and fuller picture.

My father packed up the car and headed south, to San Luis Potosí, capital of the state of the same name. I fell in love with Mexico then and there, as a young boy. I can't truly describe it, but with the colors, the smells, the warmth of foreign people who did not speak the same language but who made me feel comfortable, I would have loved to move to Mexico.

My father, however, was typical of many who think they want to move there but really aren't suited for it. He was a lawyer-turned-farmer. He had been drummed out of (or quit, no one is really sure) the legal profession in Chicago because of his inability to get along with people. He was a good farmer. He had a natural gift for it. He created new species of citrus fruits to improve his business. He was a man of few words but expressed his love for my mother by creating new varieties of roses for her. He had a few friends and was not a bad man, but he became a different person in Mexico.

We all become different people when we cross the border. For most of us, it brings out a better, less-stressed side. For him, and others similar to him, it brought out arrogance. Believe me, you had better leave your arrogance in your other suitcase at home when you go to Mexico or else you will have nothing but problems. Such people propagate the negative stories about Mexico, importing negativity and exporting deceit.

My father (God rest his soul) was the typical Ugly American. If you find yourself resembling him, do Mexico and yourself a favor and stay home. He refused to learn the language. Not only did he not learn Spanish, he expected everyone to speak English. He believed that the Mexican people all knew it and were refusing to speak it to him. He thought that if he shouted at them, they would respond better.

His plan to buy a ranch or farm (the two are used interchangeably in conversation) in San Luis Potosí came about because he had read a book written by someone who talked only about how cheap it was to live there and didn't know the culture. The book was well advertised and probably made a lot of money for the author, but it resulted in a lot of people being disappointed. At a very early age I was impressed with the power and the responsibility of the printed word. This book told my father that living in Mexico was easy, cheap, and simple. It told him that he would be a king there, living on a pauper's income.

I noticed that the Mexican people were very quiet, shy, and polite. Whenever my father spoke to them in his loud, authoritarian voice, they winced. Still, they were too polite to respond to him in kind. They were particularly offended when he said the name of their city. It is pronounced something similar to "Saan Louees Po toe seé," with an accent on the last syllable. He called it "San Louis Po toé see." It would have been an understandable mistake the first dozen or so times he did it, but, after a few days, it became obvious that he had no intention of showing even the most basic politeness.

My father had gotten an invitation to meet the mayor. This man could have done wonders for easing my father's purchase of land had my father merely been polite to the man. Instead, he corrected the mayor's halting English, shouted at him as if he were deaf, and continually mispronounced the name of the man's city. My father was not a big man at city hall.

My father referred to Mexicans, who are quite proud of their heritage, as "Messkins," a loathsome South Texan term, or "Indians," always said with derision. He was suspicious and always thought he was being cheated. He refused to learn how the peso worked. Instead, he paid for everything in dollars, asking "How much is that in real money?" He got very drunk and abusive in the bar at the hotel. People talk about how unsafe a place Mexico is. How long do you think a foreigner with my father's attitude would have gotten along in the United States without someone taking a swing at him?

He didn't know how to buy property in Mexico and just assumed (after all, he was a lawyer) that it worked the way it did at home. The best thing about the trip was that he didn't find any land he wanted or he would have squandered our savings buying land from someone who probably didn't have the right to sell it to him. When he returned, he was bitter toward Mexico and told all who would listen that they had better be careful when they went there, as he had been deep into the interior and knew what he was talking about.

There are pitfalls to buying property. See chapter three for information about how to avoid them.

He was not unlike many of the people you will encounter when you say that you are considering moving to Mexico. After all, they have been there and they will tell you all the horror stories you can take. People such as these give the country a bad reputation. If you, who may never have been there or may not have been outside the tourist enclaves of Acapulco, Cancún, etc., don't know any better, you will believe them. My father had been in the country of Mexico but he never saw it. He never got beyond his own ego and misconceptions.

I was a child. I had no ego to speak of and no prejudices. I remember waiters smiling when I asked for Dr. Pepper and one who miraculously found one. I remember Mexican kids being the same as me, except for the language, and we played together and had a good time. I remember the warm days and cool nights, the air fragrant with wild, tropical scents. I remember the feeling of adventure and the kindness of everyone we met when they dealt with me. I also remember their unhappiness when they talked to my father, but they never took it out on me. After we left Mexico, I wanted to go back.

Both my father and I had been in the same place and had the same experiences. One of us loved the country and the people and one of us hated them. Who was right? We both were. Mexico was not for my father. He would have been very unhappy there. (In truth, he was unhappy anywhere he was, but that is another story.) It is better that he did not move there, because after a few months or years he would have had to leave and would have been able to blame his failures and unhappiness on the country.

DOING BUSINESS IN MEXICO

I had a good first experience and went back to Mexico several times, eventually living there, and now I travel there on a regular basis. Many people ask why I do not live in Mexico at the moment. I will be moving back in the next few years.

When I'm not traveling for business in the States, I spend my time in Mexico. My "other life" consists of consulting over the phone with people moving or starting businesses in Mexico (800-234-3452); presenting seminars about living in Mexico (to see if I will be coming to your town, go to www.mexicomike.com, "Seminars"); conducting self-help seminars in the United States for a nonprofit group that I founded (Clutterless Recovery Groups; www.clutterless.org); starting support meetings; and selling books. I spend about four months a year on the road in the States and four months setting up those seminars. Right now, it is just easier for me to stay here and visit Mexico, as I could not do all the advance preparations for my seminars as well from there.

Selling books over the Internet (or anything that needs to be shipped on a regular basis) just works better from the States. If you have a business that requires people to call you on a toll-free number, it is less expensive in the States, although it is possible to get a number that rings in the States, then "rings through" to your Mexican number.

MEXICO IS A STATE OF MIND

Some of you readers should not live in Mexico, and some of you should not live anywhere else. As good as I (and the tens of thousands of you who bought the first, second, and third editions) think this book is, it is only a book. It will guide and educate you, but by itself it cannot predict how well you will like Mexico. We are, by nature, self-deceiving. Although you might have all the character traits of my father, you probably won't admit it (though your wife or partner will). Some of you won't know how you and Mexico will fit together until you actually go and try it out. It affects people differently. During the past decade, I have consulted with thousands of people seeking advice about traveling, living, and working in Mexico.

Mexico is more than a place. It is a state of mind.

I remember one fellow from Boston who had an expensive motor home and was the most uptight man I ever met. He had his wife, children, and grandmother with him. He was so filled with apprehension and worry about his expensive motor home that I told him he should just not go.

He was taken aback. "I thought your job was to encourage people to go to Mexico."

"No," I replied, "My job is to help people to have a good time, and you are so worried about your motor home that you will not have a good time. Do us both a favor and stay home."

He thought about it and said, "What if I leave the motor home here and just take the car?"

He did, and his two-week trip became a monthlong journey of self-discovery. I saw him when he returned and he was completely relaxed and smiling. In fact, he and his family stayed an extra two weeks, and Grandma came back several years younger in spirit.

Grandma danced in the square in Veracruz.

I have a place to stay if I ever get to Boston. That experience taught me that I should never judge whether someone will fit into Mexico, but I can make general assumptions about what might not work. Follow your heart, but take some of my suggestions to the same place.

You'll enjoy living in Mexico if:

1. You have a spirit of adventure.

Even if you are going to live in Mexico City and work for a company, life will be an adventure. You can either have fun with it or be frustrated by it. The choice is always yours.

2. You can accept that most things are out of your control.

If you think everything has to be in its place and there must be a logical explanation for everything, then you are going to spend a lot of time being unhappy. Learn to "go with the flow."

3. You are willing to accept things as they are.

There's a wonderful little prayer that says, in part, "God, grant me the serenity to accept the things I can't change, the courage to change the things I can, and the wisdom to know the difference." You may find yourself repeating this when little "Mexicanisms" get between you and getting things done.

4. You truly like people and can accept their differences.

Remember that you are never alone in Mexico. Even if— especially if—you live in a small town where there are no other gringos, you will meet many locals. They are a gregarious bunch with large families and a healthy curiosity about the bizarre ways of foreigners. Remember that many of the things we take for granted about ourselves are pretty darn amazing to outsiders. Old people and small kids will ask you questions as you travel about. Middle-class businessmen will go out of their way to help you when you need it. Strangers of all classes will show you things and help you find whatever it is you are looking for, be it a road out of town or a battery for your car alarm.

5. You have a sense of humor.

This is probably the most important ingredient in enjoying life in Mexico. If you do not take yourself too seriously, you will do much better than if you do. If you are a very serious or sad person and you have been sent to Mexico by your company, take heart, your whole personality could change for the better.

These are the main personality traits that will make your life in Latin America easier. I'm not a psychologist, and there is absolutely nothing scientific about my list. It is based on my experience and what I have gathered from the thousands of people I have talked to and observed throughout the last several years. It is only to give you an honest assessment of some of the differences of living in Mexico versus living in the United States or Canada.

¡Viva las diferencias!

COSTS OF LIVING

Asking what it costs to live in Mexico is similar to asking what it costs to live in the United States or Canada: A lot depends on where you want to live. Frugal as you might be, you cannot live in Cabo San Lucas for the same amount you would spend in Mazatlán. Your own personal lifestyle makes a big difference too.

In this edition, I've included a cost-of-living comparison chart for many cities (see pages 8–11). I've also included average real estate and rent prices, though these will change as time goes on. Use them as a guide, not as a biblically based holy word. The Ten Commandments were written in stone; this book wasn't (easier to carry that way).

Most things will be cheaper in Mexico, but not as cheap as you may think. Some things you are used to having (imported goods, for instance) are more expensive. Gasoline is more expensive. Due to the lower living wage paid in Mexico, anything that involves some human being working on it will be cheaper, such as household help, mechanics, handmade furniture, handmade clothing, and arts and crafts (except where a gringo buyer has caused prices to escalate, as with some crafts in Oaxaca and other areas), etc. Eating out can be less expensive, but not necessarily. McDonald's and other international chains are not cheap; they are luxury food. Local family-run restaurants are always a bargain. Slick, fancy restaurants can be a bargain, compared to first-class restaurants in the United States, in terms of service and what you get, but they are still expensive.

The chart below is only a general guide. Prices go up and they go down. Sometimes something that used to cost more will plummet, while things that cost less will go up. Electronics, for instance, used to cost 100 percent more in Mexico than in the States or Canada. Today, thanks to the North American Free Trade Agreement (NAFTA), they have gone down. However, import duties are subject to the whims of both governments and can change overnight.

What's Cheaper in Mexico?

Property Taxes: 80 to 95 percent

This, the same as anywhere else, is dependent upon where you live.

Household Help: 80 percent

You will be able to afford help where you couldn't at home.

Medical Care: 40 percent

Medicines are from 50 to 70 percent cheaper. Hospital costs are *closer to 50 to 60 percent less expensive. A stay in an intensive care unit costs about $1,500 a day, or $8,000 a week. Doctor exams are about $40 to $60 on average.*

Fresh Vegetables: 50 percent

If you buy from the markets, prices for local items can be as much as 80 percent, and almost always 50 percent, cheaper. Mangoes, citrus fruit, pistachios, and pineapples are dirt cheap. At grocery stores, you'll still save about 30 to 40 percent.

Fresh Seafood: 20 to 40 percent on the coasts, assuming you buy from the markets. In grocery stores on the mainland the costs will be much higher.

Utilities: 30 percent

Electricity is about the same as in the United States, or can actually be more expensive per kilowatt hour, but due to the temperate climate, you use less. Gas (propane) is relatively inexpensive. Water can be about the same or more expensive, depending on where you live in the States or Canada. It's more expensive in areas of Mexico with a water shortage than in other areas.

Coffee: 60 percent

For fresh-ground coffee, we pay $7 to $9 a pound. It's $2 to $3 in Mexico.

Booze and Cigarettes: 30 to 50 percent

Sin doesn't seem to be taxed as much here. And smoking isn't treated as sinful, though political correctness is moving in on Mexico. Canadians will find these things much cheaper than at home. Cigarettes are half price. Good Mexican or Central American cigars are $3 to $8; Cubans are $12 to $20. Cheap cigars (real, not with paper wrappers) are about $1.25 apiece, when you can find them. However, when eating out, drinks (good-quality booze) and beer, cerveza, will cost about what it does in the States.

What's About the Same?

Internet Connection (Both Dial-Up and High-Speed)

There are deals in all three countries that make comparisons difficult, but it evens out to be a little higher in Mexico. Average prices for dial-up are $20 per month, for high-speed, $50.

Eating Out

This has gone up a lot in the last few years. While small family-run restaurants frequented by locals are less expensive than back home, middle-class and above restaurants can be a bargain compared to those in the United States, but they are still expensive.

Phone Service

A phone line with dial-up Internet service runs about $40 to $50 per month. Phone service by itself is $25 to $30. Long-distance service is still extremely expensive, unless you get a dial-around service (see the section on communications, page 46. If you want high-speed DSL service, it will add another $50 to your bill. Add 15 percent tax to the above prices. A DSL modem will cost about Mex $3,000 (around U.S. $300), for the equipment.

Cable TV

About the same, where it's available.

What's More Expensive?

Auto Fuel: 30 percent

This fluctuates in all countries, but less so in Mexico. It will always be more expensive than the median price of gas in the States, though closer to par with Canada. Diesel is sometimes cheaper than in the States.

Cars: 40 percent

This applies to new cars. Used cars vary wildly, but are generally somewhat more expensive.

Luxury Goods: 50 percent

Depends on current import duties. Items from some countries may be less expensive than at home.

Electronics (Computers, TVs, Stereos, etc.): 30 percent

Postage: 20 percent

Chicken: 30 percent

Sometimes chicken can be a bargain, but traditionally has been more expensive (it used to be nearly 50 percent higher) than back home. Allow about a foul, I mean fowl, surcharge of 20 percent.

Meat: 20 percent

The quality of beef (tenderness) has improved greatly over the years. However, cuts are thinner and often not as tender as you are used to. Angus beef is available at a premium. Pork is pretty good and a little cheaper.

MONEY MATTERS

WHAT MEXICANS MAKE

Consider this: The average working-class Mexican family lives on about $400 to $500 a month (not quite double that if both adults work). There are a lot of reasons that few gringos can do this, so don't expect you will be able to live on that; you don't have the family connections or the resources to achieve this goal. And yes, more often than not, a gringo will pay a higher rate for the same service or item. For example, my Mexican friends have told me that they can rent a two- to three-bedroom house for about $70 to $80 a month, while you'll pay $300 to $400 for the same place. Accept it and don't constantly complain. After you have been a resident for a while, you'll find yourself in a better bargaining position and your living costs will go down, but most people will never be able to live as cheaply as a Mexican.

Outside Mexico City, the average private sector, lower middle-class people (assistant managers) make about $18,000 to $25,000 a year. The average mid-level government employee makes about $20,000 to $30,000. The average private sector, middle-class executive or technician makes around $30,000 a year.

For the last several years, the peso has traded in a range between ten to twelve pesos to the U.S. dollar, and seven to nine pesos to the Canadian dollar. Yet inflation has remained high. (Due to the government's policy of understating inflation numbers, there is no "official" rate of inflation you can trust, but expats and Mexicans have told me that if you triple the government numbers, you will get a pretty true figure. Ten percent per year is a conservative estimate. Some journalists have told me that true inflation is about 20 percent per year if you consider all goods and services, at least for the last three years.) Consequently, your relative purchasing power has gone down.

Should there be a devaluation, or a dramatic change in the peso-to-dollar rate, hurry down and take advantage of the situation. There can always be a sudden devaluation, intense inflation, or other factors beyond anyone's control. If that happens, don't agonize over the moral dilemma. You didn't cause the devaluation. You are actually helping the economy and Mexicans by bringing in dollars. And move quickly or the bargains will have been adjusted upward to compensate. Since most real estate in gringo environs is quoted in U.S. dollars anyway, you'll only benefit from property in small towns. But you will benefit from buying goods.

BANKING

Most Mexican banks have been sold to foreign firms. Banamex is now

Citigroup; Bancomer is now BBVA; SERFIN is now Santander; Inverlat is now Scotiabank; Bital is now HSBC; etc. Before they were sold, they changed a lot of their customer service methods and are now similar to those in the United States. I highly recommend Scotiabank and HSBC since they work well with foreigners. Avoid Citibank and BBVA; they are huge banks and the lines take forever. Deposits of Mexican checks from banks other than your own will take twenty-four hours to be credited, and from the same bank will occur instantly. However this can still vary from bank to bank. Sometimes a Mexican check can still take three to ten days to be credited. Count on waiting a week or two for U.S. checks.

For Americans who need to cash a check in U.S. dollars, they can change it at a *casa de cambio*. They might charge a small commission but will give you a good rate. The best exchange rate can be obtained from ATMs, so I always recommend to my clients withdrawing money from ATMs instead of changing cash at banks. I'm afraid that Canadian checks are still problematic to cash. Allen W. Lloyd has offered banking and investment services to foreigners for more years than I can remember and is a company I would recommend for assistance.

The banks (all of them) will nickel-and-dime you to death with incomprehensible service charges. You certainly don't want to borrow any money from them because interest rates, which vary, are currently around 20 percent! During the crisis of 1995, they were as high as 140 percent! Of course, the other side of that coin is that you can garner some hefty interest on your own shekels by getting a *cuenta maestra*, which pays you interest and allows you to write checks and use a debit card.

You can invest your money in CETEs, or twenty-eight-day certificates of deposit. The same as in your country, there are longer term certificates, up to 180 days. The days of 30 percent and higher returns on your money are gone, for now. You'll get a bit more than you would in the States or Canada at the moment, but who knows what the future holds. Mexico's inflation rate is currently about 4 percent, and the central bank raises interest rates periodically, just as in any other country.

Again, the easiest way to get money is to use your debit card from your home bank at an ATM machine. These are everywhere. Cirrus is the most popular, followed by Pulse; Visa Plus is sometimes accepted. You can also use your Visa or MasterCard for cash advances at the ATM. (If you go to a bank to use them, you will have to show a passport.) You know, of course, that there is a hefty fee for this service. Unfortunately, ATMs in smaller towns always seem to be out of cash. If you have an American Express card, you can go to any American Express office and get up to $500 in American Express traveler's checks.

EMERGENCY MONEY
Last year, $9.3 billion was sent from the United States to Mexico. Fees, however, ate up $1.86 billion. The cost of a wire transfer has dropped from

about $20 to $30 to about $11. A wire transfer can take from one to three days.

Your best bet is to have a friend deposit the money in your home account and retrieve it via an ATM. International U.S. Postal Service money orders are honored, and this is how most Mexicans working in the United States send money back home.

If you receive money on a regular basis from investments, have it deposited to your U.S. or Canadian bank account.

Traveler's Express has relationships with Banorte banks in many cites and smaller agencies in small towns (www.moneygram.com). However, their fees are exorbitant. One hundred dollars costs $15, which isn't so bad. But $500 costs $40, and it gets worse from there.

There's an online service called iKobo (www.ikobo.com) that will let you send money over the Internet. The first $500 is free of charges. In order for your recipient to get the money, he needs an iKobo card, which can be used at any Visa Plus ATM machine. They will express this card to your recipient (currently for no fee) in Mexico. It takes three to five days to arrive. Once your account is set up, you can transfer money on a regular basis for a 4 percent fee. There will also be some ATM fees incurred by the recipient.

If your friend has a bank account in Mexico, a service called Paystone charges a reasonable flat fee of $6 for up to $1,000 (www.paystone.com). There is no fee if the recipient has a Paystone account.

You can also send money via PayPal for free (www.paypal.com). Millions of people swear by PayPal; however, check out the negative comments at www.paypalsucks.com, or just type "hate paypal" into a search engine and make up your own mind.

You can get money sent to you by Western Union, and it can be picked up in a matter of minutes at 2,700 telegraph offices or 400 Electra department stores, which are open from 9 A.M. to 9 P.M. Western Union charges the sender a flat fee of about $30 for up to $1,000. However, your recipient is charged a fee at the other end that can amount to about 10 percent. It's fast but expensive.

Bank of America and Wells Fargo have relationships with Mexican banks and transfer billions of dollars to Mexico annually.

The whole process is a lot easier than it used to be.

TRANSFERRING MONEY

If you wish money to arrive through a bank or to a different destination other than the consulate, it is important that you know what wire transfer companies exist and the cost of their services. There are several wire transfer businesses or bank services to send money to people in Mexico. Some of them are Ace America Cash, Armed Forces Bank, Bank of America, Bank of the West, Check In–Cash Out, Dinero Seguro, International Money Exchange, Money Gram, Order Express, Valuta Corporation, Wells Fargo Bank, and Western Union. All of these companies charge between $10 and $30 to send amounts of up to $300 to Mexico. The money may be available in a time frame ranging from fifteen minutes to one day, depending on the type of service requested.

To send the money, you must contact the company directly. You will need a completed application, the money, and an official form of identification. To collect the money, the person will also have to present an official form of identification.

The Mexican government offers a monthly updated consumer's report on wire transfer companies through PROFECO. You may contact them free of charge from the United States at 877-868-8722 or from within Mexico at 01-800-903-1300, or you may check their Internet page at www.profeco.gob.mx.

In emergency situations only, if you wish, money may be sent through the consulate. The most secure way is by establishing a Department of State trust fund. This service is available *only* to U.S. citizens on an emergency basis. Through this, depositors establish a trust account in a recipient's name in order to send funds overseas. Upon receipt of these funds, the department authorizes disbursement to the recipient from the appropriate U.S. embassy or consulate. Overseas Citizens Services Trust (OCS) takes approximately one working day and funds are disbursed in local currency. The State Department has a $20 processing fee for this service. The forwarding of funds will be delayed if the sender fails to provide the recipient's overseas location. There are several options to make these arrangements.

Sending funds by Western Union: If the sender has a major credit card, he or she may telephone Western Union at 800-325-6000 (or 4176). Likewise, they may tell the local Western Union office that they wish to purchase a money order for the desired amount, plus $20 (State Department's fee), made payable to the Department of State. A message with the sender's name, address, and telephone number, as well as the name and overseas location of the recipient, must accompany the money order. Western Union charges a fee based on the amount sent. The money order and message are sent to: Overseas Citizens Services, Department of State, Washington, D.C. 20520. Funds are normally received electronically at OCS within several hours. The Department of State has a Western Union check writer in their office and an officer is available to receive funds during business hours.

Sending funds by bank wire transfer: It may take one to three days to process a bank wire transaction. If the sender chooses this option, they must tell the bank that they want to wire the desired amount, plus $32 to: Nations-Bank, Department of State Branch, 2201 C St. NW, Washington, D.C. 20520, at 202-624-4750, via ABA number: 114000653; account number: 7476363838; account name: Pupid State Department; Special Instructions: OCS/Trust for Benefit of (Recipient's Name), U.S. Embassy/Consulate (City, Country); and include the sender's name and telephone number. The wire instructions must include the recipient's full name and overseas location. NationsBank notifies the State Department when funds are received. The $32 fee includes the $20 Department of State fee and NationsBank's $12 wire fee.

Sending funds by overnight or regular mail: The sender obtains a cashier's check or money order for the desired amount, plus the $20, made payable to the Department of State. A letter must be attached with the sender's name, address, and telephone number, as well as the name and location of the overseas recipient. Mail to: Overseas Citizens Services, CA/OCS, Rm. 4811, Department of State, 2201 C St. NW, Washington, D.C. 20520. Regular mail can take seven to ten workdays before it is received, and even overnight mail may not reach the department for several days.

Important notice to those who receive funds at the consulate: To request funds from a trust account, office hours are between 8 and 11 A.M. The person collecting the money must present a government-issued form of identification. If the person collecting the money is other than the recipient, a written request specifying the name of the person authorized to receive the funds from the recipient to disburse the funds will be required. Should you have any further questions, please do not hesitate to call the American Citizen Services Section of the U.S. consulate in Ciudad, Juarez, at 011-521-613-1655.

Bancomer has a deal so that you can transfer money from U.S. post offices in California and Texas to their 2,400 branches in Mexico.

Wells Fargo has a deal with Banamex whereby someone in the United States opens an account for an annual $10 fee and then pays $10 for each wire transfer. Banamex automatically opens an account for the recipient. The transfer can take from a day, which is unlikely, to five days at the outside.

A simple bank-to-bank transfer can vary in cost from $25 to $45 and take between one and three days.

My personal advice while you are just traveling around, looking for your spot to land, is to take about $600 in cash, $1,000 in traveler's checks, and use the ATM card for anything else. Don't bother with the aggravation of a bank to change money. Use a *casa de cambio*, or exchange house (similar to a *bureau de change* in Europe). These independent businessmen have stands in every town of any size; find one that does not charge a commission. In small towns, I have changed money at hardware stores and pharmacies. On the road, I have gotten varying rates at Pemex gas stations.

Need more help? If you need more guidance about moving to or working in Mexico, you can call me at 888-234-3452. I make a living from offering these services, so only call if you are serious and willing to pay me for my time.

FOOD

EATING OUT

> *Eating out in Mexico can cost about 30 to 50 percent less than it does in the United States, or it can be the same as Stateside prices.*

I don't care what some people say about how it is cheaper to eat out in Mexico than cook at home. The same people say the same thing in the States and Canada; they're just making excuses for not cooking. It is always cheaper to eat home-cooked meals, but it is cheaper to eat out in Mexico, in general, than in the States or Canada.

If you want to eat out a lot, do so and enjoy it for the company and variety, but don't think you are saving money versus cooking at home. Some gringos insist that they can eat out more cheaply in the States; they're right and they're wrong. You can get inexpensive buffets of dubious quality here. Shoney's and International House of Pancakes have breakfast specials, but you'll get better quality and more wholesome food at restaurants in Mexico for much less than comparable restaurants in the States.

WHAT FOOD COSTS

Food in Mexico used to be one of the great bargains. It still can be, but only for select items. You can expect to pay 20 percent less for food in general. If you're a vegetarian, you can live on practically nothing. Fresh vegetables are not only really fresh but dirt cheap, by our standards, especially if you buy from local farmer's markets. Beef is more expensive (though some cuts can be cheaper). Better quality cuts will cost you much more. Pork is about the same price as in the United States. Flour is more expensive, since it has to be imported. Staples such as cooking oil, butter, spices, etc., are less expensive. Eggs and milk are more expensive. Seafood is cheap (compared to U.S. and Canadian prices). If you're a pistachio lover, you'll think you've died and gone to heaven.

I have to have espresso and cigars. Coffee is a bargain, if I am comparing it to fresh-ground coffee back home. Cheap Mexican coffee is still way cheaper than fresh-ground in the States.

Vanilla

Vanilla is sold by the quart and is only a few bucks. The alcohol content varies from 2 to 25 percent. Labeling laws are, shall we say, loosely enforced in Mexico, so there's no way to know the first time you buy a brand what it contains. There used to be a danger that Mexican vanilla was distilled using coumarin, an ingredient in rat poison. Now, for the most part, that isn't the case, though I can't swear that every little factory has eliminated this practice. The best vanilla comes from Veracruz state and the best of the best is made by Orlando Gaya Hijos in Gutierrez Zamora, Veracruz.

Is Mexican vanilla pure vanilla? I used to think so, but, according to www.vanilla.com/html/facts-mexican.html, I was wrong. All I know is that I buy a quart or two a year of various brands and have been using it on my ice cream for years and haven't died or turned into a rat (though there are probably some ex-girlfriends who would disagree).

The Costs of Sin

Booze is a bargain, except at restaurants. There you'll pay about what you do in the States. Canadians, however, will think they've died and gone to alcohol heaven. You'll be able to drink more for less in Mexico than you could even dream of in the States or Canada. Mexicans think all gringos drink, so you will be overwhelmed with "welcome margaritas" at hotels, restaurants, and public affairs.

Mexican cigars are not cheap. I can buy them through mail order from Thompson's in Florida for about one-third what I pay in Mexico. Mexican cigarettes, even name brands such as Marlboro, are much less expensive in Mexico than here.

Sadly for smokers, nonsmoking prejudice is catching on. While you can still smoke openly without fear of a nonsmoking militant dousing you with water (as happens in the States), you can't smoke everywhere. I was in the Mexico City airport, proudly smoking a legal Cuban cigar, when a lady cop came up and informed me that smoking was prohibited. I said, *"¿No estamos en México?" "Sí,"* she replied, *"estamos en el México Nuevo."* I went into the bathroom and found all the employees smoking up a storm. In Mexico, there is always a way.

Another sad (in my opinion) effect of *Mexico Nuevo* is that in heavily gringoized towns, gringo landlords will only rent to nonsmokers. I've yet to see a prohibition against renting to drunks.

I've included a chart with representative prices of many items on pages 16–19. These prices will change, but they will give you an idea of what your second biggest expense is after rent or mortgage payments.

You can get updated prices for darn near everything in Mexico from the government-run PROFECO site, www.profeco.gob.mx/html/inicio/inicio.htm. It's in Spanish, so go to the left-side menu, click, *"Consumor informato,"* then *"Quién is quién en ... "*, and then *"los precios"* from the side menu. Next, go to *"Precios Minimos y Maximos,"* then *"Seleccione Ciudad."* Then pick a city. You'll get a drop-down menu of major items. These prices are what you'd pay at large grocery store chains such as Soriana, Gigante, Comercial Mexicano, and the government-run ISSTE stores. Smaller, locally run stores will be pricier, but also offer more of a social experience (including the best gossip), in addition to providing foodstuffs. They will vary slightly, according to your area.

An expat-run Web site, www.mexconnect.com, also has a market basket of goods on their site. You have to pay a membership fee to access it.

Sam's, Wal-Mart, and similar stores are, of course, the cheapest of all sources to buy things, especially imported goods.

But, whenever possible, I like to buy mangoes, papayas, and locally grown produce from little stands along the highway. I once bought three mangoes for a couple of dollars and the lady didn't have small change, so she gave me two mangoes change. Ah, Mexico!

COMMUNICATIONS

There have been huge improvements in this area since the last edition of this book. Now you can actually get a *new* phone line! For those of you who have been around Mexico for a while, this is revolutionary. However, you can only get a new phone line in a new house.

Getting a new phone in a new place is no longer a matter of lighting candles to the Aztec phone god, making early Christmas gifts to the local installer, or making a stop at the Telmex office (the national phone service) to plead as part of your daily routine. Instead of waiting months to get a phone, it is a matter of days or weeks, at the most. Old-timers have been dazed by the speed of installation. Second, there are alternative long-distance carriers. Third, you can get Internet service, either dial-up or high-speed, bundled with your phone service, billed on the same bill. Fourth, the public phones now are more likely to work than those in the United States, and there are more of them. Fifth, callback or call-around services can cut your long-distance bill to a fraction of what you used to pay.

One casualty of this progress has been the *casetas de larga distancia*, long-distance offices, which used to be plentiful in every city, hamlet, and truck stop. They still exist in small communities, but are a vanishing breed. In times of yore, you could have a real human operator place a call or send a fax for you. Doesn't that take you back in time?

The cheapest way to keep in touch with folks back home is through the Internet.

What is still true is that the phone number and service are still tied to the previous resident (if you rent or buy a place that had a phone), so the same caveats from the previous editions still apply. Before you close the deal, visit the Telmex office to make sure you aren't inheriting thousands of pesos of calls to someone's Uncle Enrique in Los Angeles.

If there is a phone at an existing home you are renting or buying, make sure the bill is paid. Otherwise, you will end up paying for expensive calls to Tio Miguel in Los Angeles, California.

Pulse dialing is now mostly (except in isolated villages) a thing of the past. Millions of kilometers of fiber-optic cable have been laid throughout Mexico.

Every area code in Mexico changed since the last edition; there's no guarantee that they won't change again tomorrow. When Telmex changes area codes, the last people to know are those living in a community. To verify whether an area code is still correct, go to this nifty Web site: www.cft.gob.mx/campana/regiones.html#.

TELEPHONE SERVICE

Good news on phone service!

Phone Cards

Prepaid phone cards are required to use public phones and Telmex cards are available just about everywhere (including from my Web site; click "Phones" to order), from convenience stores to gas stations. Rates are about $0.50 a minute to the States. Calling home is far more expensive if you are using a calling card, such as one from AT&T, MCI, or Sprint.

With so many companies offering phone cards in the United States, I should warn you that *they are not all reputable*. There have been cases where their rates were higher or they had inadequate switching facilities. Buyers beware. One way they gig you especially is to offer a $0.01 or so a minute rate, but with a $1 to $5 connection fee!

Dialing Protocols

Mexicans will always give you a telephone number with "01" as the first two digits. This is the code to dial long-distance inside Mexico. To dial into Mexico from outside, you must dial "011," for international access, then "52," the country code for Mexico, then the area code, then the local phone number.

Area codes—they are a' changin'.

Area codes changed nationwide to three digits, just as in the States and Canada, except for Guadalajara (33) and Monterrey (81). However, all numbers throughout the country are now ten digits. To get an up-to-date list of area codes, you can go to my site or www.cft.gob.mx/campana/regiones.html#.

Cellular Phones

There are some choices in cellular companies, but Telcel remains the dominant company with the most reliable service. Reliable is relative, however. Expect more dropped calls than back home. In tourist areas, such as the beach resorts, the service seems to be better. There are also frequent confusing promotional deals, just as there are back home. Service has become cheaper than it was a few years ago, but prices change frequently. A rule of thumb (depending on the size of your thumb) is about a peso a minute for promotional plans (during off-peak hours). That said, most Mexicans go with a pay-as-you-go plan, rather than "X" minutes a month. Considering how complicated it is to keep up with your cell phone bill in a country where they speak your language, this probably makes the most sense. Just figure that a Mexican cell phone call will cost you somewhat more than in the States and always more than you expect (ever hear of roaming?), and make sure you understand the maps of coverage. Additional minutes are about three times your plan minutes.

I ran into a problem trying to get a Mexican cell phone when I was a movie mogul with MTV. It seems that unless you are a resident, many cell phone companies won't sell you service. While you are traveling, you will have to get one of the alternative cell phone plans listed on the next page. Your U.S. or Canadian cell phone will work in Mexico, but it will cost you. Make sure you understand how much before you leave, or you may have to sell your house at home to finance your cell phone bill when you get back.

Many U.S. and Canadian cell phone companies now offer coverage inside Mexico. But again, before you go, make sure that you understand the rates, or you might have to mortgage the kids when you get back home.

There is a service by Gorilla Mobile that lets you call Mexico from your cell phone (while still in the States) for about $0.15 a minute (www.gorilla mobile.com). They charge an annual $5.95 fee and $0.15 to connect.

One way to cut your costs is to send brief text messages, or SMS. The receiver doesn't pay for the message. Someone in the United States could actually send you a text message from his computer without it costing either of you a nickel. At the moment, this is only available from Telmex.

You can use your Blackberry in conjunction with your cell phone and get Global Positioning System, or GPS, information with Telcel as well.

Cellular Abroad offers cell phone rentals for about $30 a month, or you can buy the phone for about $190 (www.cellularabroad.com). From inside Mexico City only, incoming calls are free and about 2.2 pesos (U.S. $0.20) a minute from outside D.F. For the rest of the country, it costs about 4.10 pesos (U.S. $0.37) to get a call from within Mexico and 6.10 pesos (U.S. $0.60) to make one. Calls from outside Mexico are 13.50 pesos (U.S. $1.22) a minute. Calls to the United States and Canada are about 14.50 pesos (U.S. $1.31) a minute. This is certainly the most sensible way to have cell service while making your exploratory trips.

Some other companies are Iusacell (www.iusacell.com.mx), Telcel (www.telcel.com), Telefonica Moviles (www.pegasopcs.com.mx/), and Unefon (www.unefon.com.mx/). For a complete listing of cell phone providers, there are a couple of Web sites that offer a comparison of quality and service for major companies, www.cellular-news.com/coverage/mexico.shtml and www.cellularabroad.com/mexicocellService.html.

When calling even a local number from a cell, you have to input the area code.

Callback Services

If you already have your home in Mexico, a callback service makes the most sense for you. There are several companies that offer this, but they all work the same way. You call a phone number in the United States, let it ring once, and hang up. There is no charge for this call. The company's computer calls you back and asks you for the number you're calling. The call is placed from the United States and billed in six-second increments after the first thirty seconds. The best company I've found for this is aitelephone.com (www.aitelephone.com/callback.html). It'll cost you from $0.12 to $0.22 a minute, depending on the location, to call either Canada or the United States. It costs $0.12 from Mexico City, $0.17 from Puerto Vallarta, etc. The $0.22 figure is for all other areas besides major cities. There are no minimums or monthly fees. You can call Canadian or U.S. toll-free numbers as well for the same fee. You can prepay if you don't have a credit card, or use a credit card that can be billed as you use the service. There is a Federal Communications Commission charge (currently $0.35) for calls to pay phones, however.

Another option is the Globalphone Corporation (www.gphone.com). Rates are $0.17 to the United States or Canada. They also offer a toll-free number service so that you can get calls from customers worldwide while based in Mexico. Rates run from $0.17 to $0.23 per minute.

Voice-Over Internet Protocol (VOIP) Choices

And, of course, there is always Voice-Over Internet Protocol (VOIP). While there are companies that sell special phones that do seem to work better than the monthly services, the companies recommended below work quite well (about 95 percent of your calls will be crystal clear). Having used them myself, I would say that they are a lot better than cell phones and often have better sound quality than my landline, but there are times when you'll miss a few words from the person you are calling. Essentially, you pay a flat fee of about $20 to $30 a month (depending on the company) for unlimited calling. Not all VOIP providers have service to and from Mexico, so check it out. You must have a broadband connection to use VOIP. Also, there is a wrinkle to having just a VOIP phone that the advertisements don't tell you plainly. They currently do not work with fax machines (sending or receiving) or credit card charge machines. The companies below told me that they are working on the issue and expect the issue to be resolved "soon"; maybe they meant *"mañana."* I have Packet8 in the States and have to keep a local line for faxes. The local line is the most basic service available and costs me about $10 a month. If you don't need a fax machine at your home in Mexico, this is not something that will affect you.

VOIP is excellent as your local and long-distance phone, with this caveat: If the broadband service in your area (see below) is not dependable, your VOIP phone won't be either. If you really need to depend on your phone for business calls and are in an area where broadband isn't dependable, get a Telmex local line and a VOIP phone for long-distance calls. If you need a fax machine, you *have* to have a landline.

The best service in terms of reliability and call quality is Packet8. I use it myself and know many expats who have switched to it from Vonage, which is the granddaddy of VOIP phone services. For about $19.95 a month ($10 a month less than Vonage), you can have unlimited calling to the States and Canada and a U.S. phone number for your family to call you. Their in-country rates are quite reasonable. If you have a business, they have a $39.95 monthly plan that offers tons of features but requires a special phone. I recommend switching to VOIP before leaving your home country, so you can make your calls to Mexico at reasonable rates of $0.03 to $0.05 a minute. (Please see www.mexicomike.com and click "Phones" to order.)

Many expats still use Vonage (www.vonage.com). They were the first VOIP company and are currently doing a lot of advertising in the States. They cost $10 more per month than Packet8. Their reliability is not as good. I've gotten calls from expats using both services and Packet8 wins hands down.

Two services recommended by Roy Dudley in Jalapa, Veracruz, are Stanaphone (www.stanaphone.com) and Dialpad (www.dialpad.com). He called me on the Stanaphone connection and the connection quality was good, though we had some disconnects. He told me that he calls all over the world and usually doesn't have this problem; maybe it was the Galveston end of the connection.

Fax Machines

Even with the advances in phone services and the Internet, I still suggest you get a fax machine that prints on plain paper. It will double as a copy machine, and while living in Mexico you seem to need several copies of everything. If you're doing business, you have to have one. Mexican businessmen consider a fax more "official" than e-mail, and it is more dependable. This is the most reliable way to communicate, and it is cheaper than calls back to the States or Canada since you can send your faxes in the middle of the night and they are usually shorter than conversations.

With the increased reliability of phone lines now, you can pretty much expect your fax to go through. A few years ago, you had to follow up with a voice call. But do turn on the "confirmation page" feature, just to make sure. One thing that has not uniformly changed is that many Mexican companies still use their fax line as a voice line, so often you'll have to call and ask them, *"Quisiera el tono de fax, por favor."* Many people have told me that fax/modems are not as reliable as a stand-alone fax machine; this is also my personal experience. You should have no trouble getting a fax machine through customs, provided it is not in the box and looks a little used. (Spit on it or get your kids to put greasy fingerprints on it.) As is the case with all electronics, fax machines are a bit more expensive in Mexico.

I personally prefer a stand-alone fax machine for receiving calls. You will also need it to send a variety of documents, so get one, even if you have a fax/modem.

COMPUTERS AND THE INTERNET

The problems with the Internet and Internet access alluded to in the last edition are essentially all solved now. You can get dial-up service from Telmex for about an additional $20 a month almost anywhere, and high-speed (DSL) access for about $50 a month. Add taxes of 15 percent to those prices. Prodigy is still the strongest Mexican Internet provider; the DSL service is called Prodigy Infinitum. To set it up, call (within Mexico) 01-800-123-2356. Push 1, then 2. Ask for an English-speaking operator. (In Spanish, say *"Por favor, quiero un technico a quien hablas Inglés."*) Expats tell me that the best time to call is Monday through Friday between 6 P.M. and midnight. The reason (and this could change) is that they currently have a staff of six fluent English speakers who come on at 6 P.M. You'll have to add about $150 to $200 for installation and their modem/router.

I have to tell you that the reliability varies, depending on where you are. In some areas, especially smaller towns or places such as Cozumel, the "always on" feature seems to be "almost always on."

If you have trouble with your Prodigy connection, here's a tip: They have seventy-two hours to fix it. If that doesn't happen, report them to PROFECO. It'll take a week or longer for you to get an appointment to explain your complaint.

Some people still swear by satellite systems. They do seem to have a better connection, but not when it rains; then they seem to go into a hydrophobic mode. Again, this varies according to the location, so check with others before making a decision. There is a larger up-front cost to a satellite system.

Cable Internet connections are available through MegaRed (www.megared.net.mx). Users have told me that sometimes it is good and sometimes not, depending on your location. They're only available in major cities. You have a choice of connection speeds and options (and pricing). Residential pricing is as follows: For 64 KBPS, it runs about $20 a month; 256 KBPS for up to four computers is about $30; 1024 KBPS is about $40 for an unlimited number of computers; and 2048 KBPS, for an unlimited number of computers, is about $130. Add 15 percent tax to all of the above. Business pricing for the above services is $45, $60, $90, and $220 monthly.

Just as in the United States and Canada, there are fewer and fewer local Internet service providers, or ISPs. They may provide some extra services, however, so check them out.

Protect that DSL modem as well as your computer!

Whatever you do, be sure to buy a good surge protector and/or a UPS (uninterruptible power supply) for your computer. They're available in Mexico, though you'll pay a bit less if you buy one in the States. Isotel makes good ones and they are reasonably priced. Some of their models even guarantee protection against lightning strikes. They have a lifetime guarantee for damage of your computer equipment for up to $100,000. For now, however, this does not apply outside the United States and Canada.

Don't forget to protect your DSL modem. Power surges through the phone lines are more common in Mexico than here. Don't just get one of those cheapie power outlets. You need something that has instantaneous response time and a 1,500-joule (or better) spike suppression. Get one with modem protection (for dial-ups or DSL, whichever you have). There are few three-pronged outlets in older houses in Mexico, so get an adapter at a hardware store that converts three prongs to two. They're available in Mexico too, but even though I've bought several, I have never been able to remember the Spanish to ask for them.

Even today, power outages and brownouts occur, as does dropping power followed by a surge. Many people use surge protectors for their TVs, stereos, and VCRs as well. It is certainly a wise precaution. Be sure to back up your hard drive religiously. You can get many computer supplies in the larger cities. Mexico is a very technocratic society.

MAIL

This is one area that is still changing slowly. Mexican mail service is still slow and unpredictable. Most Mexicans pay their utility bills in person for that reason. You should too. You can do so at some chain stores in Mexico, particularly the conglomerates owned by Carlos Slim Helu, one of the richest men in the world. Since he owns Telefonos de Mexico, Prodigy, Sears, Sanborn's (in Mexico, no relation to the company in the United States), and a host of other companies, you should be able to find a Slim store near you.

You can also pay most of your bills on the Internet today, so take advantage of that. You can certainly pay your U.S.- or Canadian-based accounts over the Internet, and by all means do so.

If you want something to get where it is going and not take an extended vacation to Chiapas or Chihuahua, send it (within the country) by Estafeta, DHL, FedEx, or one of the other major courier services. UPS has a small presence in Mexico, improved since the last edition. Ask other expats whom they trust. You can also send it by Mexpost, a service of the Mexican Postal Service. I have used it nationally and internationally and have been amazed at the speed with which my packages have been delivered. (Maybe I should have said "pleasantly" amazed.) If you are sending a large package, use the bus system to get it anywhere within Mexico. However, this will only get it to the border, so this is impractical for packages to the States or Canada.

Most gringos use a mailing service to send letters to the States, where they are brought to the U.S. border, then put into the U.S. Postal Service system. Every city with a sizeable gringo population has one or two. The likelihood of your correspondence arriving before you get any more gray hairs is worth the extra cost.

Don't let your mail take a trip to Sri Lanka.

If you are sending mail to Mexico from the States, put the *codigo postal,* zip/postal code, *in front of the town where it is going.* Putting it at the end almost guarantees that some of it will embark on a journey to Sri Lanka or deepest Africa—no foolin'. (A note on addresses: C. P. stands for *codigo postal.* When addressing an envelope, it is better to use the abbreviation than to spell it out.)

Don't forget to put "MEXICO" in caps at the bottom of your address.

For mail sent within Mexico, put the *codigo postal* where it usually belongs. Until you get an address, you can have mail sent to you in care of yourself at the *lista de correos*, or general delivery. Have your correspondent write your name, "*lista de correos*," *codigo postal*, city, state, and MEXICO. Be sure to write "*correo areo*" on the envelope for airmail. Be sure to write "unsolicited gift" on the outside so your receiver does not have to pay duty. Expect that the package will be inspected. I have had mixed luck sending packages back to the United States.

For getting mail to and from the States and Canada, most towns with any gringo residents have a mail drop where you can deposit your mail and pick it up. These businesses have couriers who run to the States regularly. They are your best bet for paying bills and keeping up your correspondence. If you can arrange to have your bills paid directly from your U.S. bank account and have your checks deposited there, that is the best bet. For communicating with the folks back home (if only to "dig them" [which in Spanish slang is *chingalé*, although it really has a much worse meaning, so be careful when using it] about the wonderful weather you are enjoying while they are shoveling snow-drifts), use the Internet.

Chapter 2
THE TECHNICAL STUFF
MEDICAL CARE AND
INSURANCE COVERAGE

This information has expanded enough to warrant its own section in the new edition. It could be just that I am getting older ("not old!," he screams, with shortness of breath—SOB in medical terminology—how appropriate) and am finally paying attention to my feeble attempt to live longer.

Here's a big caveat: I am not a medical or any other kind of doctor, shaman, or healer, and never have been a pharmaceutical salesman (unless you count that time in the sixties). The advice here is a general guide. While I've consulted medical professionals and tried to take their advice (take two aspirin and get a real job), absolutely nothing I say should be taken as medical advice. Your physician is your best source of information. That said, I do believe that there is some good information here that will help you understand the plusses and minuses of medical care in Mexico.

Medical care will cost 40 to 70 percent less in Mexico.

For those of us without health insurance, medical care is one of the big plusses in moving to Mexico. You will find doctors and dentists and hospitals to be a good deal less expensive (on average, from 40 to 70 percent less expensive) in Mexico, but you will have to pay for them yourself. There are special insurance policies for expatriates (see below) and insurance is available from large Mexican insurance companies, as well as the national health plan, the National Hospital Insurance System, or IMSS. Which one you choose depends on what you can afford and what you believe. Some expats swear by IMSS, other swear at it. (See below.)

Medicare and your average U.S. insurance company will ignore your claims incurred while living in Mexico. There is a provision in American Medicare that states it will consider your claim if *"You live in the United States and the Canadian or Mexican hospital is closer to your home than the nearest U.S. hospital that can treat your medical condition regardless of whether an emergency exists."* That would not do any of you living in Mexico any good, but it might explain why some people say they have been reimbursed by Medicare for services in Mexico: They were (or were able to prove) that they were just tourists. Some Medicare supplemental policies do offer coverage outside of the United States, but you had better check the fine print before depending on them.

You'll find many English-speaking physicians throughout Mexico. Some have done their residency in the United States or Europe, and those who have will have an excellent command of English and of our culture.

Your doctor will have the time to get to know you.

Although this varies from doctor to doctor, just as it does in any country, local practitioners are often less rushed (can you say "HMO"?) and are able to devote more time to being with their patients. Most of your appointments will be longer, and Mexican doctors will have the time to talk to you about your life in general and get to know you as a person. The experience is often more rewarding for the patient.

Even in small towns, good *medicos* are available. Although they may not speak English in small towns, I have had good luck with them (see story below). However, let me be frank (no, wait, I am still Mike, this is just my Frank persona), there are also some bad doctors. In a small town, ask the richest-looking businessman you can find who he uses. That's no guarantee, but it stands to reason that the best doctor in town charges the most, though some pretty good doctors are altruistic and treat poorer patients. And sometimes there may only be one doctor. In that case, your decision is made for you.

Are you better off getting treated for a serious condition in Mexico or returning to the States? Ask your doctor and take the advice in *Mexico Health and Safety Travel Guide*. I cannot overemphasize what a good book this is and how valuable an addition it is to the resources for anyone traveling or living in Mexico.

True, most doctors' offices don't have as much modern medical equipment as you may be used to, but patients are referred to local clinics or hospitals that are usually well equipped for lab tests, MRIs, and more advanced procedures.

Although this is less true now than it was for the earlier editions (and not true for hospital-based physicians), a few doctors still make house calls, but this is getting rarer and rarer, especially in big cities. The ones that do still make house calls (which cost $25 to $50, depending on the location) are very good.

A doctor's visit will range from about $25 to $60 on average (although my friend in Chapala says his doctor charges $100 an hour and is worth it), depending on the location. In gringo towns, doctors who specialize in treating expats will be at the higher end of the scale. Some reasons for the lower costs overall are the lack of malpractice insurance (which bothers some people—if a doctor makes a mistake, there is no recourse), less paperwork, and, therefore, less overhead.

Medical care a big plus for moving to Mexico.

The accessibility of advanced medical care in Mexico has improved tremendously during the past few years. Cardiac care has improved to the point that there are now more than fifty hospitals that can perform cardiac catheterization to open-heart surgery. Angioplasty can also be done. Some hospitals can perform transmyocardial laser revascularization. (This information was provided by Dr. Efrain Gaxiola-Lopez, interventional cardiologist at the Hospital Bernadette, Guadalajara, as interviewed in *Mexico Health and Safety Travel Guide.*)

Dialysis is another example. A few years ago, I would have told you to be wary of living in Mexico if you require dialysis, based on my Mexican friends who came to McAllen, Texas, from Mexico for treatment. But now you will have no problems in the major cities of Mexico.

INSURANCE COVERAGE

INSURANCE IN GENERAL

Some hospitals, such as the ABC Hospital in Mexico City and others in large cities (and even a small hospital in Lake Chapala), offer private insurance. Some U.S. carriers will cover emergency treatment, but not routine medical care. Grupo Angeles is a large nationwide chain of good Mexican hospitals.

Some folks have told me that their Stateside insurance will pay claims incurred in Mexico, but these insurance companies are very specific about what paperwork they accept and then only pay a part of the claim.

Insurance Services of America has a great deal with both medical insurance and emergency medical evacuation (401 N. Alma School Rd., #9, Chandler, AZ 95224; Phone: 602-821-9052 or 800-647-4589; Fax: 602-821-9297; www.worldwidemedical.com). Global Medical Insurance offers major medical coverage on an annual basis for about $1,000 a year for a fifty-five-year-old single, and $2,000 a year for a couple in the same age range (www.solutions abroad.com/a_healthinsurancemexico.asp).

Another medical insurance provider is International Insurance Group, Inc. (www.internationalpro.com). They offer a variety of products at reasonable rates.

For a variety of expat or travel health insurance providers, see www.medtogo.com/preparation/pg-health_insurance.asp.

U.S. INSURANCE COVERAGE

If you have a high deductible on your insurance policy, you may find out that it is unlikely you will ever reach it, unless you are really seriously ill. I would never advise anyone to drop their medical coverage, but you should make sure that it will pay off for you. You should also consider that you may elect to return to the States for treatment, and then, brother, you'd better have some kind of coverage. Check with your insurance carrier before you go.

Air Evacuation Policies

In my opinion, the best and most affordable company offering medical air evacuation is SkyMed. While the other company I mention has a fine reputation, SkyMed does not quibble about evacuating you. Most company policies read that you must be evacuated to the "nearest medical facility that can effectively treat your condition," SkyMed simply takes you "home," which is wherever you want to go. Their philosophy is that you should be treated by your family physician and be surrounded by your family in the event of an illness or accident. Of course, if it is medically preferable to go to the closest facility in Mexico, then that's a medical decision. Otherwise, you go home. SkyMed is only one company that offers repatriation of your pets, should you need medical air evacuation. Their service begins the day you specify and is effective as soon as you are 100 air miles from your home, so they protect you on your way to Mexico. You can sign up on www.mexicomike.com. Click "Heath" and you will see "Air Evac." If you don't have a computer, their contact info is SkyMed International Inc., 4425 N. Saddlebag Trail, Scottsdale, AZ 85251; Phone (United States and Canada): 888-234-3452. A one-year policy (for an individual up to seventy years of age—they also cover those over seventy at a higher rate) costs $156, plus a $48 application fee. They also have daily rates for short-term trips at about $6 a day. A family can be covered for $300, plus a $48 application fee. Unlike the company mentioned below, Medex, they do not charge more for expatriates. A family plan includes two adults (marriage not a requirement) living at the same address and any children under twenty-four years of age, even if they are in school away from home.

Another excellent international medical air evacuation plan is available from Medex (1447 York Rd., Ste. 410, Lutherville, MD 21093; www.medex assist.com). Their TravMed policy includes emergency medical care and medical evacuation. The cost (for an individual up to seventy years of age—they also cover those over seventy at a higher rate) is $225 a year ($350 if you are an expatriate). They do not have a family plan. Each person costs extra. Two people will pay $450 a year ($700 for expatriates). Daily rates are about $5 a day per individual. Many auto insurance companies also offer air evacuation insurance to their customers.

There are also a lot of unscrupulous outfits that offer great deals but don't pay off. Frankly, you are better off getting one of the companies above for the same price and knowing what you are getting. Please investigate thoroughly before you spend your money for any medical or air evacuation plan. Ask how long they have been in business, get references, and check with the state they are licensed in, as well as with other expatriates.

Medicare Supplemental Insurance
The authors of *Mexico Health and Safety Travel Guide* have this advice for Medicare recipients: "We suggest that you apply for a Medicare supplement called Medigap. For more information on a Medigap policy that includes foreign travel emergency coverage, call 800-633-4227 in the United States."

Hospitals Affiliated with the United States
Cima, in Hermosillo, is owned by a U.S. company and has strong affiliations with Baylor University. Several hospitals in Monterrey are affiliated with Texas hospitals and some of their best students train in the United States and then return. Amerimed has hospitals in Puerto Vallarta, Cancún, and Cabo San Lucas.

CANADIAN INSURANCE COVERAGE

Health Canada touts the portability aspect of their coverage, but I haven't met a Canadian who got reimbursed, except perhaps for an occasional 8 or 9 percent.

Medipac International offers out-of-country insurance (180 Lesmill Rd., North York, ON, M3B 2T5; Phone: 416-441-7070 or 888-633-4722; www.medipac.com). Rates vary and are on their Web site. For coverage for up to $1 million in comprehensive emergency medical benefits, a person age fifty-five with a $1,000 deductible would pay Can $415 for a 183-day policy (183 is the limit Canadians can stay out of the country and not lose their Health Canada benefits). Ontario and Newfoundland residents can purchase up to 212 days. Annual policies are available. Benefits include emergency medical evacuation and are endorsed by the Canadian Snowbird Association. They have relationships with hospitals in Mexico, and, in most cases, can pay the hospital directly. Both lower and higher deductibles are available. The coverage is good in the United States, as well, or anywhere in the world.

MEXICAN INSURANCE COVERAGE

You should also consider getting medical insurance from a Mexican provider. A Mexican friend (age fifty) said he is very happy with his coverage that costs about $2,000 a year for unlimited coverage, from hospital stays to doctor visits—although one forty-three-year-old man claimed he got a quote of about $400 a year with a $1,000 deductible for a similar plan. Some of the largest insurance agencies are Seguros Tepeyac, Grupo Nacionál Provincial, and Seguros Monterrey Aetna. Their rates vary greatly, so shop around. If you are over sixty-five, they won't cover you, and if you get coverage under that age, you'll be dropped at around age seventy-five. The rates for insurance coverage are a fraction of what you'd pay in the States or Canada—probably about one-third. A forty-two-year-old man got quotes from $200 to $400 a year for pretty good coverage.

The National Hospital Insurance System (IMSS)

The National Hospital Insurance System, or IMSS, is available for holders of FM-2s and FM-3s (see pages 69–77) for more information on these permits). It costs (currently) $340 a year, and there is a waiting period of six to nine months. You can only apply between January and February or July and August. There's a bit of bureaucracy to the application process. However, there is no medical exam. Once you are in, you're in, as long as you pay the annual premium. Once accepted, you have to go to an IMSS hospital or clinic. For detailed information about this service, see www.medtogo.com/preparation/pg-health_care_system.asp.

There are drawbacks to IMSS coverage. If you don't speak Spanish, you're likely to have problems. Although some of the IMSS doctors do speak English, it's more likely that they won't, or will only speak limited English. You do not get to choose your doctor, so you will probably see a different one each time you go. Normally, there are a lot of people waiting to be treated and you'll wait a long time. The doctors are under time constraints, so your exam is likely to be a lot shorter than if you saw the same doctor in private practice. When I have to use the emergency room for treatment while living in the States, it's a similar situation. Unless I am bleeding profusely (I've thought about getting those pill wrestlers and actors use), I can count on a five- to eight-hour wait to see a physician. Sometimes that's true in IMSS hospitals and sometimes it's faster. You're dealing with government bureaucracy, which is seldom a leisure-time activity most people look forward to.

Some gringos get both private and IMSS coverage. IMSS is everywhere. In an emergency, they know they can get treatment. They don't mind the wait. If they're in a hurry, or dissatisfied with the IMSS treatment, they go to the private doctors. I don't know, it seems like overkill, but I've talked to enough expats who do this to include the option. You decide.

TREATMENTS AND COSTS

It's possible to pay similar prices to what you'd pay in the States to visit some private clinics and doctors in Mexico. Some general practitioners charge $100 or more an hour. Some clinics charge $200 per visit.

Should you need to make an emergency visit to a clinic in a small town, you'll probably pay about $20 to get a hand stitched up. The clinic doctors will do the best they can. However, please have the wound looked at by a doctor in a larger town as soon as you can. My friend, the musician Joe "King" Carrasco, cut his hand in a small town badly enough to need stitches. A local clinic fixed him up and he went on his merry way. He needed more advanced care to avoid nerve damage. He has spent many hundreds of dollars in the United States trying to get his hand back to normal so that he can play the guitar.

You can avail yourself of inexpensive medical care by joining IMSS. It costs $255 a year. Applications are accepted in January, February, July, and August. There is a six- to nine-month waiting period.

Malinchismo

Why do rich Mexicans come to the States for medical care? A Mexican friend of mine explained it this way.

"Let me explain you about hospitals these days. There are really good hospitals with magnificent doctors that manage kidney transplants, etc. I don't know the reason why many Mexicans travel to Houston to get treatment. I have many doctors in my family, and they have told me that many patients they have in Monterrey will, instead of getting treatment in Monterrey, go to Houston for treatment, and most of the time the same doctor treats them but charges U.S. dollars. This might sound stupid, but maybe they will show their society that they can afford to get treatment in the USA.

I guess that it is more like cultural things, that people think that things are better outside of Mexico. We call this malinchismo, *when people don't trust national things. But we do have great hospitals in Monterrey, Mexico, D.F., Guadalajara, Saltillo, Querétaro, etc. A really big hospital chain in Mexico is called Grupo Angeles, which has several hospitals around Mexico.*

I had a Mexican friend who was dying of cancer. He was rich. He had insurance. He came to the States to be treated. By 'living' in a bubble room, and [receiving] other treatments, his life was extended for perhaps six months. Oddly enough, when his health insurance ran out, he was told that there was nothing more the doctors could do for him."

LAB TESTS

Lab tests will cost about one-third of what they do here. The work is generally good. I know many people who swear by them and have no desire to spend three times as much back home.

DENTAL CARE

Dental work is absolutely fantastic. Many "winter Texans" and snowbirds flock to Mexican dentists across the borders from Texas and Arizona to have everything from fillings and cleanings to plates and dentures done. Dental care, in particular, is a bargain: The cost is less than half of the cost in the United States, though ask around for a recommendation. I went to one dentist who said I had seventeen cavities; she also mentioned that she was helping her daughter through dental school—I guess I was the scholarship of the day. I went to another and found out I had gingivitis. In any border town, dentists and pharmacies are the two most popular businesses. I find it worthwhile to drive several hundred miles just to get my own dental care done on the border. A filling costs about $20; X-rays cost about the same. A root canal ranges from about $300 to $500. Bridgework and dentures cost about one-third what they do in the States.

A wife of a dentist in Chihuahua told me "Like all dentists, some charge more than others do. My husband is an orthodontist here and he is American Board Certified and got his degree at LSU [Louisiana State University]. Braces here are less expensive, $1,500 compared to the $5,000 you will pay in the States."

A number of Mexican physicians have trained in U.S. or European hospitals. Some U.S. doctors have trained in Mexican medical schools, notably in Guadalajara. Mexican doctors are more prone to diagnose by feeling and touching and (remember this?) actually listening to you, rather than by automatically requiring extensive lab tests, but they do order tests when necessary.

DISABLED PERSONS

If you are physically challenged, you'll find living in Mexico, well, a challenge. Except in cities such as Mexico City, Guadalajara, and Monterrey, there is very little accommodation for people with disabilities. Yet there are probably more people in wheelchairs or blind people in Mexico than in the States and they get by, about the same way people did in the States twenty and thirty years ago. My one temporary experience of having a broken foot (small potatoes to one who is wheelchair bound) caused me to interview several Mexicans with mobility issues. They told me that, yes, they'd heard that the United States was easier to navigate than Mexico, but that they had talked to Americans who told them that they preferred Mexico, even with all its shortcomings.

What my wheelchair-bound friends tell me is that there are some plusses. For one, you are treated with respect, not ignored or pitied. And while it may look hard to access many buildings, Mexicans will appear out of nowhere and lift you and your chair to wherever you want to go. The reason is one of culture. Many Mexican families have a family member with some challenge, so they are more used to, and more understanding of, those with disabilities. Whether this will compensate for your decreased independence or mobility is a very personal decision.

Street crossing is rarely facilitated for the blind. Invariably, a Mexican will help you cross when it is safe. The streets are cobblestones in many places; sidewalks are narrow and uneven. Steps abound and wheelchair ramps are the exception, not the rule. Bathroom stalls (except in newer hotels and tourist attractions) are seldom wide enough to accommodate wheelchairs. Entrances to shops and older public buildings are too narrow to accept chairs.

NURSING CARE

Nursing care in hospitals is still less than perfect. Try to have a family member get instructions from the doctor on what follow-up care is needed and have them there to make sure his orders are followed.

If you have serious medical conditions that require special equipment, it is now possible to get comparable care in Mexico. This has been a major change since the last edition of this book. In fact, there is a book, *Mexico Health and Safety Travel Guide* by Drs. Robert and Curtis Page (Meditogo Publications), that lists nearly 200 English-speaking, mostly board-certified doctors and credentialed hospitals in forty vacation destinations in Mexico. The Web site is www.medtogo.com.

A Personal Story
I had some kind of forgotten ailment during a trip. It was a fiesta day in Acayucan, a small crossroads town. The only place I could get to was a Red Cross office. The nurse was fairly competent and gave me a shot and recommended I get another in a couple of days. My companion hadn't the slightest interest in sticking a hypodermic in me (probably a good thing), so, a couple of days later, while we were on the Gulf Coast road near Esmeraldas, we pulled into a doctor's office on the side of the highway. It was a real doctor, and although he didn't speak English, he was quite intuitive. I got poked, then we started talking. He had an interest in locally prevalent skin infections, but didn't have a good

camera. I had an extra Nikon. I felt good about helping him out and doing good for a community. I made a friend for life. That's the kind of thing that can happen in Mexico, if you are open to the possibilities.

BLOOD TRANSFUSIONS

I regret to say that the likelihood of tainted blood is greater in Mexico than in the United States, Canada, or Europe. Personally, if I were in a life-or-death situation, I would get one. But if I were scheduling surgery, I would request that my blood come from donors I knew.

DRUGS

LEGAL

For some people, the lower cost of medicines they need is a good reason to move to Mexico. If you pay one-half what you pay here for the same medicine, that effectively gives you 25 percent more money to spend on enjoying life instead of being an indentured servant of the pharmaceutical companies. So enjoy those margaritas, cases of mineral water, and visits to the symphony or jazz clubs on your drug company!

Drug prices are, theoretically, controlled by the government. You'll see a price stamped on each bottle. These recommendations are routinely ignored. On the border, in larger cities, and cities with a large gringo population, prices are often discounted. Then there is often an "immediate" discount for buying from that store. Seldom (but it has happened) have I seen drugs sold for more than the recommended prices. Be sure to ask if there are any *descuentos especiales* before you buy. Be absolutely certain to check the expiration date of any drugs you purchase.

The largest national pharmacy is Benavides. Chains such as Sanborn's, Gigante, Auchan, and others also have pharmacies in them.

Almost all drugs you are used to are readily available from the same manufacturers that produce drugs in the United States and Canada. Some have plants in Mexico, though most drugs seem to be produced in Puerto Rico. You will also see drugs not available in Canada or the United States that are imported from Europe.

But not *all* drugs are available in Mexico. On your scouting trip, bring an adequate supply of drugs you need to take. Take them to local Mexican pharmacies and verify that they are available in Mexico. Then find a physician and discuss your medical needs and whether moving to Mexico is a viable option for you.

You don't generally need a prescription for most prescription drugs, although the instructions on the package will say, "Dosage: Take according to your physician's recommendation." What's really cute is that these drugs have written plainly on the side, "Available by prescription only." That's Mexico. The bureaucracy has been complied with, and people do what is expedient. Most prescription drugs generally cost between one-quarter to one-half what you are used to paying in the United States. One thing I should warn you about is that the dosage in Mexico is sometimes different from what you are used to—they may have higher concentrations of the main ingredient, for example. Creams are often combined with different ingredients than what you got back home.

Concentrado de *sheep dip?*

For instance, I use a cream for my psoriasis. The same cream is available in Mexico. However, instead of a 0.5 percent concentration of the active ingredient, there was a 2 percent concentration. Since this was going on a sensitive spot on my anatomy, I declined. While I have never actually seen this on a label, I have sometimes felt that some ointments and creams contain *concentrado de* sheep dip as a major ingredient. Just because a person has on a white coat doesn't mean they are really pharmacists: so does the guy who cleans the elephant cages. There are great bargains on drugs in Mexico, but you also have to be aware and do your homework.

Getting the wrong dosage or combination of drugs for psoriasis is unlikely to be life threatening. However, one physician advised me that he has known of cases where insulin was sold in the wrong dosages. That is serious. It's your life, use diligence.

For an updated list of the costs of medicines in Mexico, go to www.profeco.gob.mx/html/precios/queretaro/medics.htm. This happens to be for the city of Querétaro, but it's a pretty good source. (You can choose from several other cities as well.) It's in Spanish, so go to the left-side menu, click, "*Consumo informato,*" then "*Quién is quién en.*" Then choose "*los precios*" from the side menu, then "*Precios Mínimos y Máximos,*" and then "*Seleccione Ciudad.*" Then pick a city. You'll get a drop-down menu of major consumer items; choose "*Medicinas.*" (At present, there's an easier way, just choose "*Quién is quién en los precios,*" on the front page, but this may change.)

Viagra, Claritin, and Generics

Viagra and other erectile dysfunction drugs ("not that I personally use them," he said macho-ly) are available over the counter and cheaper than in the States. However, a medical evaluation should still be called for. These drugs can be dangerous when taken with some heart, high blood pressure, or prostate (talk about mixed messages) medications that contain nitrates. They come in different dosages. If you want these medicines, buy the larger dosage and cut it in half. In the old days, this wasn't always a guarantee of getting half a dose, but doctors have assured me that today's medications are well mixed.

Oddly enough, you may be asked for a prescription to get this type of drug (or so I have been told—okay, I actually did buy some once). Don't despair. Just keep going to other pharmacies and you will get it.

Pharmacies in larger cities are less picky (although several pharmacies in Toluca didn't seem to think I needed it, though I suspect that it had something to do with cultural preferences. My Toluca fiasco may also have had to do with not knowing the dosage. I said I wanted 100-milligram pills. Talk about an inflated, er, ego).

Please, be aware that Viagra (and other erectile dysfunction drugs) can cause severe problems or death if taken with drugs containing nitrates. Doctors are inexpensive in Mexico; your life isn't. Please see one before taking Viagra on your own.

Not all drugs are cheaper. Claritin (which I admit to taking) is more expensive than in the States. But it's cheaper in New Zealand, even with postage to the States. Now that it's available over the counter in the States, the generic versions are cheaper here than in Mexico. Things change.

This brings up generic drugs, which are relatively new in Mexico. I've tried them; I don't necessarily recommend them. A Mexican pharmacist and a Mexican doctor told me that the standards for their production are more lax than for name brands. My own experience has agreed with this. You can't count on the dosage being the same. Those who use it tell me that Viagra in the generic form is a waste of money.

What you can do, however, is buy a bottle of the generic and a bottle of the name brand. Then, if it is not something that will harm you by missing a dose or make you sick by taking too much (Claritin, for instance), take the generic, and it if doesn't work, switch to the name brand. Some bottles will be fine; others will be weak. I have never found one that is too strong, but it could happen. Use your better judgment and ask for advice from others who take the same medication.

Frankly, what many people do to save money on drugs in Mexico is to buy the double dose, then cut the tablets in half. See the caveat from a physician below.

A Caveat about Cutting Pills in Half
Dr. Page, coauthor of **Mexico Health and Safety Travel Guide,**
thought it was important to insert this caveat: "Many newer brand names are extended-release tablets that have a timed release system based into their layers. Cutting the pill in half may cause immediate absorption of all the active ingredients and leave nothing for later on. A good rule to follow is that if the tablet is scored, you can cut it in half. Many other meds that are not scored can also be cut in half. Consult with a doctor. I wouldn't advise consulting with a pharmacist, generally. Some know what they are talking about and some don't."

So, generalizations, such as the ones in this chapter, can get you (or me) into trouble. I'm not a medical man, and although I've taken pains (no pun intended) to obtain accurate advice from those who do know, it's always best to spend a few bucks and ask a medical doctor.

AIDS Medications
Many of these drugs are now available in Mexico. There are private clinics

(mainly on the border and in big cities) that purport to specialize in AIDS treatment. Many are rip-offs. Be very, very careful. Ask for recommendations, and then take them with a grain of salt. One physician told me that he wouldn't trust any medical care from a provider whose main clientele came from American tourists unless that provider was recommended by someone he knew and trusted.

AIDS is considered a "gay gringo disease," so be prepared for some preju-dice. (And, as far as prevention, in the old days Mexicans told me not to depend on Mexican brand condoms. They recommended buying U.S. and European brands, which are more expensive. Whether the Mexican brands are of a lesser quality, I can't say for sure. I do know that all public schools in Mexico have implemented a sexuality course and am sure that they recom-mend the national products.)

Cancer Clinics

There are many private clinics that claim to treat and cure cancer. Many times the "medicine" is either a placebo or a well-intentioned herbal treatment. While I do believe that herbal medicines have value, I wonder about these clinics. Some people have told me that their cancer was cured by Mexican clinics. Obviously, those who died cannot tell me a thing. What have you got to lose? Your money. But if you have exhausted all available means and want to try, perhaps you'll get lucky. If nothing else, the rationale is that they offer hope. My opinion is that it is false hope.

Controlled Drugs

You can get some controlled drugs over the counter in Mexico. Since they are addictive, use some common sense. If they've been prescribed for you by your physician, that's one thing. If you're just looking to have a little recreation, that's another.

Don't try to bring them back without a U.S. prescription. You will be busted. Antidepressants are readily available, at half U.S. prices. Although some people swear they have bought codeine, my opinion and personal expe-rience is that it takes an act of *Dios* to get it. Most physicians even will not prescribe it, and some have told me that it is not even available in Mexico (I doubt this). I was dying from a cough (okay, well maybe it just felt as if I was dying) and went to a physician in Cabo San Lucas. She said she could not prescribe a cough medicine with codeine. When I have dental work done in Mexico, dentists prescribe the equivalent of Aleve. To get a real pain pill, I have to have a doctor or dentist on the other side of the border. Here's my opinion on why the "dangerous" drug of codeine is so hard to get in Mexico:

Generalissimo Antonio de Lopez de Santa Ana (1794–1876) is prob-ably responsible for this. He was the general defeated by the Texans in the battle for Texas independence from Mexico. He was, at one time, a democratically elected president of Mexico, but he decided that Mexico was not ready for democracy and declared himself dictator. One of his faults was that he was a codeine addict. Some say that is why he lost half the country. My belief (not supported by any factual evidence) is that this is why codeine is not available in Mexico.

A Drug by Any Other Name

I know that many thousands of gringos cross the Mexican border to get medicines. And it would seem encouraging that the *Physicians Desk Reference (PDR)* is sitting on the pharmacist's counter. After all, you can read about the side effects yourself and make your own decisions, right? Wrong, *kimosabe.* Consulting with a physician in Mexico is not a big expense; getting the wrong combination of drugs can be deadly. A pharmacist may suggest an alternative drug to the one you're taking, saying, "It's just the same, only better (or cheaper)." Stick with your physician's recommendations, whether he's from home or Mexico. I've tried to read the *PDR* and tend to skip over the big words that I don't understand. The problem is, those big words may make for big trouble. And things change. New drugs are taken off the market on a regular basis because new side effects are discovered. The *PDR* is published annually and the one in the pharmacy may be years out of date. Trust a person, not a book.

If you take a lot of prescription drugs, you could save a fortune buying them in Mexico. But use common sense.

Just make sure that you are getting the exact dosage and combination of drugs you need and that your doctor prescribed. If you want to gamble, go to Vegas. I'm a gambler, and this is one area where I play it safe.

To find out if drugs you need are available in Mexico, the best source is the official consumer protection agency of the Mexican government, PROFECO (www.profeco.gob.mx). You won't find PROFECO through a search on the Internet for medicines in Mexico, but you will find several online Mexican pharmacies.

Speaking of the Internet, be wary of these online Mexican pharmacies. I will not recommend any of them because of my personal prejudice, but you can find them by doing a search for "pharmacies + mexico," and see what they have to offer. I did some comparison shopping for antibiotics and found their prices to be considerably more than what I paid in Mexico. Unlike online U.S. and Canadian pharmacies, they don't require a prescription, however. Whether you can actually get drugs delivered is subject to change and to the whims of our respective governments.

Tropical Medicines

If you want to know what's up with tropical diseases, you can go to www.istm.com or www.cdc.gov. The first site has listings of specialists in all fifty states who are up on tropical diseases. The latter is somewhat alarmist. For the most part, unless you're adventuring into the jungles of Chiapas, you don't need to take any special precautions (though obviously that can change if an epidemic occurs, so check the sites and work with a physician who knows). It's better to buy the medication you might need for something than to take the chance on it not being available when and where you need it.

I do know of at least two diseases you should take preventative steps for. Dengue fever (colorfully and correctly called "bone-break fever") is a lot more common than you would expect. The pesky mosquitoes that carry it seem to love me (I hear it's the female that bites: That explains it). I've had it three times. The first was in Puerto Escondido and I was too cheap to get a doctor; I toughed it out—I do not recommend this. When you move, even the slightest bit, it feels as if you are breaking a few bones. My landlord brought me chicken soup, but it didn't seem to do much good. The second time was in Teácapan when I was being interviewed by *The Wall Street Journal* (yeah, I'm famous, and that and a dollar will get you a cup of coffee). Fortunately, the reporter left just before my willpower was overcome by the symptoms. I holed up in Tepic and saw a doctor. The last (?) time was in Cancún. I holed up in a nicer hotel.

The other is West Nile virus. We Texans don't have an exclusive on this one; it's in other states and Mexico too. The prevention for both of these is pretty simple. Always use mosquito repellent with deet. Wear long-sleeve shirts and pants when possible.

ILLEGAL

Don't. I know that those of you who want to use them will, but try to focus (as hard as that can be when you want to get high) on the fact that if you get caught, you will immediately go to jail and be found guilty. There are drug checkpoints on every highway and the enforcement officers use dogs. Your chances of getting caught and prosecuted are greater in Mexico than in the United States—even for small amounts. I know of one case where a trio of college students was arrested for having too much Valium they had bought legally (with a Mexican doctor's prescription) at Mexican pharmacies. If you do get caught, see if you can resolve the situation immediately *(mordida)* with the cops before they take you to jail. If not, do not start shelling out money to a jailhouse lawyer recommended by one of your keepers. You have the right to contact the U.S. or Canadian consulate and you should do so. Although the consular officer will not get you out of jail, he or she will give you a list of recommended lawyers. They are more reputable than most.

PERMANENT VISAS

TOURIST CARDS AND VEHICLE PERMITS

Some people can be confused about visas. First of all, you don't need a visa to travel to Mexico as a tourist. You need a tourist card, called an FM-T. It is no longer free (except in Sonora). Although the cost of it varies according to the peso and does go up periodically, it will set you back about $25 (that's today—the cost will only go up). Sonora has a "Sonora Only" tourist card that you need to get, and, theoretically, you need a tourist permit for Baja, but the enforcement of this rule is sporadic at best. If you are traveling for seven days or fewer in the rest of the country, you don't need one. Technically, you can only be a tourist in Mexico for 180 days out of 365. Technically, and often practically, if you try to return to Mexico after your 180 days are up, you will be told to go home.

It used to be that you could get as many tourist cards as you wanted. Now, thanks to computerization, the government can keep track of you (conspiracy theorists, unite!). They keep a database of everyone who enters and for how long, therefore you should be careful about how much time you request on your tourist visa. Don't ask for 180 days unless you need them; otherwise, you might not get back in for a year. Get a few days extra, to allow for the unexpected, but don't get more than a week's extra time if you want to come back again soon. Be sure to turn your tourist card in, either at the airport (where the ticket agent will insist that you do) or at the *Migracion* office near the border. Finding these is always a challenge, but worth it.

If you're moving to Mexico, but (the same as me) can't get an FM-3 because you can't prove enough income, all is not lost. There is a way around this, but I don't feel comfortable putting it into print. (You do run the risk of not being able to get back into Mexico if you return home.) Things change and I don't want you to blame me if you get thrown into the *carcel.* A service I offer for a fee is to consult with you over the phone (888-234-3452) for current ways to get around this challenge.

Your car permit is a different story. *Hacienda* (the tax man) keeps real good track of these. A car permit will cost you about $37 now and will probably cost more when you read this (it went up while I was writing this edition). You have to pay by credit card (Visa, MasterCard, American Express, or Diners). You need the title or registration and a notarized letter of permission to take it into Mexico if it is financed. Be darn sure you turn this permit in before leaving Mexico. Otherwise, the next time you come, if it is expired, you'll have to pay a pretty stiff fine. (See the chapter on driving for further details.)

That said, some people have told me that they didn't turn their permit in and got back into Mexico anyway. Others have told me that they were detained at the border. Still others had to pay a rather large fine. *Hacienda* states that the penalty for not turning in your car permit is $33, plus $5 a day for each day it has expired. There are ways around this, but, again, I don't feel comfortable putting them into print. As mentioned above, a service I offer for a fee is to consult with you over the phone (888-234-3452) about loopholes (if there is one for your situation—there may not be). It's better to be safe than sorry.

The maze of visas.

FM-3 VERSUS FM-2

The state of Sonora has lightened up on FM-3s. Their requirements, especially for starting a business, are considerably less stringent than anywhere else in Mexico. You can even get information from their Arizona tourist offices.

Do not rush into getting a permanent visa. Live in Mexico for at least six months as a tourist before deciding if you want to move there and obtain one. The requirements listed below are subject to change, and they probably will, although they have been pretty consistent for the last few years. In recent years, the Mexican consulates in Canada and the United States have been quite helpful with updated information. A caveat, however: Prices for some visas have gone up 60 percent since the last printing. Others have gone up a lesser amount. Don't ask me to pay the difference if they cost more. Of course, if they cost less you can always send me a check, or take your spouse out to dinner.

THE ADVANTAGES OF AN FM-3, OR *VISITANTE-RENTISTA*

An immigrant document known in Mexico as an FM-3 may be applied for by an American or Canadian citizen residing in the country. The advantages of having FM-3 status are mainly that you do not have to leave the country every six months as you do on an FM-T (tourist permit), and that you may also keep your car in Mexico without returning it every six months. (Note: Periodically, there are some miscommunications between *Migracion* and *SCT*, or local *Transito* officials. These are really a pain for expats, but they happen. The rule stated above is correct.)

Most people get an FM-3. Although it does not entitle you to become a resident of Mexico, an FM-3 allows you to do just about anything an FM-2 does. Should you opt for the FM-2, there are limitations on how many times you can leave Mexico during the next five years. (Both of them have to be renewed annually, but at the end of five years, you can apply for permanent status.)

This is the official explanation of what an FM-3 will do for you, from an official Mexican government Web site:

Current Mexican Immigration Law includes an immigration status for *"Visitante-Rentista."* This law applies to those foreigners who wish to reside temporarily or permanently in Mexico as pensioners and live on funds or pensions brought from abroad, or on any other permanent income obtained from Mexican fixed interest–bearing securities. Such persons are not entitled, however, to engage in any remunerative activity in Mexico. A foreigner meeting the requirements may acquire retiree status for a year, which must be renewed on a yearly basis. After five years, the individual may apply for permanent resident status as an immigrant.

Household Goods

A person with retiree status may take his/her household goods into Mexico duty-free by obtaining a permit from the Consulate nearest their place of residence. This permit must be obtained when bringing the goods into Mexico but no more than six months after the retiree's first entry. The *consular fee* is equivalent to $120 in U.S. or Canadian funds.

You must present a list of your household goods that details the electrical household appliances by label and serial number, along with a letter addressed to the Mexican embassy stating your last address and, if possible, your new address in Mexico.

Note: When bringing your goods into Mexico, everything has to be on a bill of lading. If there is even one item that is not listed, your entire shipment will be delayed. And please, please, please do not pack guns, ammunition, drugs (including legal drugs), plants, or your cat. I'm serious about the cat. I've known people who have tried to illegally immigrate their cats in a packed box and it was a mess (no pun intended).

"Household goods" can mean anything that goes into a house. I knew one man who owned a small hotel in Mexico and wanted to import his millions of dollars of antiques. It just wasn't going to happen through regular channels. However, when he declared them as "household goods," they zipped right through customs and on to Cuernavaca.

Technically, if you leave Mexico without renewing your FM-3, your goods are supposed to leave with you.

You cannot rent a U-Haul or trailer your own goods into Mexico. You'll have to hire a service that does the hauling for you. There are several out there, but only one that I feel I can personally recommend without hesitation, Cetra Relocations. They're based in Mexico City, but can help you move anywhere in the Republic. I consider the general manager, Jesus Garcia, a friend and a straight shooter (Within Mexico Phone: 01-152-555-261-4390; Fax: 01-152-555-261-4310; jesus.garcia@cetra.com.mx; www.cetra.com.mx). He is extremely knowledgeable about all of Mexico, honest, friendly, and goes way beyond the call of duty to help make your move to Mexico a good experience. One thing Cetra makes sure of is that only one carrier handles your household goods from start to finish. I personally know people who used other services with multiple freight carriers and it was not a pretty picture. When things didn't arrive, or were broken, it was always the other guy who was responsible. Don't let that happen to you, even if you don't use Cetra.

Other Advantages

I've talked to expats and government officials who swear thàt, unless you pay an import tax, you will have to renew your car permit every six months. Others (including government officials and other retirees) say you do not have to renew your car papers. That's the way I read the law. They say that your car is legal as long as you are. They tell me they have been stopped by cops or *Hacienda* officials and have shown them their FM-3s and been told they were okay. At the moment, gringos are being stopped and their cars impounded in the Guadalajara area. That will be ancient history by the time you read this, but it could happen there or somewhere else in the future. These things happen from time to time.

My advice? It may depend on your locality. Because this is subject to change (and perhaps interpretation), you should find out what other expats recommend while you are in country. What is without question is that you can come and go (even without your car) for as long as your FM-3 is valid.

If you own property, there are additional advantages. Once you have your FM-3, you are given a six-month period to bring in any personal possessions, including household furnishings. After that initial six-month period, your importing is extremely limited. Requirements for FM-3 status vary slightly from Mexican state to state (although one obtained in your home country is valid in the entire Republic. My advice: Check at home first and go with the method that suits you better) and you should check with the local immigration office to see exactly what your state requires.

The following guidelines are for the state of Guanajuato where San Miguel de Allende is situated. These are as of April 2004. A renewal may be applied for up to thirty days prior to the expiration and at least two weeks beforehand. (The FM-3 cannot be renewed outside of Mexico).

FM-3—Canada and the USA

HOW TO GET AN FM-3 FOR AMERICANS AND CANADIANS

The Short Version—
Obtaining an FM-3 in the United States or Canada

The short official version of what you need to get an FM-3 in the United States or Canada follows. Note: The current requirement of $1,000 income, single ($1,500 for a couple), has fluctuated from $1,000 to $1,200 ($1,500 to $1,800 for couples) during the past several years. Use it as a guideline and check for the current requirements.

To download the two-page application, use these links. For a complete list of Mexican consular offices in the United States, go to www.nafinsa.com/consulatedir.htm. For a complete list of Mexican consular offices in Canada, go to www.embamexcan.com/DIRECTORIES/DirectoriesSubMconsul ates.shtml. Click on your city on the map to get the address and phone numbers.

All documents requested must be originals and notarized; photocopies are not allowed.

- A passport valid for at least one year.
- An application form, either typed or clearly printed (available online or at the consular office).
- Two identical passport-sized frontal photographs (1.05 sq. in.).
- Proof of financial resources. Income must be equivalent to $1,000 per month, per applicant, plus $500 per dependant.
- United States: Consulate offices in the United States insist that you must also provide a letter from the bank or financial institution that must state the source of your monthly income, which, minimally, should be $1,000, plus $500 for each dependent. The letter must also specify how the money is going to become available to the applicant(s) while in Mexico. It must be notarized.
- Canada: Documents accepted as proof of financial resources (bank statements showing monthly interests, a social security letter, or pension receipts). The documents submitted must be notarized.
- Pay the consular fee.
- United States: Pay the consular fee of U.S. $126, either with cash or money order, payable to the Consulate General of Mexico in (your town). Personal checks and credit cards are not accepted. (Some U.S. offices insist on cash just as in Canada.)
- Canada: Pay the consular fee of U.S. $127 in Canadian funds (cash only). (This amount covers the migratory card and the visa fees.)
- A health certificate issued by the family doctor, typed on the doctor's stationery, stating that the applicant is free of any contagious diseases. Must be notarized.
- A police clearance letter, issued by the applicant's local police department. Must be notarized.
- (Unofficial) If you are divorced, provide proof, especially if your name is different from the one on your birth certificate.

FM-3—Mexico

The Long Version—Obtaining an FM-3 in Mexico

I'm indebted to Sherry McFarlane of San Miguel de Allende for this current information about obtaining an FM-3 in Mexico. (She does folkart tours of Mexico that are head and shoulders above anyone else's. Contact her at mexfolkart@hotmail.com.) The differences between getting an FM-3 in the States or Canada versus in Mexico are in bold. The cost of obtaining an FM-3 in Mexico is about the same as in the States or Canada. You do not need a lawyer to get your FM-3. In many areas of the country, the *Gobernación* officials speak English. However, as Sherry suggests, it's probably worth hiring someone to help you with the forms.

- Step 1. You must obtain a letter of solvency from the nearest U.S. consulate **(N/A in your home country)** or a local bank. This letter must state that you have at least U.S. $1,000 in monthly income, plus $500 per dependant, from various sources. Sources can include social security, retirement income, investments, etc. As long as money is flowing into your bank, it doesn't matter where it comes from. A copy of statements of those sources used for your solvency must be included. Be sure to then make a copy of the letter for your files if needed later on.

- Step 2. You will need to obtain what is known as an SAT 5 form from a local solicitor **(N/A in your home country)**. This form assures that you have paid the fee necessary for processing. You then take this form to a local bank and pay the required fee, currently Mex $1,038 (roughly U.S. $98). This is returned to you marked paid for submission to the *Migracíon* offices.

- Step 3 (a multipart step). Make copies of the last three months of your bank statements **(six months in your home country)** to verify that you have income coming into that account. You will need a complete copy of your U.S. or Canadian passport, including all pages and your current visa. If it is a renewal, you will need a complete copy of your current FM-3.

You are required to show that you have some permanency in Mexico, such as your most recent property tax statement and a copy of your utility bills in your name **(N/A in your home country)**. If you are renting, you will need a letter from your landlord stating that you are renting and paying "X" in rent monthly, and for how long. If the utility bills are not in your name, the letter must state that although they are in the name of so-and-so, you, by name, are paying them and are the responsible party.

You will also need a letter stating why you wish to live in Mexico. This is a very precise instrument and can be written up by a notary or a man usually located near the immigration offices. **(In your home country, ask the Consulate what they require to be in it.)** It must be typed and contain certain information you will be asked for.

Finally, you must have a *solicitud official.* This is a form from the immigration office that you will fill out stating exactly what status you are applying for and if it is a change from the last time you applied. If it is your first application for an FM-3, the procedure is more involved, including questions about your parents' names, what color hair and eyes you have, in Spanish (they had fun with reddish blonde and hazel), and even your thumbprint. They will help you with this form. If it is your initial application for an FM-3, you must also present three pictures **(two pictures in your home country)** taken by a local photographer in the exact size needed.

- Step 4. You submit all of these papers, photographs, and forms, along with your original FM-3 (if it is a renewal), and they will give you a form to pick up the new papers in approximately two to three weeks **(this could be as fast as forty-eight hours in your home country)**.

If you need to leave Mexico for some reason during this time, you have to apply for permission **(N/A in your home country)**. A departure application form must be filled out, along with a new SAT 5 form, and paid for in the amount of Mex $231 (about U.S. $22). This must be presented one week before your departure date and picked up three days before you leave. Failure to do this can prevent you from boarding your plane!

In most Mexican cities, there are local people who can help you get your FM-3 **(N/A in your home country)**. They can take you through the whole procedure step by step, and usually cost no more than $50; be careful of any who want to charge you more than that. Once you have your new FM-3 status, breathe a sigh of relief that you no longer have to leave the country every six months but can stay indefinitely, as long as you continue to renew it!

Working in Mexico? What visa is right?

BUSINESS VISAS

There are many different flavors of FM-3s. For short business trips, get a free *visitante representante comercial* at the border or airport, which is good for thirty days.

If you are going to be there longer, or repeatedly, get the FM-3 business visa, *visitante hombre de negocios.* Apply to any Mexican consulate. You'll need a letter on your company letterhead, addressed to the consulate general of Mexico, saying why you are going, how long you will be there, and that you will receive no salary while in Mexico. (Obviously, this doesn't mean you don't get paid at home, so don't let your bookkeeper try to skip your paychecks while you are gone.)

You must apply in person at a Mexican consulate and present a valid passport, good for at least six months; two passport-sized pictures; a letter of credit from your bank; and a copy of your business license. Then you have to fill out an application form at the consulate. The FM-3 business visa is valid for one year and costs $96, payable in cash, whether in the States or Canada. It entitles you to conduct business meetings but not to work or earn wages in Mexico.

TECHNICIAN OR ENGINEER FM-3

If you are invited to Mexico to repair, maintain, or install machinery (this includes computers), train or advise personnel, or to take tools or machinery into Mexico, you've got to fulfill all of the above requirements, plus pay a fee of $156, as well as have a letter from the Mexican company requesting your services.

VISAS FOR STUDENTS, MISSIONARIES, AND OTHERS

The other types of FM-3s are *visitante: transacciones comercial, inversionista* (investor), *profesional, cargo de confianza, dependiente familiar, artista* or *deportista, consejero* (consultant), *estudiante, distinguido* (I will never get one of these), and last but not least, *ministro de cultura.* People traveling through Mexico to Central America need a *transmigrante visa,* or FM-G. You only need to know about the last one if you are traveling expressly to Central America, particularly if you are bringing a lot of stuff with you. (So, if you are taking a car to sell in Central America, technically you need this. If you are moving to Central America, you definitely need it.) Requirements for this change, but you can expect to pay a fee of at least $200 and can only get it at the border. You no longer need to produce a police letter stating that you are not a criminal and your car is not stolen. (The U.S. border cops got fed up with the extra paperwork and the camps of Central Americans waiting in their cities. They convinced the Mexican government that it wasn't right for them to do their work. Score one for the gringos.)

FM-2—Is it for you?

An FM-2 (*inmigrante rentista*) is similar to a green card, or resident alien card. It entitles you to many of the rights of a Mexican citizen (except voting) and entitles you to work. Officially, you must live in the country for five years, without working, and then make a *declaratoria de inmigrado,* and if it is approved, you can work. You will automatically receive this visa after five years of having an FM-3, if you also apply for it. It has certain drawbacks, such as only allowing you to drive a Mexican-plated car and a limitation on the time you can be out of the country. You must make an application to the Delegacíon de Gobernacíon. Most expats have told me they avoid getting this visa and go for the FM-3.

Student Visas

You've got to have a valid passport, two passport photos, a letter from a Mexican school authorized to accept foreigners, and a letter (notarized) from your parents proving you'll have at least $300 a month income while in Mexico.

Missionaries

Missionaries need a special visa.

You must have a special visa that entitles you to preach at a specific church. If you are caught preaching without one, you could be deported, at the worst, or asked to leave town, at the best. To get it, you must apply at a Mexican consulate, present the same documentation as for other visas, and provide a letter from the church where you are going to preach. Also, I might mention that you should not plan on bringing down a lot of clothes or medicines unless you are willing to pay the customs duty on them. Periodically, the government goes on an antimissionary crusade. It's enforced differently at different border crossings. Sometimes you can't take a bus with your church name on the side. Sometimes you can. Check with someone you know on the border to find out what's going on at the moment. Charles Nelson of Nelson Insurance, in McAllen, Texas, insures a lot of missionaries and always knows the ins and outs of your situation. Contact him (800-638-9423; www.nelson travelinsurance.com).

Need more help? If you need more guidance about driving through, moving to, or working in Mexico, you can call me at 888-234-3452 or e-mail mexicomikenelson23@mexicomike.com. I make a living from offering these services, so only call if you are serious and are willing to pay me for my time.

Chapter 3
WORKING and LIVING in MEXICO
WORKING IN MEXICO

This section contains advice for those being transferred by their companies, those who want to start their own businesses, and those who want to work for Mexican employers. Perhaps you've been "downsized" by your company. If you have gotten a good-sized severance package, maybe you would rather "retire" early where it will cost less to live. The possibility of working in Mexico exists, though it will take perseverance and determination. I don't want to encourage anyone to drop out, but if you feel as if you've given it your best shot and aren't getting anywhere, what have you got to lose?

Many of you move to Mexico not to retire, but to start a business, because you were transferred by your company, or because you want to work for a Mexican company. First, I'd like to discourage a couple of groups of employment seekers. Then I'll get into who should work in Mexico and how you can do it. I'll also give you some cultural clues so you won't make a fool of yourself when doing business.

BAD IDEAS

OPENING A BAR
About half the calls I get for consulting are from people who want to start a business in Mexico. Many calls on Monday come from someone who wants to buy a bar after spending a weekend in Mexico. Gee, I wonder how that came about? If that's your idea, take two Alka-Seltzer, wait until Wednesday, and if the idea still seems good, call someone else.

WAITING ON GODOT, ER, GRINGO
Another group that calls is those who want to work as waiters, bartenders, or cooks. Save your nickel. Here's some free advice: Don't even think about it. I know, you just got back from Cancún or Vallarta and met a gringa or gringo who was doing just that. Chances are there is more to the story. There's probably a love interest involved, though it may be one-sided. And, she (or he) is working illegally. You cannot move to Mexico and take jobs away from Mexicans. Period. Before you start howling that it isn't fair, that Mexicans move to the States and take jobs away from Americans, think about it. Without getting into the debate about whether they are taking jobs at salaries that our citizens

won't take, the reality is that they are working illegally too. In Mexico, the unemployment rate is horrific or else Mexicans wouldn't have left their families to come to the States. Mexico is a lot more serious about enforcing their labor laws. Actually, money sent back to Mexico from the United States is the third largest source of income for Mexico (behind petroleum and tourism) and makes a couple of billion dollars for U.S. firms (and the USPS) that transfer the money. So, political rhetoric aside, there are economic interests at work here that keep this cycle going.

HAVE TOOLS, DON'T TRAVEL

Skilled craftsmen, such as carpenters, plumbers, mechanics, or those with any connection to construction work (except architects and designers), should forget it. Mexicans have those jobs sewn up. However there always seems to be an exception lurking somewhere. I consulted with a skilled carpenter. He wanted to start his own business in Mexico. He was able to land a job with a Mexican/American company building houses in Puerto Peñasco, Sonora, based on his experience and expertise. From that basis, he learned how to do business in Mexico and eventually started his own business. But this was Sonora. This plan might also work in Baja, if you have the right connections. In general, though, I don't recommend you even think about it.

RUB-A-DUB-DUB

The last group that seems to want my help is massage therapists. They've got a shot. There are many spas in Mexico that cater to foreigners and they are able to legally hire massage therapists. But be aware that the jobs don't pay much, there is tremendous turnover, and tips are not usually generous. I know. I ran a spa reservation business for years.

COMPANY TRANSFERS

If you work for an international company that transfers you, the hard part will be done for you. Your company will have to get an FM-2 or FM-3 for you, which gives you permission to work in the country. While technically the FM-2 is the "working" visa, the FM-3 is more commonly used. When MTV seduced me with the glamour of "being in the film industry," they got me an FM-3. (Hollywood called, I answered, and got dumped when they hired Mexicans who worked cheaper. See, things work that way on both sides of the border. It's called greedy capitalism. After firing me at five in the morning, they were so cheap they wouldn't even buy me a bus ticket from Veracruz to Mexico City. Let's just say that everything you've heard about Hollywood being cutthroat and inhuman is true. If Hollywood calls you, put them on hold.)

Your company probably also has a human relations person who will help you find housing and help your family to acclimate. The housing part is easy. They'll find you something in an "executive" part of town, which will cost way more than most of my housing price ranges.

RELOCATION OR MOVING SERVICES

Life will go a lot smoother if they hire a relocation company to coordinate your move. There are several out there, but only one that I feel can personally recommend without hesitation, Cetra Relocations. They're based in Mexico City but can help you move anywhere in the Republic. I consider the general manager, Jesus Garcia, a friend and a straight shooter (Within Mexico Phone: 01-152-555-261-4390; Fax: 01-152-555-261-4310; jesus.garcia@cetra.com.mx; www.cetra.com.mx). He is extremely knowledgeable about all of Mexico, honest, friendly, and goes way beyond the call of duty to help make your move to Mexico a good experience. One thing Cetra makes sure of is that only one carrier handles your household goods from start to finish. I personally know people who used other services with multiple freight carriers and it was not a pretty picture. When things didn't arrive, or were broken, it was always the other guy who was responsible. Don't let that happen to you, even if you don't use Cetra.

FAMILY AND SOCIAL ADJUSTMENTS

The hard part to living abroad in any country is helping your family adjust to living in a new culture. New in this edition are suggestions for helping kids to adapt. Spouses will need help too. Joining a newcomer's club will help ease the transition. Learning to fit in with your Mexican associates in both business and social situations is a necessity. Family is very, very important in Mexico. Your career can be made or broken by how well you assimilate.

The most important thing is to learn some Spanish. While Mexicans don't expect gringos to be fluent, they do appreciate the effort to communicate. When I worked for a Mexican company, I made the mistake of giving a presentation to the board in Spanish. I hope my Spanish is better now, but I still wouldn't do that again. As I saw the pained looks on my employers' faces, I realized I'd made a mistake. One of them finally politely said that perhaps I could communicate better in my native language. Your Mexican associates will understand English far better than you will speak Spanish, unless you are already fluent.

USE YOUR POOR SPANISH SPARINGLY

Throw in a few Spanish words and phrases (correctly—have someone check the nuances before you use them) and you'll do just fine. I got into trouble in Ecuador when I was at a potential girlfriend's family dinner. I tried to excuse myself to go home because I was "muy casada." Her mother left the room with her and her brothers were ready to have a long talk with me. Finally, I figured out that although "cansada (or 'o')" means tired, "casada," which sounds very similar, means "married." Don't say "married" when you mean "tired."

You'll make mistakes, but sometimes humor can defuse the situation. A good friend of mine, John, owned a factory in Monterrey and spoke pretty good Spanish. However, before he got fluent, he made a slight mispronunciation. In a meeting with other Monterrey businessmen, he thought he'd make a joke. He did, but not the joke he thought. The table in the meeting room was long and rounded at both ends. He thought it looked similar to a sausage and said so—almost. *"La mesa esta como un salchichi,"* was what he said. He meant *"salchichicha,"* which is Spanish for sausage; *"chichi"* means "tit." What he'd said was the table was like a salty *(sal)* tit. The businessmen at the table were silent for a moment, then burst out laughing. They laughed so hard that tears came to their eyes. From that day forward, John had made some good friends because they saw he was trying and we all make mistakes. Mexicans are more understanding of grammatical errors and errors in pronunciation than their American counterparts.

Be careful with regionalisms. Knowing them can show that you are trying to understand the culture and language, but use them with *un grano de sal.* While most of Mexico refers to people from Mexico City as *Chilangos,* and even residents of the city refer to themselves this way, you should not, unless you have known someone for a while and they use the word themselves. (An older, more polite word not as much in vogue is *chapulin,* literally, "grasshopper," but I think it has died out.) Although they may use it themselves, be wary. It can be acceptable in polite conversation if you already know someone, but it's similar to calling someone of Polish extraction a "Polack," or someone with Italian heritage a "Dago." Would you do that at home? As with anything else, it depends on the person and the situation.

Guadalajara people are called *Tapatios.* There's nothing derogatory about that. People from Monterrey are called *Regiomontaños.* They are proud of the title. In fact, *Regiomontaños* have more of a distrust of *Chilangos* than an affinity for them. Monterrey has often been on the short end of the *Distrito Federal's* stick and are fiercely independent.

Occasionally, you'll hear a comment about, well, let's just say an expletive placed before gringos. Your host will immediately turn to you, put his arm around you, and say, "But I don't mean you, John. You're okay." Mexicans differentiate between the country and the individual. It's something that most of us, Canadians and Americans, could learn from them. I've done business in Mexico when our governments were squabbling. My Mexican *compadres* (see, you know more Spanish than you thought) always told me that I wasn't like that "(expletive deleted) *Norteamericano* government."

A *Norteamericano* is what an American is, technically. Both the United States and Mexico are part of the Americas. This distinction isn't as important as it used to be thirty-five years ago when I first started doing business in Mexico, but every once in a while, you'll be corrected by an older Mexican for calling yourself an American. We are all Americans. Mexico is officially the *Estados Unidos Mexicanos.*

Canadians are *Canadienses.* Japanese are *Japoneses* and Chinese are *Chinos.* Although there are, of course, specific names for people from each country, anyone from outside Latin America is a gringo.

Knowing a little culture kept me out of jail.

If you happen to be a fan of any countries in Central America, don't say so. Mexico considers herself to be superior to Central America. Cuba is another story. It's probably best to keep your mouth shut about Cuba. One time I was in big trouble—we had hit a child with a car we were driving. The child wasn't hurt, but we didn't have auto insurance. We were in a small town on the Gulf Coast. After the townspeople surrounded us and marched us to the local jail, the officer in charge began interviewing me, since I at least spoke a little Spanish. Things were looking quite dismal. I noticed that the jefe had on a pair of very nice boots. I complimented him on them, then showed him mine. In Spanish, I said, "But, of course, mine are inferior. They were made in Guatemala." I swear that's what turned the tide and kept us out of jail for the night. We paid our fines and the medical care for the little girl and some compensation all around and were on our way the next day. This just goes to show what a little understanding of the culture and the language can do for you.

ADVICE FOR WIVES

In all honesty, women will have a harder time, whether they are the executives or the spouses. There is still prejudice toward women executives from their coworkers. If you are a spouse, the other wives will often be cliquish. Perhaps this is from a deep-seated jealousy that a new gringa will try to take away their husbands, I don't know. I do know that a gringa wife (or girlfriend) is often considered a trophy for some macho men. The wives need to allay those suspicions quickly. Be friendly to your husband's associates, but try not to get into one-on-one conversations with them at parties. Try to have your husband always present.

When talking to the other wives, go with the flow of the conversation. Even though you might have a Ph.D. and definite ideas on business, if the conversation is about household matters and kids, stick to those subjects. Develop a rapport with one other wife. She'll help you understand what's going on, and when the conversation slips more and more into Spanish (usually on about the third margarita), she will bail you out. Also, if you just politely ask the group to explain something they're all laughing at, they will be happy to help you. Mexicans are very polite. That they slipped into Spanish wasn't meant (generally) as an insult. It was just more comfortable for them and they may have assumed you know more that they thought.

For God's sake, learn some Spanish. If the other women start talking Spanish exclusively, try not to nod affirmatively and say "*Sí*" to everything. Listen and try to catch the general gist of the conversation. My last (I hope) ex-wife came home in tears after our social events with my Mexican bosses. She refused to learn Spanish and it showed. She never fit in. This led to conflicts at home, and it probably will in your case too.

TAXES

Why can't I get a receipt?

U.S. Citizens

Getting a receipt for tax purposes takes an act of God, or entering another level of bureaucracy. One reason for this is that many Mexican businesses keep two sets of books (gee, as if American businesses don't). Every receipt they give out has to be accounted for and reported to the government. They will ask you for your RFC, or *Registro Federal de Compobante*. This is a business identity card that Mexican businessmen have, and you probably don't. If you are living in Mexico and doing business, you'll have to get one from *Hacienda* (the tax man cometh in every country). Meanwhile, if you are just doing business in Mexico, are still living in the United States, and want to deduct your expenses from your income tax, why not do it the easy way? I lose receipts, and even a laptop and a Palm Pilot couldn't save me. Use the official U.S. State Department per diem rates (www.state.gov/m/a/als/prdm).

I'm not a tax advisor, and you certainly should consult someone more competent than me to verify that this applies to your situation, but these are the general rules about taxes and the IRS.

One company that specializes in helping Americans who live abroad is (although this gentleman has a prestigious last name, he is no relation to me) Nelson's U.S. Expatriate Tax and Legal Services (Don D. Nelson, attorney at law, C.P.A., Nelson's U.S. Expatriate Tax and Legal Services, 34145 Pacific Coast Hwy. #401, Dana Point, CA 92629; Phone: 949-481-4094, Toll-free: 866-712-0320; Fax: 949-218-6483; ustax@hotmail.com; www.taxmeless.com).

In your Mexican gringo community, there are usually retired accountants, C.P.A.s and IRS people (yes, they are people too—my mother was one) who have little businesses to help you out. In any case, you absolutely have to file a tax return. Although I've read that people who don't make the minimum income don't have to file a return, there's a "gotcha" to this. If you file a return, the statute of limitations runs out. If you don't file one, there is no limitation as far as how long the IRS can go back to investigate you.

If you live abroad for 330 days out of a calendar year, the first $74,000 (currently; double that amount for a married couple) of earned income is exempt from U.S. taxes. If your income is passive, i.e., from investments, real estate, etc., it is taxed at the regular rates. If your income is greater than the exempt amount, you may get a tax benefit if your rent exceeds the guidelines above. However, if the source of your income is from doing business in Mexico, you'll still have to pay Mexican taxes.

The IRS has another "gotcha," though. The above applies if you are an employee. If you're self-employed, you may still have to pay the self-employment tax! Go figure.

The IRS actually has inspectors who haunt the expat communities in search of scofflaws. There aren't many, but the most bizarre case I know of was an inspector who came all the way to a little village in search of an eighty-nine-year-old woman who lived on social security. You just never know when you're going to become a blip in their radar.

Canadian Citizens

Canadians have a whole different set of tax situations that come with being an expat or on income derived from working in Mexico. I wouldn't even presume to understand the Canadian tax system, but, fortunately, you have some better sources of information. The Canada Customs and Revenue Agency (CCRA, formerly Revenue Canada) provides online information to help you determine your status (www.cra-arc.gc.ca/menu-e.html).

One thing that seems clear (as if any tax code could be so) is that Canadian residents, whether living in Canada or abroad, have to pay taxes on income earned anywhere in the world. And if you earn income in Mexico, you'll have to pay taxes on that. Just as Americans do, you have to file your taxes when living abroad.

Keep that RRSP!

It also seems clear that your RRSPs (Registered Retirement Savings Plans) are still sheltered from Canadian tax as long as you hold onto them, no matter where you live. Some Canadians are afraid that they have to cash them in when they move to Mexico. Experts have told me it isn't so. If you do cash them in, you pay (currently) 25 percent tax on the whole thing. The good news is that as long as you maintain tax residency in Canada, you may (I'm not going out on a limb here, consult a tax expert) be able to keep making contributions. If you become a nonresident, you can't contribute unless you have Canadian income that would entitle you to RRSP deductions.

There's a pretty good discussion of the tax ramifications of living abroad at www.escapeartist.com/Offshore_Finance_Canada/Moving_Abroad.html. A general purpose site with several links is www.geocities.com/canadians_abroad/taxes2.htm. A group of Canadian accountants who specialize in expats is www.compasstax.ca. From time to time, *CRA Magazine*, an online magazine, has articles on dealing with your tax situation on their archives (100 York Blvd., Ste 600, Richmond Hill, ON, L4B 1J8; Phone: 905-709-7911; Fax: 905-709-7022; www.canadiansresidentabroad.com).

SOCIAL CUSTOMS FOR DOING BUSINESS

One of the most aggravating things gringos do that offends Mexican businessmen is to jump right in and discuss business. Take your time. Make small talk. Ask about the family, but be sincere. Any insincerity will be detected in a heartbeat. Let him take the lead about when to begin discussion of the topic at hand. Another mistake is to insist that contracts be signed and deals made on the first meeting. There are exceptions, of course, especially when you've flown in for a single meeting, but that in itself doesn't give you the right to dictate terms. Without sounding like an ignorant gringo myself, this has nothing to do with a *mañana* attitude. Mexican businessmen are quite possibly the smartest on the planet. They have to deal with high interest rates on borrowing money, corruption, complicated labor laws, strong unions, and a host of nuances that we gringos will never completely understand.

Mexicans believe that anything important should be approached slowly and deliberately. They often have to consult with people you know nothing about. They have to take in the cultural ramifications of any decision.

And perhaps there is just a bit of xenophobia involved. The United States has taken advantage of Mexico for centuries.

Psychological Bias

A word to the wise: Even Mexican businessmen who have dealt with Americans for years have a little psychological bias. (Since my last three books were psychologically oriented, and lots of my friends are shrinks, I have a tendency to analyze things, but also to ask for expert opinions to validate my own.) Mexicans (in general) often believe that Americans (in general) have more money than they do. This attitude doesn't seem to carry over to Canadians as much, so you have an advantage over your American counterparts.

Canadians are viewed differently from Americans.

There is also a deeply hidden feeling of not quite inferiority, but perhaps a somewhat "less than" attitude. Very often there's a feeling of "us versus them." While they're looking out for ways that the gringo will take advantage of them, they're also looking for ways to outsmart the gringo, thus proving that the Mexican is superior. The interesting thing is that they are. Eight times out of ten, the Mexican businessman does find an advantage that slips right by the gringo.

Layers of Documentation

One other reason it takes time to get deals done in Mexico is that most Americans don't understand how Mexican businessmen want proposals done. If you want your idea to be seriously considered by your Mexican partners, be ready to do a lot of paperwork. In Mexico, it is customary for proposals to be lengthier than they are here. Everything must be documented, complete with footnotes. Include lots of graphs, spreadsheets, and charts. The best investment you can make is in an assistant who is good at Excel and PowerPoint presentations.

Several board meetings will probably take place where your proposal will be reviewed by committee. Mexican businessmen like to talk things through with others.

Projections Turn into Stones

Don't let your projections become millstones.

When I was an executive with Citibank, and later with a hospital, I had to make projections on the profitability of my department every month. They were estimates, based on my best knowledge and an Ouija board. I knew that if we didn't make the estimate, as long as I had a good explanation for the causes, I could keep my job. The estimated earnings of U.S. companies are often wrong, as any Wall Street investor knows.

No so in Mexico. When you make an estimate, you had better be right. Once it's on paper, it is treated as a fact. If you don't make it, you are in trouble. If you exceed it, everyone will be happy, but they will want a darn good reason why it was so low in the first place.

I've known enough businesspeople to know that this is true, yet I ignored my own advice one time (and only once) when I worked for a Mexican corporation. I had worked for them for years and was put in charge of a big project. I made a series of projections that were, shall we say, a little optimistic. Instead of making several hundred thousand dollars, we lost a few thousand. Not too long after that, I was fired. Excuses don't count.

A friend of mine was a newspaper editor in Mexico. He made the same mistake. Even though letting someone of his experience go hurt the paper, the board fired him.

Another friend was in the insurance industry. Same story. I could go on, but I hope you get the picture.

Trust and Politeness

Trust is the cornerstone of doing business in Mexico. If your Mexican partner does not trust you, you can get all the assurances in the world, but the bottom line is that nothing will happen. This is a double-edged sword. Before inking a deal, no matter how sincere-sounding and gallant your potential partner is, try to find out his reputation. I can't count the number of gringos who have partnered with Mexicans without understanding the culture. Often this works out, but when it doesn't, it really doesn't. You can bet your bottom dollar that he has investigated you.

If trust is the cornerstone, then politeness is the mortar of doing business in Mexico. "Yes" may mean "Possibly," and "No" may mean "Not at this time." When I lived in Los Angeles, California, I came to understand that this way of thinking is not limited to Mexicans. L.A. is a passive-aggressive town. People (and not just Hollywood scoundrels) don't like to say "No." It's less stressful for them to say "Yes," and mean "Maybe." Yeses are often followed by delays. If you're smart, you'll figure this out and cut your losses without becoming belligerent. Saving face is the brick of getting along in both cultures. (We've now exhausted my construction metaphors.)

Bridges Are for Building, Not Burning

When a deal doesn't work out, don't burn your bridges. The same person may come through on another deal. Make an enemy and you have made an enemy for life. Once, I seriously offended a Mexican executive I worked for in private industry. While this may be an extreme example, it's probably not too far-fetched. This man so hated me that for ten years, whenever my name was mentioned, he got angry. When he was dying of cancer, mutual friends confided to me that the only thing keeping him going was his hatred of me. While this could happen in any country (we all know people like this), it's good to keep in mind when doing business in Mexico. The veneer of polite-ness makes it unlikely that a Mexican will let you know how deeply you've offended him. In fact, you may go on blissfully ignorant, thinking things are hunky-dory.

If you make an enemy, you may not know.

Another time, I made this mistake by being arrogant with a government official. After all, I was a hotshot, sent by my company to get a job done. For the next ten years, whenever some piece of business slipped right out of my grasp, the offended official was at the heart of things. While these are personal stories, I've known enough bilateral businesspeople to know that it is a pretty accurate generalization.

Government Officials

Speaking of government officials, never dismiss one because he has lost power. Regimes change. Bureaucrats don't die, they just change departments. I main-tained a friendship with a man who was the head of his department when I met him. Years later, he had some menial job and was taking the bus instead of flying to a conference. I agreed with him that it was a better way to see the country and congratulated him on his decision. A few years later, he was the head of another department and did a lot for me.

> **Mañana** *doesn't mean what you think it does.*
> **Mañana** *doesn't necessarily mean "tomorrow"; it means "not right now." Time is relative. Although business meetings tend to start on time, social events don't always. If something is set for "eight o'clock," people could arrive at 8:30 or 9:30. You might as well arrive on time, just in case, until you get your sea legs. If something is scheduled "en punto," then that means at the scheduled time.*

Eating Meetings

Much business is conducted over meals. Breakfast is the best choice, as lunches can turn into cocktail hours. I know that the three-margarita lunch is being phased out in Mexico, but it still is more common than here. Don't expect much business to be discussed until the end. You'll often be invited (or should do the inviting) to what you think are gringo restaurants, such as VIPS or Sanborn's. These are where business is conducted.

If you get invited to a really good Mexican-style restaurant, consider yourself honored. Follow your Mexican friend's lead on ordering. I made the mistake of ordering pancakes instead of *huevos rancheros*, or some other Mexican dish, and immediately knew I had made a mistake. Tacos are considered a low-class food. Even though I think they are among the best of Mexican foods, there is a social stigma about them for business. Tortillas are considered by some as inferior to white bread. Follow your host's lead. The variety of salsas that will be automatically included with your order are perfectly acceptable. (The *pico de gallo* is generally mild. The red and green sauces may surprise you with their spiciness.) A meal without some sort of sauce served on the side is *muy triste,* very sad. While it's common to squeeze lime onto foods in informal settings, don't automatically do it during a business meal. I did this just once. My host winced, as we were eating gourmet Mexican food. If water is served at the table, drink it. You can bet that your Mexican businessmen are no more going to drink unpurified water than you. Don't make a big deal of it. Go with the flow, so to speak.

In Monterrey, it is acceptable to go to a *cabrito* (roast goat) restaurant, thank God. If your friend asks where you want to eat, and you know the local specialty, it is okay to suggest a restaurant that specializes in it. The protocol is that the person who is selling something should pay. For meetings among equals, the one who does the inviting is expected to pay. Do not offer to split a check; this is the height of impropriety.

ALTERNATIVE WAYS TO WORK

BUSINESSES THAT COULD FLY

Read the paragraphs above, as they apply to anyone doing business. Businesses that could fly in Mexico include Internet-based businesses (provided you can work out the shipping details if you sell products—that's not easy. If you have a partner in the States or Canada to do the actual shipping, that would be best.); consulting; working with Mexican companies that want to expand into U.S. or Canadian markets; engineering consulting (While you are unlikely to be hired as an engineer for a firm, you could provide consulting expertise.); import-export (obviously); medical professionals (You have to be extremely fluent in Spanish to work in your field. You'll have to be certified by the appropriate Mexican boards. Skilled nurses could work, but you will find that the working conditions are not what you are used to. You will not, with some exceptions, get the respect you're used to here. Think nursing thirty years ago. Chiropractors seem to be able to set up shop. Physicians have no problem. Medical techs can obtain employment.); tourist-based businesses (Provided you employ mainly Mexicans. I know of a guy who started a yacht cruise company. I told him his chances were slim, which goes to show that even I don't know everything, he said sheepishly.); manufacturing (I know a fellow

who built a plant to extract shark cartilage and bottle it.); computer technicians (This is harder, as there are plenty of Mexican technicians. Your best bet
is to form a corporation and hire Mexican techies. The pay scale is less than
half of U.S. and Canadian standards, but a lot higher than places such as
India.); realtors (This will be rather hard, as you'd better be able to interpret
Mexican real estate law, but in gringo areas, there are plenty of gringo real
estate salespeople.); time-share sales (You don't need to be fluent in Spanish,
know a darn thing, or do anything but be able to sell. Expect prejudice from
your Mexican competitors, er, coworkers.); advertising executives (While there
is competition from Mexican advertising agencies, gringos are believed to be
good at this.); copywriters (While this field is dwindling, it's a little easier to
get into in Mexico than in the States or Canada.); artists (There is lots of
competition from Mexican graphic artists, but you could bull your way into a
position.); journalists (Gringo papers such as the Mexico City *News*, the
Guadalajara Reporter, and other smaller papers hire gringos. *The News* is considered a training ground for reporters. However, if you think journalists in your
country are underpaid, wait till you get to Mexico.); and English teachers (You
don't need to be certified as anything to teach English in many private
schools. All you need is to be able to speak English—American, Canadian, or
British varieties. A high-school degree is about all you need. If you have some
teaching experience or a couple of years of college, it's a plus. But having an
ESL degree is not going to mean much, in most cases. The field is open to
English-speaking Europeans as well. Pay is just enough for you to survive, and,
in some cases, enough to live comfortably, but not large. It ranges from about
5,000 to 10,000 pesos a month [U.S. $500 to $1,000]. You make extra money
tutoring. If you are applying at a school that specializes in teaching executives
and their families, you'll probably need some experience. There are a lot of
scam companies that promise to get you jobs. I trust only one, InterNetworks
[555 S. Sunrise Way, Ste. 200, Palm Springs, CA 92264; Phone: 800-426-0161;
teach-english-mexico.com]. Mark Farley, the founder, has been doing this for
a decade at least and is 100 percent honest. They're a member of the Better
Business Bureau and have never had an unresolved complaint. I could tell you
horror stories about some other services.)

STARTING YOUR OWN BUSINESS

It is possible to form your own corporation while you still have your FM-T, or
tourist permit. If you do, you will not be able to receive any pay from the
corporation except for dividends or bonuses. You must hire Mexicans to work
for you and you cannot work at the location of your business, although you
can visit it to oversee the operations. Another way to work here is to marry a
Mexican citizen and then put the business in his or her name and get him or
her to hire you. Another way is to get yourself sponsored by a Mexican business and get hired. Then you can work, but only for that company. The
smartest way to work is to get an FM-3.

The Internet

The simplest way to work in Mexico is to do so without setting up shop and have your money paid to you in the United States. If you are a consultant and can do much of your work by computer, then you can do it from Mexico, with an occasional commute. Indeed, with the improved Internet service available in Mexico today, including high-speed, there's no reason why many of us can't operate from our homes, wherever they may be. Good Internet access is available in all cities and many smaller towns.

SEASONAL WORK

Another alternative is for those who can to do some sort of seasonal work back in the States and live in Mexico in the off-season.

WORKING OFF THE BOOKS

Many gringos work "off the books" in Mexico until they become legal. The drawback to this is that if you get caught, you can be deported, and everything you own can be confiscated. The likelihood of that happening really depends on where you are and how blatant you are about what you do. If you are in competition with a national and he gets jealous, he will turn you in. Therefore, do your best not to cross anyone. If you have made your *solicitud* for a working permit and it is in the works, you can usually operate. If your application is denied, close up shop right away. I have been told that work permits are harder to come by in the Baja.

If you teach English, you should have few problems, though you should have an FM-3. If you want to set up shop as an electrician or carpenter, forget it. If you do some sort of consulting work, you should get the *consejero* or *hombre de negocios* FM-3.

I know people who work illegally and say that it is simply a matter of keeping a low profile and getting along with everyone. But since it is now easier to get an FM-3 than it was ten years ago, why not go ahead and do it?

DRIVING CARS TO CENTRAL AMERICA

I get asked about this a lot. Yes, it can be done, and no, it is not a get-rich-quick scheme. When you are driving down a southern U.S. highway leading to Mexico and see a small caravan of pickup trucks filled with bicycles and assorted junk, know that they are heading to Central America and are generally driven by Central Americans. (Important note: You cannot tow a vehicle through Mexico, though you sometimes see this done. Don't even think about it.)

Some people eke out a living driving cars to Central America to sell. There is nothing illegal about this, but it requires contacts and patience. (Forget about Costa Rica—they raised the duty, making it unprofitable.) In some countries, you may make one-and-a-half times your money, but you must be patient. The people who want to buy cars know that you need money to live and will stall so you will lower your price. If you don't have deep pockets, they will win.

Only buy four- or six-cylinder vehicles, preferably Toyota or Nissan pickup trucks. I tried to sell my eight-cylinder, four-wheel-drive Dodge Ram Charger, thinking, "What a deal. They need four-wheel-drive vehicles in Belize." Even though I had a whole family in Belize to help me out, and one of them came to Galveston, he wouldn't take it. Gas is just too expensive (more so even than in Mexico). Once again, I showed my tremendous business acumen. The only profit from the deal is what you will get by not following my example. My last ex-wife did manage to sell her six-cylinder Ford truck without any papers (it's a long story, but the bottom line was it wasn't paid for) to a Guatemalan for pennies on the dollar. The truck died on the trip, but the Guatemalan didn't hold us responsible. A deal is a deal.

IMPORTING—LEGAL

Advice from the Whip King of New Orleans

Importing handicrafts from Mexico or Central America is commonly done with a tourist visa. The chances of your getting caught are limited to traffic police. If they look in the back of your van and see several hundred serapes, that could make things sticky. Many people ship their packages back from Mexico via FedEx, Estafeta, DHL, or on the bus lines to avoid this. If you get stopped, a little *mordida* will usually do the trick. The cop doesn't really want a lot of Indian handicrafts, but he surely could use the money. Then it becomes a question of your bargaining ability. Decide in advance how much your load is worth to you. If you don't get stopped, keep that amount aside for another trip; eventually, you will be stopped.

Another good idea is to talk to U.S. customs officers and find out what is and is not duty-free. They will also tell you what paperwork is required to bring your treasures back. For instance, the goat fur cushions fiasco described below was aggravated by the fact that I nearly didn't get them back across the border. There is (or was) an allotment of how much cotton could be imported into the States: The cushions were filled with cotton. The customs guy looked at me, smelled the wet goat fur, and told me to get the hell out of there and never bring any more back. Sage advice.

From my personal experience as a failed import-export impresario, I strongly advise you to talk to shop owners before you go and find out what they want. Don't fall in love with your own taste, even though it is probably a thousand times better than mine. I once cornered the market on goat fur cushions because I thought they were unique; there was a reason I hadn't seen them in any stores—nobody wanted them. To add insult to injury, mine got wet. I don't know if you have ever smelled a wet goat, but I hope you don't have to. I never got the smell out of the upholstery of my first ex-wife's car— but that's another story, available in some of my other books. I was once the Whip King of New Orleans, but I only sold them. Don't ask, don't tell. Anyway, I found out what the market wanted and got a good deal on them. I am

ashamed to admit it, but I also made a lot of money on velvet Elvises—
something I never would have thought of on my own.

My friend Joe "King" Carrasco, the king of Tex-Mex rock and roll
(www.joeking.com), cornered the market on leather patches that said "Joe
King," but he didn't want to pay duty on them, so he asked me to smuggle
them back. I was paranoid. It took a woman who was with me to snort, "Men!"
and bring them across. The moral here is that women are better smugglers
than men. The other moral is that there would have been no duty. So find out
before you corner the market on anything.

FINDING WORK WITH AN EXISTING COMPANY

If you're an executive, go through a headhunter agency. All of the major international agencies have offices in Mexico. Stick with a known name brand.
Expect to pay a fee of around $1,000. These people get a lot of inquiries from
people who are a cut above the guy who wants to start a bar in Vallarta, but
the principle is the same: You have a great vacation and think Mexico would
be a great place to live. Be serious about wanting to move and read this book
before you plunk down big bucks.

There are employment agencies in Mexico that will help you find a somewhat lower-echelon job, but it's a long shot. You can try contacting them
ahead of your move, but don't expect immediate results. The American Cham-
bers of Commerce in Mexico's three largest cities can help you, though they
will charge a small fee. The Web site for all chapters is www.amcham.com.mx.

- **Mexico City**
  American Chamber of Commerce Lucerna No. 78, Colonia
  Juarez, 06600 Mexico, D.F.; from outside Mexico Phone: 011-
  52-555-514-3888 or toll-free in Mexico: 01-800-711-0078;
  Fax: 011-52-555-570-32911; amchammx@amcham.com.mx
- **Guadalajara**
  Av. Moctezuma No. 442, Colonia Jardines del Sol 45050
  Zapopan, Jal.; from outside Mexico Phone: 011-52-333-634-
  6606; Fax: 011-52-333-634-7374;
  direccion_gdl@amcham.com.mx
- **Monterrey**
  Rio Manzanares 434, Oriente Colonia del Valle 66220 Garza
  Garcia, N.L.; from outside Mexico Phone: 011-52-818-114-
  2000; Fax: 011-52-818-114-2100;
  socios_mty@amcham.com.mx

A final note on finding a job: While you may be able to find an executive
job while still living in the States or Canada, for other types of jobs the field is
crowded and you may have to spend months looking after you arrive in
Mexico. It will not be easy, and the important thing to remember is that you
must offer something that a company could not get by hiring a Mexican.

See the section on visas to understand what you need (pages 69–77).
While you are seeking employment, you can travel on a tourist visa. If you are

temporarily working, you'll need a business visa. Theoretically, if you are attending a business meeting, you'll need a business visa.

LABOR LAWS

Mexican labor laws are complex and subject to interpretation. While it's relatively easy to hire someone, firing them is not. Invest in a Mexican labor attorney before you do anything. Some of the laws you need to know are:

- You must provide health benefits through the National Hospital Insurance System (IMSS).
- You must contribute to a retirement fund.
- Your workers are entitled to a small percentage of your profits. The percentage may change, but it's currently around 10 percent.
- Your workers are entitled to a bonus of fifteen days worth of wages at the end of the year. Plus there are several paid holidays a year.
- You must contribute to the Infonavit housing programs for workers to buy their own homes.

For personal advice about working in Mexico and setting up a corporation, I recommend a company that specializes in it: John Schick with Mexico Consulting Group has the expertise and connections to help with establishing medium-sized to large-scale multimillion-dollar businesses (info@mexico consulting.net; mexicoconsulting.net). I've found him both personable and professional. His and his company's knowledge of and contacts in Mexico can save you a lot of heartbreak. They'll tell you if your idea is worth pursuing, and, if it is, will help you navigate the treacherous waters of Mexican business. Mexico Consulting Group was founded in 1978. They provide services to clients on a fee basis. Any company that wants to add value to their enterprises by developing successful businesses in Mexico should talk to them. Although most are midsized firms, they work with funded start-ups, and nearly one in five of the Fortune 500 have been clients of theirs.

In fact, if you do plan to work in Mexico, you should also have a business plan and show the amount of money you are going to invest in the country when you make your application. The states of Baja, Quintana Roo, Sonora, and Guanajuato are particularly open to foreign investment. The trick is not to open a business that is in direct competition with existing Mexican businesses, although you are not precluded from doing so.

The government is concerned that you aren't a freeloader who will be begging on the streets in six months and that you will pay taxes. By the same token, they don't want to put Mexicans out of work.

DRIVING IN MEXICO

CHECKING OUT THE COUNTRY BEFORE MOVING

Please, please don't read this book, pack up everything, and move to Mexico tomorrow. Try it on for size first. To do this, simply go as a tourist on a tourist visa and drive around for a while. Find a place you might want to live and stay there for a few months.

Visit first.

WHY DRIVE?

I recommend driving over any other way to see the country. Buses, although very comfortable and far more first-class than the ones in the United States and cheaper than driving, are not my favorite way to travel, nor are they cheap. A ticket from the border to Mexico City, for instance, will cost about $150. Not so many years ago, it cost about $25. Driving, for two people, will cost more. Tolls alone could equal bus fare, and gasoline is currently around $2.60 a gallon and it goes up a few cents every month. Still, the freedom and flexibility and the chance to really see Mexico make up for it. When you go looking for housing, it's a lot better to have your own car than a taxi.

I've driven at least half a million miles in Mexico and never had any problems. Don't listen to those who will try to talk you out of it. Whether you're driving a car or an RV, driving is safe and a heck of a lot more fun than any other way of traveling.

HELP PLANNING YOUR TRIP

If you need guidance planning your driving trip to Mexico, or about moving to or working in Mexico, you can call me at 888-234-3452 or e-mail mexico mikenelson23@mexicomike.com. I make a living from offering these services, so only call if you are serious and are willing to pay me for my time.

MAPS

If you want a good map, many people swear by the *Guia Roji* maps. You can get them in Mexico at newsstands in stores, at some gas stations with a big convenience store attached, or before you leave from Treaty Oaks Maps (P.O. Box 50295, Austin, TX 78763; 512-326-4141; maps@treatyoak.com; www.gone tomorrow.com).

YOUR STUFF

You can bring in a *reasonable* amount of personal effects as a tourist. This varies according to the customs inspector. True, there is an official list of what is permitted, but it is seldom followed. As long as you do not have too much stuff, don't worry about it. Laptop computers are no problem. Desktops, which used to cause problems in entry, aren't as big a deal as they were years ago. I'd take mine if I didn't have a laptop.

Exceptions

That said, everything is subject to the customs inspector's whims. You may end up paying a duty on your computer of about 20 percent. Or you could pay a *mordida* of about $20. It's up to you. Try storytelling. One time I was having a hard time with a computer until I told the official that I was a writer. "What kind of stories do you write?" he asked. "Like James Bond, 007." He beamed and waved me through. Or try another shift or crossing. I've known people who had been turned back from one border crossing, drove to the next border crossing or waited for the shift to change, and got in. New clothing with the tags still attached, even a couple of shirts, will almost always cause you trouble.

Mordida—*The Little Bite*

I might as well mention **mordida**, *which means "a little bite." It is a* **Mexicanismo** *for "bribe." It used to be a way of life on the border. The government periodically tries to stamp it out. In recent years, they have been more successful than before. Frankly, a lot of the success depends on how well the economy is doing and how close Mexico is to a presidential election. The end of an administration is seen as a time of every man for himself. The beginning is when the laws are enforced.*

Although I cannot encourage anyone actually to pay a bribe, and certainly don't suggest it, if an official makes it plain that there might be an easier way to deal with your situation, he is showing you that he is amenable to some token of appreciation for his extra services. At that point, you have to decide what you want to do. Under no circumstances should you offer anything without being encouraged. The new, young, idealistic crop of border officials will be insulted. I find it best to play by the rules, smile a lot, and be friendly but dumb. It helps if you forget all your Spanish, unless you tell a story.

Once, I had a new shirt with the tags on it and the customs officer at the secondary stop (approximately twenty-one kilometers from the border) insisted that I pay duty on it. I talked my way out of it by saying that my girlfriend thought I had such bad taste that she bought me a new shirt. Some of you may be saying, "Yeah, that's easy for him to say, he speaks Spanish. I don't." Most visitors to Mexico do not speak Spanish. Most customs officials speak some English and many are fluent. Don't worry about it.

SPEAKING SPANISH

Sopa *isn't soap.*

When driving, speaking Spanish comes in very handy, even if only a few phrases. You'll be dealing with a lot of different classes of people, and not all will speak any English.

If you really want to learn Spanish before you go, get the U.S. State Department's *Foreign Service Institute Language Course*, sold in bookstores. There are a couple of companies that package it, but Multilingua is the least expensive. A great book for those who already know a little Spanish is *Breaking out of Beginner's Spanish* by Joseph J. Keenan (University of Texas Press).

"Mexico" Mike's **Spanish y Slang** *Book*
If you just want to learn enough Spanish to communicate and enough slang to sound as though you understand the culture, get my e-book, **"Mexico" Mike's Bastante Español, Modismos Y Slang (with enough slang to make you sound cool).** *It's available online at www.mexicomike.com; just click "Books." I'm not a linguist, cunning or otherwise. I've taken the most common mistakes (mostly learned the hard way) and given you easy ways to avoid them. There's a lot of humor in this little book. For instance, don't confuse* **sopa,** *soup, with* **jabon,** *soap, just because they sound similar in English. I did and it was hilarious.*

Instead of boring you with a lot of grammar rules and phrases, such as, "The red vase is on the table," or "Your mother makes good tortillas," I'll give you the common questions you'll get, such as "Where are you going?" from the drug police. I've found that confusing "Where are you going?," "¿A donde va?", with "Where are you coming from?," "¿De donde viene?", seems to upset them. If you're heading south and you say you're going north, they either think you are crazy, lost, or lying. Cops being cops, they usually opt for the latter. The best answer to "¿De donde viene?" is "los Estados Unidos," (or **Canadá***). If they tack an* **"anoche"** *on the end, it means "Where were you last night?" Try not to smile lustily and look at your traveling companion.*

Knowing what others are saying is more important to foreigners than what they're going to say. Naturally, I'll cover every driving situation you'll run into (or hopefully won't run into). I will keep you out of trouble. For instance, instead of asking a butcher if he has **huevos,** *you'd better ask him for* **blanquillas,** *if you don't want to offend his manhood. I found this out the hard way, since all my Spanish books had only* **huevos** *for eggs.* **Chichis** *is an impolite way to refer to a woman's breasts (among others). Use* **senos,** *which is rather clinical, or, more commonly,* **pechos** *instead. Don't get confused and say* **sueños** *(dreams), though this may be accurate if they are the breasts of your dreams. The polite way to say "penis" is* **pene.**

TOLL ROADS

Driving in Mexico is no more dangerous than driving in the United States, but it is more challenging. Since the last edition, it is now possible to drive just about anywhere you want to go via four-lane toll roads that (for a price) can make you feel as comfortable as if you were back home. (You can get the current toll rates from www.sct.gob.mx.) The two-lane roads vary in width and conditions, so that some of them are usually in great shape and others are often full of potholes.

RULES OF THE ROAD

Check that side-view mirror!

A left turn signal on the highway is used to tell the vehicle behind you that it is okay to pass you. In towns, it means you are turning left. I worked for MTV as a driving consultant on their show *Road Rules*. One driver forgot that rule and the one about checking the side-view mirror before passing. Fortunately, we only lost a mirror; we could have lost much more.

Don't drive at night, even on the toll roads, as there are often animals on the road; cows don't wear taillights. Watch out for *topes*, speed bumps, in every town. They begin just as you enter a town and there are many in between. Slow down in rain—the roads are slicker, due to the blow-off from the big trucks, and it takes several hours of a heavy rain to wash it away.

Truckers are usually friendly and will use the aforementioned left turn signal to give you the go-ahead to pass when you cannot see around them. Traffic cops are more honest than you have been led to believe, but some are looking for bribes, especially in Mexico City. When this happens, stand firm and tell them you want to go to the *comandancia*. Periodically, Mexico City begins programs to eliminate corrupt cops, but I don't think they've won the battle. Telling them you'll report them to PROFESCO, Procuraduría Federal del Consumidor, might have some effect. You can't drive in Mexico City on certain days, depending on the last number of your license plate. Every toll road close to Mexico City has the days posted. I didn't put this in the book this time because the rules could change. This also applies to rental cars; the rental companies will have a list.

You will not go to jail for having a traffic accident, unless you do not have insurance or are drunk, high, or argumentative. If the accident is serious, you could go to jail, or you and your car could simply be detained until the matter is settled. That's why it is a good idea to have a legal-assistance policy.

Flashing your headlights at a car in front of you indicates that you want to pass them. If you drive with your headlights on during the day, you will be flashed by oncoming drivers because they think you left them on by accident. Now that newer Mexican cars come with DTRs (daytime running lights), this is becoming a hassle of the past.

RV Driving Tips

You aren't in Kansas anymore.

Be sure your tires are in good shape, as the roads can be rough on them and half-size tires are rare in Mexico. Invest in a set of heavy-duty springs. Don't overload your rig. You are going to do more bouncing than you would in the United States. There are many toll roads in Mexico, but some are bouncy. For a complete guide to RV parks, order the *Traveler's Guide to Mexican Camping* by Mike and Terri Church (www.rollinghomes.com/Authors.htm) from their site, a bookstore, or my Web page. Some books will tell you that there is a special toll rate for RVs. Forget it. That was one of those ideas that lasted for a few weeks and then was forgotten about. Tolls are high and based on the number of wheels you have—except in Sonora. A representative toll (very much subject to change) is about $250 to drive from Nogales, Arizona, to Mazatlán, Sin. You can take the free roads, but the wear and tear on your vehicle and the aggravation, particularly if you are a first-timer, will make you wish you had spent the bucks. If you break down, don't worry. Mexican mechanics are among Mexico's hidden treasures. They can fabricate parts if they don't have them—in most cases.

The Green Angels will probably find you and help you. They are mechanics who work for the tourism department. They patrol the highways looking for people who need assistance. Their help is free, but a tip is appreciated.

COPS

Cops—The Good

The Good News

Corrupt cops are not as common as you think. In my now nearly forty years of driving in Mexico, I have met four cops who tried to shake me down; two succeeded. Most cops give tourists a break. I totaled my truck in Torreon. I did not go to jail, paid no bribes, and was helped out by the officials of the toll road. The highway patrol was polite and efficient. They gave me a ticket for being stupid, and I had to pay for damaging the toll road (quite a lot, the toll roads are quite dear), but that was it. Many times I have been lost (yes, it happens to the best of us) and a cop helped me on my way, refusing payment, saying, "I am only doing my job. Enjoy Mexico." I have heard ten of these stories for every bad-cop story—honestly.

There are corrupt cops on both sides of the border. Most of the stories you have heard are blown out of proportion. If a cop is corrupt, he is not out to hurt you or rob you. He is merely looking for a privately financed pay raise. You have the power to grant that raise or not. You are the *patrón*.

I do not mention the following to justify their actions, but so that you will understand the system. Local *transito*, transit, cops make about $150 to $250 a month, depending on the town. *Policía Federal de Caminos*, Federal Highway Patrol, are the elite of the police forces and are well trained and well paid. Their salaries start at about $1,200 a month. They can make two times that with time and promotions. They do not stop people for shakedowns. Many of them are trained at the FBI Academy in the United States.

State cops, *judiciales*, are somewhere in between—in terms of honesty, pay, and courtesy. They have bad reputations. The PJF, or federal judicial police, are what people call *Federales,* and they make $500 to $600 a month. They are the villains of most horror stories. Mostly they are at drug checkpoints wearing black T-shirts and baseball caps with PJF (which stands for *Policia Judiciales Federál)* on the front. They are very thorough and no-nonsense, but not terribly impolite. The army also mans drug and weapons checkpoints. They are usually polite and efficient. There is nothing to fear.

Cops—The Bad

The Bad News

Now that I have given you the good news, I have to add that, in some places, local or state highway cops will shake down motorists. We gringos think this applies only to us, but we are not so unique; they happily shake down their countrymen. The states of Hidalgo and Mexico are noted for this, by my own personal experience and that of others. They will say you can't drive in their state on certain days; this is not true. The "day-without-a-car" program applies only to Mexico City, but cops will tell you differently. Argue the point. Mexico City cops used to be the worst, but Hidalgo and Mexico states aren't far behind.

If you are stopped, give the officer a copy of your papers and driver's license. If he is a scoundrel, he can't hold your papers hostage during the ensuing negotiations. Don't pay a bribe and do play dumb. If that doesn't work, say you want to go to the *comandancia y hablar con su jefe.* It is not perfect Spanish, and it is not supposed to be. Making it difficult to communicate is part of the game and one of your weapons. Stand firm for about thirty minutes and he will get disgusted and let you go. Always look for the officer's badge and write down his number, as well as the number of his patrol car. One lady, who was unjustly stopped, did this and the cop offered to trade her driver's license, which he had illegally taken, and documents for the paper with that information on it!

As in Mexico City, telling them you'll report them to PROFESCO might have some effect. If you have really broken a law, the cop will take your license. You will have to appear at the police station or municipal offices to claim it by paying your ticket. On weekends, you will have to wait until Monday. You can drive with the ticket but must return to appear by the appointed date. With legal-assistance insurance, you will be a lot better off. Get it. (See more information at www.mexicomike.com.) The legal system is slow and complicated. It even tried my patience the few times I have used it. If there is an easier way to handle the situation, find it.

DRIVERS' LICENSES AND CAR PERMITS

INTERNATIONAL DRIVERS' LICENSES

Don't bother obtaining an international driver's license. If you see a Web site that offers it, avoid it. In these days of terrorism, anything similar to this is suspect. Forget the AAA ones. If you want to see a Mexican cop chuckle, hand him one.

As a defense against a crooked cop taking your license for a bogus offense, some people carry a second legitimate driver's license from their home state. I'm including this for your knowledge only and am not endorsing the practice. You cannot have two licenses legally, but as long as you only use the more recent (duplicate) one in the States (I assume Canada has similar restrictions), you aren't really breaking any laws. Use the original in Mexico, so that if it is taken by a crooked cop, you'll still have the duplicate to drive home with. I cannot guarantee that you won't end up in some Mexican database for skipping out, if you've really committed an infraction; if you do encounter a corrupt cop, I don't think there's any danger of his entering anything into a database. Still, use your own good judgment.

TOURIST PERMITS

Sonora has a "Sonora Only" tourist card that you need to get (no charge), and, theoretically, you need a tourist permit for Baja, but this is rarely enforced. For the rest of the country, there is now about a $25 fee (which will keep going up) to get a tourist permit (which you'll need whether flying, driving, or bicycling), but if you are going to be in Mexico for seven days or fewer, there is no charge. Your tourist permit (it's not really a visa—you don't need a visa to visit Mexico) is an FM-T. The law has always read that a tourist can only visit Mexico for 180 days in each 365-day period. In the past, this was routinely ignored. Now (subject to the whims of the government, of course), this is being enforced. It is getting harder and harder to get a 180-day permit. Officials are also being pickier about documentation. They really want to see a passport (which is not a bad idea to have when coming back to the United States), but a voter's registration is still accepted in lieu of a passport. If you are pigheaded like me, you can insist on using a notarized statement of citizenship, but it's a lot of hassle. If you are politely insistent, you can still get a 180-day permit. Say you want to tour all of Mexico.

But only ask for one if you intend to be gone that long. I'd allow about a week more than I expect to stay. If you use up your 180 days right away, you may not get up to the plate again. The government keeps a database of everyone who enters, so make sure you turn in your papers before you leave the country. There are ways around this 180-day rule, however (see below). If you're moving to Mexico, but (like me) can't get an FM-3 because you can't prove enough income, all is not lost. I'm not going to put the tricks in print, because things change and I don't want to mislead you. Please consider spending the money to consult with me for what works. Call 888-234-3452.

VEHICLE PERMITS

You don't need a vehicle permit to travel in Sonora or Baja. Your vehicle permit will cost about $37 (this actually went up during the writing of this book, so expect it to go up again), payable by a credit or debit card to *Hacienda* (the treasury department). You'll have to have the title or registration (though officials seem to prefer the title, or duplicate title). If the vehicle is financed, you'll need a notarized letter of permission from your lien holder. You also must have Mexican automobile insurance. Some insurers are now able to write Mexican insurance through a Mexican carrier, but you'll usually get the best rates and most dependable service from International Insurance, the only one I recommend anymore. They're dependable and reasonable. There are bargain insurance companies, but you get what you pay for. You can get a quote online at their Web site (www.mexpro.com, or by clicking on the banners on www.mexicomike.com) or by phone (888-467-4639). Tell 'em "Mexico" Mike sent you. AAA also sells Mexican auto insurance, but their prices are higher, and their coverage isn't any better. Their Mexico guidebook is fairly good, but you get that just by being a member.

If your financing institution isn't familiar with the letter of permission, have them call your insurer and speak to the manager or claims adjuster. He will reassure them that the chances of the car being stolen or involved in an accident are minimal and that if it is, the insurance company will pay it off. You must have a credit card—Visa, MasterCard, or American Express. You cannot sell the vehicle in Mexico and must surrender this permit before you leave the country. You can't do it at the bridge or border crossing in most cases; you have to find the *Migración* or *Hacienda* offices (in the same place). Some crossings, such as the one back to Pharr, Texas, have the offices near the bridge, but they are on the opposite side of the highway. Bottom line: It ain't easy, but it has to be done. If you don't turn in your permit, there is a $147 fine for every thirty days you didn't turn it in, starting with the first day it is late.

That being said, some people have told me that they didn't turn one in and got back in anyway. Others have told me that they were detained at the border. Others had to pay a rather large fine. It's better to be safe than sorry. Call me for a way around this.

Only one vehicle per customer.

RVs

RVs are subject to the same regulations as automobiles. However, see below for a special deal for trailers in Sonora. You're only allowed one vehicle per person. If you're towing a vehicle, it should be entered in the name of your spouse or traveling companion (as long as his or her name is on the title).

Trailer and Boat Exemptions

Unlike many areas of the country, in Sonora the RV market is growing. You can get a ten-year permit for your travel trailer or boat and leave it (good only in the state of Sonora). You get this next door to the same place you get your tourist card, and it's only good for as many days as you tell them you'll be in Sonora, for up to 180 days. In other words, you have to bring your car back, but can leave your trailer.

BUYING A MEXICAN VEHICLE

Should you buy a Mexican vehicle? Most expats don't. You vehicle permit is good as long as your FM-3 is, so you don't have to run back to the border every six months. Are U.S. and Canadian vehicles singled out by corrupt cops as a way to add to their kids' college fund? Yes, though not as frequently as you've been led to believe.

Many of the vehicles you buy in the States were made in Mexico, so there's not a quality issue with Mexican cars. However, there is a price issue. I know, you'll see people on the Internet who talk about the bargains they got by buying Mexican vehicles. They aren't lying, they just aren't aware that pricing in Mexico is a moveable feast. New vehicles should cost more. There is a Mexican tax of about 40 to 50 percent tacked on to vehicles sold within the country. This, of course, is passed on to the consumer. Plus you pay a 15 percent sales tax for the privilege of buying it. Bank financing is high, currently around 25 percent, though dealers can offer incentives, just as they do here.

When the economy is good, prices stay high for new and used vehicles. When the economy tanks, dealers are flooded with returns because people can't make the payments. It's during those times that you find deals. Then a used vehicle might be sold for less in Mexico than in the States. I've seen $18,000 vehicles go for $9,000.

One way to find a bargain in a new car is to inquire if any were made and ordered for export and not delivered. If you find one, jump on the deal.

As a general rule, the same used vehicle in Mexico should cost about 15 to 20 percent more than in the States. Plus, the one in the States will be in better shape. Potholes are a way of life (still) on Mexican city streets and non–toll roads (the *libres*).

HOUSING IN MEXICO

The craziest thing that new foreigners do is to buy property with no idea of the area, or even talking to local residents. If you talk to locals, they will all say the same thing: Rent before you buy. Talk to people, learn the neighborhoods, and prevailing costs. Yet many barge in and repent later.   —*"Cabo" Bob, long-time Mexico expat*

Much has changed in this area since the last edition. Most importantly, financing can now be obtained to buy a house, condo, or business investment anywhere in Mexico (see www.mexicomike.com/realestate/mexico_real_estate_index.html, or just click on the "Real Estate" button on the main page). The other thing is that housing costs have gone up. This shouldn't be a surprise. Houses in the United States have gone up about 8 percent on average over the past several years. In some places in Mexico, it has been about that, and in many, prices have increased about 40 to 60 percent. This growth is unsustainable (if you will take advice from a man who sold the only house he ever owned for a loss, and made and lost several million dollars in the stock market—buyer beware).

At some point, prices will come down, but I've been waiting for that opportunity for years. If there is a devaluation of the peso, they will—but only in the areas not dominated by a dollar-based economy. (I found that out the hard way.) You probably shouldn't wait and should buy a house when you're ready to move.

In the city-by-city sections, I've included a range of costs for renting, buying houses and condos, and buying RV spaces. These are only guidelines to compare one location with another. They will change and will probably go up. Yet they were accurate at the time of printing.

PRICE RANGES

BARGAIN HOUSE PRICES LISTED—A DISCLAIMER

Bargains still exist.

I'll go into details about bargain houses in a few paragraphs, but here is an overview. I've included the "bargain" house prices of $20,000 to $25,000 in a few locations (and more often $40,000 to $50,000), because that's more in line with what a Mexican will pay for a house. You won't find these in gringo communities or be able to find them without a lot of effort and contacts. For some, they are just fine. I've put them in because some people just want to live in Mexico and don't expect many frills. God bless you. You can do it. (See the caveat in the next chapter.)

Before you get your hopes up, look at your own area. In some parts of the

United States, you can still find houses in the $40,000 to $50,000 price range (for instance, in Galveston, Texas—and they'll soon be a distant memory now that we've been "discovered"), but be prepared to make some sacrifices. Most of us want to live in silk-stocking houses on a hole-in-the-sock budget.

Generally, you won't find anything near that price in most of the United States. Since I am not a Canadian, I won't try to compare your prices with either country. You know what houses cost at home. See the paragraph below that starts with, "As a rule of thumb," to get a feel for how this relates to Canadian prices. Canadian and American thumbs seem to be about the same.

MID-RANGE PRICES

The average gringo will pay in the middle ranges quoted. A few special (but know that in Mexico, when someone refers to you as "special," they mean odd) people such as myself will find these bargains—and be willing to put the work into the finding process. To my way of thinking, too many Americans and Canadians (and other foreigners) expect to buy a house for nothing because it is in Mexico. On the other hand, too many gringos will contend that only the inflated gringo prices they pay are real.

Of thumbs and rules ...

As a rule of thumb (and only you know how big your thumb is), if you figure that you'll pay about the same for much more house in Mexico than at home, you'll be safe. If you figure you'll pay 60 to 70 percent of your local going rate for more house in Mexico, you'd also be right, if you find bargains. It all depends on where you home is and where you're going to settle. Don't expect to pay Little Rock, Arkansas, prices for beachfront property.

VALUE VERSUS PRICE

I've seen a lot of properties in various price ranges, and cost doesn't always equal quality. Some areas of the country are just inflated. One hundred and fifty thousand dollars will buy you a house of some sort just about anywhere. Twenty thousand dollars will buy you a house of sorts in many towns. Is the $150,000 house seven times as good as the $20,000 one? Sometimes.

It won't be hard to find a house under $100,000 away from the beach; that amount will buy you more house in Mérida than in Cancún. It'll buy you more in San Felipe, Baja California Norte, than in Cabo San Lucas, Baja California Sur.

TYPES OF HOUSING

BARGAIN HOUSES

Bargains exist.

Twenty thousand dollars to $25,000 is sometimes listed as the bottom of the house-buying range. While these houses do exist, they are rare. In most areas, $40,000 to $50,000 is the rock-bottom price. In some ways, it's unrealistic to expect to find houses at these prices. However, I included them because some people have the perseverance and luck to find them. But it takes a lot of legwork and connections to get them before they are gone.

When you buy a house at the lower end of the price spectrum, it will often be without a stick of furniture or light fixtures, and is sometimes missing the kitchen sink. At the medium and higher end, the fixtures will probably be there, and often some furniture could be included, especially if it's being sold by a gringo who doesn't want to cart that stuff back home. And, as I pointed out before, in any price range, the phone line that comes with the house may have an outstanding bill, so make sure you check.

More often than not, houses at the lower end of the scale are very simple concrete structures with one bedroom, a basic bathroom, in a part of town where your neighbors will be Mexicans, not gringos. The houses are often in need of repair. (A note about repairs: They'll cost you double or triple the estimated cost, but can be done piece by piece. In fact, despite the contractor's promises, that's how they'll be done anyway.) They may be in undesirable neighborhoods. Or, they could be gems in the rough. You just have to go see for yourself.

A house in this range will be small, in a local Mexican neighborhood, have old-style plumbing (you won't be able to flush toilet paper, for instance), and a shower, not a tub. The shower might be a pipe coming out of the wall and there will be a tiny (if any) ledge to keep water from getting all over the bathroom floor (it doesn't). Cooking space will be limited. There might only be a connection for a tabletop propane stove. There will seldom be screens on the windows or the door. You will generally have no yard, and often your front door will open directly to the sidewalk. However, I have lived in just such houses and they were acceptable to me.

RENTING

Renting is cheaper than buying.

Renting is always cheaper than buying. Rents have gone up in most areas, though not to the same degree as the cost of buying houses. I've included low-end rentals of $200 to $250 in a few towns. My really cheap friends tell me that they can find something acceptable to rent in the $200 to $250 range anywhere except Baja or Cozumel. Maybe. It all depends on how you define acceptable. It's more likely that you'll always find something decent in the $500 to $700 range. There are bargains in the $400 range, if you have the time to look and some connections. I even know a lady in Cozumel who pays $450 for a one-bedroom apartment. Miracles happen.

Actually, these rental estimates have gone down in some areas from the last edition. There's been more building, and when supply goes up, rental prices go down. If you are in a gringo town and want to be in the "community," then you can expect to pay $600 to $1,500 a month, depending on your tastes and luck. If you want to live on the ocean, count on paying a minimum of $1,000 a month. If you want to live in Baja, Mexico City, Monterrey, or Cozumel, you can figure that it will cost you about 40 to 60 percent more to live there than it will in the rest of the country, with exceptions. In Cabo San Lucas, for instance, most rents are about as high (as well as the general cost of living) as in Southern California (I listed some bottom-end prices throughout Baja, so it is possible to rent for not much more [20 percent] than on the mainland). These prices are for two-bedroom condos and some two-bedroom houses away from the beach areas.

If you want to live in a gringo town but get away from *gringolandia,* then you can figure on spending $250 to $600 a month. This is for a one- or two-bedroom apartment or a small house in a Mexican community. It will be perfectly safe and your neighbors will be working-class Mexicans. If you rent a room from a family, you can expect to pay $120 to $250, depending on your negotiating skills and luck. At this price, meals may sometimes be included, but that's negotiable. As I said in the previous edition, if you choose a small town with few other foreigners, you can find abodes for $100 to $150 a month, which is still true in this new edition.

You have to do the footwork for a reasonably priced rental.

Finding an Apartment—The Mexican Way

Finding a rental house or apartment in Mexico is not the same as finding one in the United States: You ask. You ask everyone you meet, from the bellboy to the gas station attendant to the hotel manager. You ask other expats. There are those who are living cheaply and those who are living large. Take the advice of either, as you prefer.

Look for signs in the windows of houses you would like to rent. The sign may not be for that house, but it will lead you to someone who has a house to rent. Go ahead and check out the local newspapers, it can't hurt. In gringo towns, you will find notices put up where gringos congregate: restaurants, laundries, RV parks. I got my place in Puerto Escondido because one of the owner's sons came up to me on the beach.

You'll find more rental property in the local newspapers than before,
but don't rely on them for the best deals.

For students, writers, painters, etc., there is a different option, called *pensiónes,* which is a small one-bedroom apartment attached to a house. Imagine a widow or an old couple that owns a big house. They might rent out two, three, or four bedrooms in their house for approximately $150 to $300 per month. That money you are paying will make a big difference to the family renting to you. (This is in Mexico City, so in smaller cities they will be cheaper.) They provide an excellent way to get to know the culture of real Mexicans, and some people feel they are paying for an education. Try it, and if you don't like it, you can always move.

Credit History

If you're one of us whose credit report causes apartment complex managers and real estate agents to frantically ring for security, you can hold your head up high when renting in Mexico. Nobody (except for those renting executive houses) is going to pull a credit report on you. Mexico is the land of second starts.

However, the flip side of this (isn't there always a flip side?) is that you will have a hard time getting auto insurance, and even electricity service, if you return to the States, because a bad credit report and having lived abroad make you a double risk. When you come back, say you were living with your brother. (This is from the horse's mouth, not the other end.)

Smokers

It used to be that in Mexico nobody hassled you about smoking. The times are a' changing. While there is not the same degree of antismoking intolerance among Mexican landlords as you're probably used to at home, you'll run into it once in a while. This is particularly true if you're trying to rent from a gringo. They'll rent to drunks, but not smokers. Don't worry, they aren't the only game in town. You'll find a place where you can smoke your stogies in peace, but you may have to look a little more.

RV PROPERTY

RVers can buy their space in some RV parks and put up a *bodega* (a permanent structure) or even leave their trailer there (if they have an FM-3, not just a tourist permit—except for in Baja, where you don't need a permit, and Sonora, where you can get one good for ten years). There's one problem with this: RV parks are disappearing, except on the West Coast of Mexico. As land becomes more valuable, owners are selling out to developers. This same sad story is being played out in the States. Poor, elderly Florida residents are being forced out of their trailer homes by rich condo developers. Fie on them and fie on the ones in Mexico. But that's progress for you.

In some areas, such as Baja, there are permanent RV developments. You're probably safe there, but that's still no guarantee. Buyer beware. Even when you can rent a long-term space, it is sometimes as expensive as renting an apartment. If you are a full-timer and your RV is your home, then go ahead. If you're thinking of spending hundreds of thousands of dollars on a new rig to park in Mexico, think twice.

FINDING A PLACE TO LIVE

INTERNET REAL ESTATE

With the advance of the Internet, it is now possible to get a good idea of what's available before you leave home. Almost every town of any size has a realtor with an Internet page. You can do a search for "Mexico real estate in (your town)" and pull them up. But be aware that, generally, only the high-end properties are listed. I've also found that *fantasmas* (ghosts) or bait-and-switch bargains are listed. That's life, so keep your dreams of cheap living in check until you actually see the place. I know real estate agents in New York City who do the same thing. The really cheap places are not going to be listed on the Internet or with realtors.

Seeing a need for people-to-people real estate (buying or renting), I've added an advertising section to www.mexicomike.com for real estate offered by owners. Some are by gringos, some by Mexicans, and some are shared housing arrangements. Check the site often. There are sections for "wanted to buy/rent" and "offers to sell/rent."

Cheap real estate isn't on the Net.

WANT A BARGAIN? DO SOME FOOTWORK.

Use the above to get a general idea, but keep your mind open. Only by living in a town for a while will you find out what's a good deal and what's not. Although there is a national Mexican real estate association, membership doesn't guarantee that the realtor is right for you anymore than membership in real estate associations in Canada or the States does. Ask around.

You can sometimes get better deals from local realtors than you can from the papers, and vice versa. Not all the properties that a realtor may have are listed on the Internet. If you're buying property, you're better off using a realtor. A good realtor is an invaluable ally who will steer you clear of houses of dubious value. He'll also help you with the paperwork necessary to buy a house, but don't rely on him alone. Make sure everything is signed off on by a *notario publico* (more about them later).

I don't care how "hot" a real estate boom is going on wherever you want to live. Don't settle on a place from the Internet, even if you've already been to a town and know you want to live there. The only exception to this might be a home or condo in a development you've personally seen and like. Take your time.

After you settle in, you will find that all your new expatriate buddies will have tales to tell of how they found their perfect habitat. As a newcomer, you'll eat these stories up. After you've been around for awhile, you'll have your own story. Just to get you started, I will tell you how I ended up in my home in Puerto Escondido, Oaxaca.

A Personal Story about Finding a Home ...

In the South, we have a song about a boll weevil (a bug) who was forced out of his home. I was as low as that bug when I began my journey.

I didn't intend to end up in Oaxaca. When I left New Orleans, feeling about as down in the dumps as a man could who had just lost his girlfriend, his father, and his fortune in the same month. I didn't know where I wanted to go. My cat had even flown the coop (talk about a mixed metaphor). All I knew was that life had given me a wonderful opportunity to start over because it had taken away everything I had. I knew I wanted to write a book and didn't want to work in the real world while I did it. I went to a friend's house near Mobile, Alabama, and lived for free in his boathouse for a few weeks. I very nearly rented a place on the beach in Alabama for $300 a month, because I was afraid to take the leap and move to Mexico.

I had fallen prey to the negative stories about Mexico. That was before I was "Mexico" Mike. After all, the weather in Alabama was almost warm enough for me and it would have been less hassle. Had I done that, I would have cheated myself out of a wonderful experience. Never let the easier, softer way keep you from your dream.

Follow your heart.

I finally followed my heart and not my head and headed south. A friend told me about a paradise—Tuxpan, Veracruz. I left with high hopes. Tuxpan is a nice enough place to visit, but the beach is gray and it gets some cold weather. I moved on. The moral here (and who am I to be telling anyone about morals?) is that you have to find your own place. What's right for others may not be right for you. That's yet another reason I suggest you live somewhere for several months before jumping in and moving.

After checking out several other places, one night I found myself on a bus going to Acapulco. At least I thought it was going to Acapulco. My Spanish was pretty poor and I didn't realize that it wasn't going in the direction of Acapulco. It stopped for the night in Puerto Escondido, Oaxaca. Something came over me when I saw the lights ringing the horseshoe bay. I fell in love. I knew this was to be my home.

Everywhere I asked for a place to live. The local *medico*, who owned a pharmacy and spoke English, said he had just the place for me. It was nice, all right. It looked similar to the place in Dothan, Alabama. It also cost more. I told him it was too expensive, so he showed me his second set of monopoly houses. These were thatched-roof huts with one room and a dirt floor.

He magnanimously offered one to me for a mere $250 a month. I was really sad. He was disgusted with me and informed me that if I couldn't afford that price, I would never find anything. Chances are you'll run into the same type of landlord (or gringo) giving you advice. Ignore them. He was just trying to sell me what he had and charge me what he thought the market would bear. If he didn't rent to me, there would be some other sucker tomorrow. (In the business section, I warn against making enemies. That doctor is now one of the muckety-mucks in Puerto, and last time I was there, he remembered me. Let's just say he didn't give me an *abrazo*. The only good news is that years later I met a very unhappy gringa. She'd married the doc and found out that he courted better than he married.)

Discouraged, I thought I'd have to abandon my dream of living in Mexico and writing my great book. I was on the beach, taking one last sunbath, when a small kid approached me. He made me understand that he knew of a house for rent. How he knew I was looking for one is a testament to the Mexican grapevine; a gringo is never unobserved. I followed him over the road, across the bridge, down a ravine, across a stream, and up a dirt hill. At the sleeping pig—literally, there was a pig that always seemed to sleep in the same place on the path—we turned left. Great, I thought, this has got to be a dump.

Mexico is the land of dreams come true.

It wasn't. It was a comfortable, large, one-room concrete house with a concrete floor and my own bathroom. It even had a sink and a two-burner propane stove! It overlooked the bay and had a hammock on my front porch where I could watch the sunset. Man, it was heaven. The rent was $90 a month. (This was a long time ago, but the principle is still accurate. Everyone will tell you that you can't find something in your budget. Keep looking and you will. That is Mexico. It is a land of hope and dreams that can come true if you don't give up. Go with it.) Because the owner wanted to be paid in pesos, and the peso was devaluing at about 20 percent a year, my rent could only go down. I took it.

I stayed there for the better part of a year. I wrote my book and then, one day, it was just time to leave. I'd fallen in love with a woman instead of a place and she lived in Seattle. Interestingly enough, I found a shared housing situation that cost me $100 a month and had hot water! *¡Que lujo!* (What luxury!)

The moral of this story (there I go again) is twofold: Don't set your hopes on a town until you have seen it, and don't get discouraged if you don't find what you want and can afford right away. It pays to shop and to be patient.

RV LIVING

There are lots of full-timers living in Mexico, mainly during the winter months. If you have an FM-3, you can leave a trailer in Mexico and go home. Otherwise, it has to leave the country with you (except for in Sonora and Baja—see above).

There are fewer RV parks today than there were when I wrote the last edition. RVers aren't traveling as much, property has become too valuable, and the existing parks vary a lot in quality and price. Some are quite nice, with concrete pads, storage sheds, club rooms, activities, Jacuzzis, and electric, water, and sewer hookups. Some are primitive, merely places to park. Most are somewhere in between. The upscale ones will cost about $350 to $550 a month. The mid-range ones will run about $250 to $350 a month. The basic ones are about $125 to $175 a month. In the Baja, there are still some basic places with no facilities for about $100 a month. You can also park on a beach there for nothing. (I don't recommend this in other parts of Mexico, but the Baja is a different case.) Electrical current is variable, with surges and dips, so it is a good idea to protect yourself from that. Also, you will need a very long extension cord, 100 feet ought to do it, although 150 feet couldn't hurt. The electrical outlets are not necessarily polarized, and sometimes they are hooked up backwards, so bring a voltage tester and an inexpensive adapter (sold in U.S. and Mexican hardware stores) that will convert your three-prong plug to a two-pronger.

In the Pacific Coast towns such as Kino Bay, San Carlos, Guaymas, Mazatlán, Puerto Vallarta, Melaque/San Patricio, and Manzanillo, the popular parks tend to fill up during the winter, but there are always spaces at some of the less popular ones. You can also buy your lot.

In the Baja, the parks between Tijuana and Ensenada are often full of permanents, year-round. In Bahía Los Angeles, Mulegé, La Paz, and Los Cabos, there will be plenty of room, though some parks can be full during the winter. Prices are high.

On the Gulf Coast, there is always room and the prices tend to be lower, but there aren't many parks. There are still enough to make a trip there enjoyable. Try the Emerald Coast between Tecolutla and Veracruz.

In the Yucatan, there are still a few parks on the beach. Property has just become too expensive. Prices tend to be similar to the Baja parks. I'd be leery of buying a space here.

BUYING PROPERTY

BUYING UNDEVELOPED LAND

Be aware that the property taxes on undeveloped land are considerably higher than on developed property. They can go as high as 26 percent and increase 2.6 percent per year that the property is undeveloped. Construction costs are about as high as in the United States, and sometimes higher.

PITFALLS OF BUYING PROPERTY

As I promised, I am not trying to sugarcoat the joys of owning property in Mexico. While most real estate transactions are aboveboard, you have to do your due diligence. Please don't take the negative stories below as the big picture. They are isolated incidents in a larger universe of happy stories about buying property in Mexico. They are here not to scare you away from living in Mexico, but to make you a better-informed consumer.

A little due diligence will save you from undue distress.

Most everyone has heard of the largest land fraud case in Mexico's history—the $25 million eviction of 150 gringos in 1999 from the Punta Banda area in Baja California Notre (near Ensenada). The scandal occurred in a development known as the Baja Beach and Tennis Club. I covered this as breaking news on my Web site for several months in 1999. The developer, Carlos Teran del Rio, has been cast as a demon or a dupe, depending on whose account you read. The short version of the story is that the land was in dispute long before the property was sold to Americans. The dispute occurred in 1974, when the property was removed from *ejido* maps, and the land was recognized as being owned by a group of eight Mexican families. Mr. Teran negotiated with the *ejilitarios,* based on a 1973 map showing the land as being under their control. Sales began in 1987. In 1988, the orginal owners filed suit to recover their land. Prospective buyers were assured by Mr. Teran that the suit was frivolous and gringos continued to "buy" property from him under a bank administered *fideicomiso.*

According to a news story in *hispanicvista,* www.hispanicvista.com/html/001106sd.html, by Patrick Osio Jr., "The true victims are those who entered into contracts between the years 1988 and 1991. They were apparently given every assurance and even entered into *fideicomiso* (bank trust agreements)." But in 1991, the bank canceled the trust, and did not enter into any new trust agreements. The year coincided with the first court victory for the legal owners.

A number of attorneys in Tijuana and Ensenada report that numerous Americans checked with them before entering into contracts, and were all advised to not enter into the agreements due to pending ownership litigation. Most Americans, however, went through with the contracts, because "it's so cheap," since nothing comparable to this was available in Southern California for the price.

Another story at www.sandiegometro.com/2001/feb/connection.html, also by Mr. Osio, stated this:

It is clear that many of the Americans who purchased through bank trusts and in good faith were victimized. Yet there are many instances where, as an attorney in Tijuana says, buyers "wanted to hear what they wanted to hear." Many Americans seeking advice simply failed to listen when told not to buy in Punta Banda. Many who did would say the salespeople were assuring them the claimants had no case, and besides, where else could they get beachfront property that cheap?

A reprint of the *Los Angeles Times* story is available at www.bajaquest.com/bajanews/archives/archv005.htm.

The lesson here, in my opinion, is that although some of the buyers were duped, the problems were well-known before most of the unfortunate Americans spent their money. Several had consulted attorneys and were warned to stay away, but ignored the advice. I would suggest that you pay heed to these unfortunate people's plight and do a lot of investigation before buying anything. If there is even a hint of dispute, walk away, no matter how "cheap" the deal is, unless you are willing to lose your investment.

Beware of buying on a "contract of usage," or on land that used to be part of an *ejido.* Do extensive research before buying or leasing land anywhere in Mexico. While there *may* be nothing wrong with a "contract of usage" deal, just be sure you know what you are getting into. Sign up for my bulletin board and newsletter for breaking stories on such things. *Stick with property that has a clear title. Even if property can be put into a bank trust, it is not a guarantee that everything is okay.*

Property prices are all over the board. The definition of a "lot" seems to be fluid. I didn't include lot prices in my city listings. See the area you're interested in to get a range.

Beware of ghosts—again.

Do not buy property under another's name (i.e., a Mexican citizen, called a *Presta Nombre*) or an assumed name. Some people will advise you to do this to get around the *ejido* restriction. It is illegal and you will lose your property, maybe not today, but eventually. Some people have bought property under assumed names of Mexicans throughout Mexico, which is blatantly illegal, and lost their land.

Do not buy property on a lease. Leases are good for ten years minus a day, no matter what your contract may say.

Do not buy property under a rental contract. Although the contract may state "for an indefinite period," under Mexican law, a residential rental contract is valid for one year, then renewable on a monthly basis—at the lien holder's discretion.

In 2004, the mayor of Pochutla, Oaxaca, got a little greedy selling land that wasn't his. A *notario publico* in Cuernavaca signed off on real estate transactions that were on *ejido* land and people lost their investments. A politician desired the land of a friend of mine in Nuevo Leon and had it taken away by using the absentee landlord provision of the law. Several people I know bought property and investments with a Mexican partner and were squeezed out due to technicalities of their arrangement. This discouraging news is not meant to scare you off, but to encourage you to be very careful when buying property.

FINANCING REAL ESTATE

Hooray! You can now finance a home or commercial purchase in Mexico. (Excuse me for repeating the information in the overview, but doggone it, not everyone reads every page!) As we go to print, there are a few companies purporting to offer financing to gringos and one that says they will finance anyone who can prove Mexican heritage. I am leery of these companies' claims and am investigating them thoroughly before recommending any of them. Please check www.mexicomike.com for real estate updates.

This is a big change since the last edition of this book. You can now finance property all over Mexico through an American collateral mortgage company, both for residential and commercial property. While there are a few companies offering this service, as a developer for a large housing project who called me for advice said, "I've talked to several people who claim they can finance property in Mexico. As they say in Mexico, they were *fantasmas*."

Only deal with the real.

Literally, *fantasma* means "a ghost," but it is commonly used to describe ideas or people whose promises are insubstantial, or who promise more than they can deliver. I learned this word from the owner of the spa Ixtapan de la Sal, who was leery of my reservation service (www.spagetaway.com) representing them because so many people claimed to have such businesses and few did. There's a lesson here for those of you who want to start a business: Gringo businesses come and go in Mexico, so expect a little hesitancy from Mexican businesses. It took me three years to get a contract with Ixtapan.

Check my Web site (www.mexicomike.com/Real%20Estate/collateral_mortgage.htm, or just by clicking the menu for "Living/Travel") to get a recommendation for honest companies. Generally speaking, you'll need about 50 percent as a down payment, though it is possible that some companies will be willing to finance you for a mere 20 to 30 percent down. The interest rate will vary, and be a couple of points higher than if you were purchasing property in the United States or Canada, but will always be less (about half) than you'd pay with a Mexican company.

Mexican banks can now finance real estate for a fairly reasonable interest rate. It used to be that interest rates could run as high as 27 percent for large purchases in Mexico, but now, although they are considerably higher than U.S. or Canadian banks, they are no longer exorbitant. Still, you will get a better rate with an international financier. Mexican banks generally (although there are a lot of changes going on in this area right now) will only finance your home purchase for five years.

Before you consider buying anything, please buy this book: Dennis John Peyton's *How to Buy Real Estate in Mexico* (2220 Otay Lakes Road, Ste. 502, East Lake, CA 91915; Phone 800-LAW-MEXICO; www.lawmexico.com). Dennis is a lawyer (approved to practice in both Mexico and the United States) and his writing style is more lawyerlike. He covers details that you might never think of.

REALTORS

I am not going to go into the step-by-step details of purchasing property as a realtor will, but here is a general guide. The most important thing to remember is buyer beware. Mexico is a different country with different laws. There are some very good, honest realtors in Mexico, and many of them are members of the Associatión Mexican de Professionales Inmobiliarios, or AMPI. The real estate industry in Mexico is not as highly regulated as in the United States. In fact, some municipalities allow someone to call themselves a realtor with no licensing. The members of this association are generally regarded as subscribing to higher ethical standards than nonmembers. Still, this is no guarantee that there are not some unscrupulous people in the bunch. Also, just because a realtor is a member of Century 21, or some other name you are familiar with (I am not singling them out), that doesn't mean that he subscribes to the high standards of the parent organization in the United States. The Mexican company has bought a franchise, and in your contract it will state that you cannot sue the parent organization if something goes awry.

The best way to protect yourself is to ask for references from other buyers. Then check them out. Also, ask several other foreign property owners whom they deal with and what their opinion is. People are always happy to give their opinion of other people. Then trust your own judgment. Some gringos assume that because a realtor speaks English, he is honest. I have never found that language skills had anything to do with integrity.

You can buy property from another gringo or Mexican and bypass the realtor. Again, don't assume that the other party is angelic. He could also be selling you something that he doesn't completely own.

Once you have decided that a realtor is working in your best interest, don't be in a hurry. That is considered bad form by Mexicans. Sellers who know you are a gringo and see you are in a hurry expect to get top dollar. Wait a while and see if the price doesn't come down.

CLOSING COSTS

Closing costs vary according to the area of the country. Generally, you can expect to pay anywhere from 5 to 8 percent of the assessed value, which may be lower than the selling price. Sometimes the costs will be even higher. Find out what your realtor charges upfront. There are other fees. They vary so much that I can't give you estimates, so ask your realtor what they will be. There will also be an appraisal fee. The appraisal must be done by a *perito valuador* (usually an architect). There's a Foreign Relations Permit, notary fees, title search, and insurance fee, and, of course, the bank administrative fee. You have to pay a deposit (generally about one-half the estimated closing costs) before the *notario publico* will begin the process of researching the title.

There is a fee for setting up the *fideicomiso*, dependent on the value of your property. A rough guide is that it might cost $2,000 to $3,000, or more. Then there will be annual administrative fees, generally a few hundred dollars a year. Mexican banks used to have a reputation for being inhospitable and bureaucratic. They deserved it. This has changed. They are now more competitive and more customer service–oriented. Shop around. Find one you like. Banks are still sometimes a pain to deal with, but they are a lot better than they used to be. The bottom line on the fees and closing costs is that you can expect to pay about 6 to 8 percent of the real value when all is said and done.

THE *FIDEICOMISO,* OR BANK TRUST

Fideicomiso—*Friend or Foe?*

If you are buying property on mainland Mexico, away from the restricted zone, you can get a title and the *fideicomiso* does not apply to you.

First, a little history. After Mexico lost a big chunk of its land to the Republic of Texas and the United States during the nineteenth century, it was justifiably suspect of foreigners buying property near its borders. So it was put into the Constitution that foreigners could not own property within the "restricted zone." The restricted zone is any land within fifty kilometers (thirty-two miles) of the coast or 100 kilometers (sixty-four miles) from the border. All of Baja is included in the restricted zone.

By the 1990s, Mexico realized that it could profit from foreign investment and passed the Foreign Investment Law of 1993, permitting foreigners to buy property in the restricted zone, yet not thwart the constitution because the "ownership" has to be approved by the Secretary of Foreign Relations. Gee, since the development of the mega beach resorts occurred soon thereafter, I wonder if there was any correlation?

If you buy in the restricted zone, then the title will be held for you in a trust by a bank. In these areas, you will be given a *fideicomiso*, or real estate trust. (For a translated page of a detailed explanation of this, go to www.translate.google.com/translate?hl=en&sl=es&u=http://www.soler.com.ar/general/inftec/2000/otros/fideic/fidei.htm&prev=/search%3Fq%3D fideicomiso%26hl%3Den%26lr%3D%26ie%3DUTF-8.)

A Mexican bank is set up as the trustee and holds the title for you. The bank is the owner of the property but you are entitled to enjoy the rights of ownership as if you owned the property. You can sell or will the property to whomever you wish at its fair market value for a period of fifty years. The trust is renewable up to three times. The existence of a *fideicomiso* does not protect you if there were irregularities in its formation. Have your own *notario publico* research it back to its formation.

Some people have a fear of this. Yes, there is a danger that the banks could be nationalized and all foreign investments could be declared null, but this is incredibly unlikely. There is that risk in any foreign country, but it is so small that I wouldn't worry about it. Should a bank become insolvent, the law states that any *fideicomisos* under its control will be transferred to another bank; I'm sure they mean a solvent bank.

Because the trend today is for the globalization of Mexico and the privatization of banks and other former government-owned businesses, I don't foresee this happening. If it did happen, it wouldn't make any difference if a bank held your deed or you had it under your mattress. In fact, I think that you are better off in this unlikely scenario if you have a bank to go to bat for you.

Some say that there is another advantage of a bank holding the deed. If you are an absentee owner and will be gone for long periods of time, there is the possibility that squatters could take over your house and land. If they know that the bank is the owner, they are not likely to try this. If they did, the bank would take care of evicting them.

However, a Mexican friend of mine scoffed at this theory. He doesn't think the bank cares about anything except collecting your money. You ask two people and you get two different answers. Who's right? I tend to side with my Mexican friend. The best thing to do is ask other expats what their experience has been—and then trust your own instincts.

SQUATTERS

There is a very real possibility of squatters taking over your land. Dating back to the Revolution, there is a prejudice in the law against absentee landlords. Thus, in Mexico squatters have far more rights than in the United States or Canada. I have known people who have owned property outright in Mexico, only to lose it when squatters took it over. The solution should be simple: Never leave your estate untenanted. (Although, I should put in the caveat that my friends who lost their ranch in Nuevo Leon lost it to their ranch manager, who lived on the property.)

Some people have other gringos house-sit for them while they're gone. Many people (especially those with ranches or large estates) have a resident caretaker who lives on the property. Ninety-nine percent of the time, this works. However, in the interest of telling you the whole story, that's exactly what my friends did. A local politician desired their land (it was a ranch), so he bribed the caretaker to lie in court and act as the squatter. While it was theoretically possible to fight a long court battle and win (after all, my friends were in the right), they gave up after spending more than a few thousand dollars. Just as in other countries, being right doesn't guarantee you'll win a court battle. Money talks.

NOTARIO PUBLICOS

Okay, now that you've found your dream home, the fun begins. You don't need an attorney as well as a notary public. The notary can do all the paperwork for you. Patience is a virtue here, as you have entered the bureaucratic zone, not unlike the twilight zone.

A *notario publico*, or notary public, is a licensed attorney who is also a de facto representative of the government. He will have something called a *cédula profesional.* This is his professional license that has his picture on it. Although he does not represent the government, he is responsible for seeing that real estate transactions are legal. He is responsible for making sure that all legal niceties are taken care of, that the seller has clear title to the land, that it is not part of an *ejido* or public land grant (this system is being dismantled as we speak, but there is still a chance that old land claims could conflict with your purchase), and that all taxes are paid. As you can see, there is no correlation between the "notary" title in Mexico and the same title in the United States.

While most *notarios* are trustworthy, there have been cases where they did not perform their jobs adequately, either through incompetence or malfeasance. Check out their reputations.

All of these things are going to take time. You will have to deal with a host of Mexican officials in preparing your paperwork. Do not be in a hurry and do not be arrogant. Treat each of the people you meet with the utmost respect. Do not belittle the people involved in the seemingly endless bureaucracy that you have to deal with. These people have a job to do and they will do it their way in their time. If you get angry or show your frustration, you will only slow the process down or bring it to a complete standstill. Patience is not just a virtue in Mexico, it is a necessity.

Condos: Good or Bad?
*Condominium ownership will be a little more streamlined because there is often an American-based company at the back of the deal. You will still have to provide various documents and go through many of the same procedures—or you should. Just because someone is selling you a condo doesn't mean he has clear title. It always pays to have a **notario publico** check out any deal you get involved with. Find out what the condo fees are now and how they have increased in past years. Although this is absolutely no guarantee that they won't double tomorrow, it could give you an idea of what to expect. My feeling about condos is that the greed factor is an ever-present reality.*

Need more help? If you need more guidance about driving through, moving to, or working in Mexico, you can call me at 888-234-3452 or e-mail mexicomikenelson23@mexicomike.com. I make a living from offering these services, so only call if you are serious and are willing to pay me for my time.

MOVING YOUR STUFF

Gotta have my stuff.

Whether you're going to rent or buy, you probably want to bring your stuff with you. Or do you? It is expensive. Many items can be purchased in Mexico for less than the cost of transporting them, but that's up to you. Here's a guideline to moving costs, from www.cetra.com.mx. Chicago to Monterrey is a good example because it is about in the middle-distance range, mileage wise. Moving the contents of an "average" three-bedroom house will cost about $10,000. Washington state to Oaxaca would cost between two and three times that amount. If you figure the distance from your point of origin to destination and compare it to Chicago to Monterrey (about 1,700 miles), that should give you a multiplier to figure a ballpark cost of the move. If you can ship your stuff from a seaport, you'll save a bundle, as explained below.

Clutterless Recovery Groups, Inc.
If, similar to me, you are one of those people for whom getting rid of possessions and making decisions about what's important and what's not is difficult, you may want to see the Web site of Clutterless Recovery Groups, Inc. (a 501(c)3 nonprofit support group), www.clutterless.org. We have an online newsletter and support groups nationwide. We call ourselves clutterers. The reason we can't get rid of things is psychological, not organizational. That's why organizing tips and tricks haven't worked for you in the past (they didn't, did they?). I've written three books on the subject, Stop Clutter from Stealing Your Life *($15),* Clutter-Proof Your Business *($16), and* Stop Clutter from Wrecking Your Family *($16), all available from the Web or by calling 888-234-3452. (Or you can order them by sending a check or money order, U.S. funds only, payable to: Clutterless Recovery Groups, 508 N. 10th St., Ste. C-10, McAllen, TX 78501. Include $5.50 shipping and handling.)*

If you decide that you would rather buy Mexican furniture and appliances and all you want to bring are personal items, you can load up your car with them. It might even pay to buy a used travel trailer to transport them (no cargo trailers allowed). Another alternative is to cart your stuff to the border, then ship it all in on a Mexican bus, though you might have to pay duty on some items. If you're using up your FM-3 allotment, you need to make a decision of what to send in one fell swoop.

A new wrinkle in storage is that you can rent cargo containers in which to store your stuff. Thus, if you use a moving company, they can load the container into their trucks and save you a bundle.

International Moving is figured on a weight/volume scheme. Whatever is bigger is what they will charge for, and, in most cases, it will be volume, since furniture is not too heavy but it does occupy lots of space.

Now what do you have to consider during a move? Packing material is required. If the moving contains lots of small items, it will be more expensive, since more packing material will be used, other than only packing large furniture. When packing small items, we don't only wrap everything, but it is then packed into boxes, using a lot of material.

Transportation is another factor. If someone is moving from Chicago, as an example, shipment must come via truck, and trucking is expensive since it is charged by weight and mile, meaning that depending on the weight/volume they will give a rate per mile, and that can increase the price a lot. If a shipment is coming from Houston, Los Angeles, Miami, or New York, it will come by sea, and sea shipments are a lot cheaper, almost 50 percent cheaper. So, depending on where it's coming from, special transportation is needed.

Cost is figured on a combination of weight/volume. Add to that a charge from Mexican customs. I wish I could give you a figure, but the cost varies wildly, based on how much time it takes them to inspect your goods. Having a detailed, and I mean *detailed*, list of items helps; don't just put "dishes." Instead, list: "8 plates, 8 saucers, 8 cups, 4 frying pans," etc. I would allow at least $1,000 for customs fees. To that, you'll have to add fees for warehousing your stuff while they inspect it until it is loaded back on the truck.

Transportation in Mexico also varies a lot, depending on the destination. Cities that have a lot of commercial traffic going to them, such as Mexico City, Monterrey, etc., have cheaper rates, but if a shipment is going to a remote city, such as Oaxaca, Zacatecas, etc., prices will be higher.

Unpacking services operate similarly to transportation in Mexico, except that big cities have international moving companies. I don't recommend using a local unpacking service if you can avoid it since, should anything be damaged, the insurance company will not cover it, and the company hired in the United States will insist that you use the services of a certified moving company, which will have to come from the closest city, and this will increase the price.

Need more help? If you need more guidance about driving through, moving to, or working in Mexico, you can call me at 888-234-3452 or e-mail mexicomikenelson23@mexicomike.com. I make a living from offering these services, so only call if you are serious and are willing to pay me for my time.

FRANK TALK ABOUT RELATIONSHIPS AND SEX

This was one of the more popular chapters in all previous editions. Who doesn't like to at least talk about sex and love? (Sorry, there's no discussion of chocolates, but I like them too.) It was also one of the most controversial. Please don't take it out of context. I'll never forget the anonymous reader who lambasted the last edition with the comment "I'm not a woman, gay, in a twelve-step program, or looking for a girlfriend. This book was worthless." Gee, I must have touched a nerve in this apparently celibate, never-challenged-by-addictions, homophobic gentleman. Everybody's a critic. Fortunately, there must have been enough people who welcomed some honest information about our natural instincts to keep the book a better seller than any of the competition over the long haul.

If reading some observations you won't get from any other book of its kind don't interest you, then skip this section (and the one for those in twelve-step programs). Take what you need and leave the rest. If, however, knowing a bit about the differences between relationships in Mexico versus the United States or Canada would be valuable to you, then read on.

CANDID ADVICE FOR WOMEN

Is Mexico the fountain of youth?

Some women who live in Latin America shed years and become younger in their attitudes. They find the challenge of living in and adapting to a foreign culture invigorating.

There are many women who have settlements from divorces or the sales of their houses who flock south to live. In fact, the ratio of female-to-male foreign residents varies from two to one (average) to four to one (Lake Chapala). Most single women who've moved to Mexico have a wonderful time and find a new life that is much happier and fuller than the one they left behind. Many of them who had spent years in unhappy relationships find themselves and experience a joyful life for the first time.

Single women can enjoy life much better in Mexico than at home.

In a gringo community, there are many social events, clubs, and activities that make fitting in quite easy. It's a different experience than in the United States and Canada. Not having a date is not uncommon. Bonding with other women similar to you is easier. Should you choose to date, your male expat friends will be able to talk about something you both have in common—living in Mexico—instead of their jobs. There's still no guarantee that they won't talk about their exes; men are still men.

Couch potatoes are rare (potatoes grow best in cold climates) and workaholics have to give up their addiction cold turkey. A workaholic in Mexico (among expats) is someone who works more than four hours a day. There's just such a feeling of fun and adventure to living in Mexico that the old petty things, such as having to have a man around the house, are secondary. If you need something fixed, you ask your handyman. You pay him a few pesos and don't have to cook and clean for him or put up with his grumpiness. Not a bad deal.

Unfortunately, there are two other scenarios that can be played out. Both can happen to men, with a few slight changes in the story line.

Watch out for negativity.

The first seems rather inexplicable on the surface. After a few years of living as expatriates, some women become negative and bitter. Perhaps it is a reaction to the fatalism of the Latin culture, or frustration at the difficulty of getting things done. Maybe it stems from the double standards found in such a male-dominated society. Machismo is very much alive. There are good sides to this as well, but it can be frustrating for a liberated woman. Quite a few gringas become cynical and concentrate on the negative aspects of life around them.

I've seen young women become old in spirit in only a few years. To avoid this, I strongly recommend a few visits back home or to Europe each year and having a trusted friend let you know when you start crossing the line. A strong competitive nature when you didn't have one to start with is a bad sign, as is a need to be right all the time over unimportant issues. I don't know the cure, but if you find yourself seeing only the bad, ordering waiters and other help around imperiously, and bragging about events in the past that gave you pleasure when everyone else is talking about the present, maybe it's time for you to relocate to Canada or the States for a while.

RELATIONSHIPS

Relationships can be a challenge in any culture. Latin men are great family men and have a charm gene that American and Canadian men didn't get. There are some very good Latin men and some marriages that have lasted for many years between gringas (or *gueras*, which means blondes, but is used as a synonym for gringas) and Latin men. One difference between Mexican men and those back home is that they don't attach the negative stigma to women just because they have a few extra pounds. In fact, some men prefer a woman who has some meat on her bones to a skinny model-like woman.

A few extra pounds? It's considered a plus by many Mexican men.

Gringas who marry responsible Latin men are often quite happy with their new life. As I say to men (about Latinas, that is), just be aware that when you marry a Latin man, you marry the whole family. If you thought that your mother-in-law was interfering in your marriage back home, you might have a hard time adjusting to a Mexican marriage. *Mamá* and *la abuelita*, grandma, will continue to exert tremendous influence over the males in the family. Chide your husband about this and you will be the loser.

KIDS

You'd better like kids. A Mexican marriage without children is, in general, viewed as a failure on somebody's part. When I told Mexican friends that I had no children, even though two women were insane enough to marry me, they just gave me a look of tremendous pity and sadness. When I married my second wife while working for a Mexican company, the *jefe* gave us a wonderful wedding gift and put his arm around me saying, "Now you are a man! Soon you will have children and grandchildren." (It never happened.)

It does take a village in Mexico!

While with middle-class Mexicans things have changed a great deal over the years, Mexican men are likely to be doting fathers, except when it comes to changing diapers or the day-to-day management of the household. *Mamacíta* will have a lot of input into how the children should be raised. So will the rest of the family. In Mexico, it truly does take a village (or at least a big family) to raise a child.

If you marry later in life, you will inherit a family that includes nieces, nephews, grandkids, and so on. You will be expected to like them. Fortunately, Mexican kids, in general, are better behaved than their U.S. or Canadian counterparts, though they still look similar to each other; MTV and Hollywood dictate fashion worldwide. Fortunately, they're more likely to listen to their elders, be quieter in restaurants and public places, and respect their teachers. All in all, if I ever were to have kids, I'd rather have a Mexican kid than an American one by a long shot. (Then I could prove to my Mexican friends that they needn't pity me because I was shooting blanks.)

BEWARE OF BUSINESS AND RELATIONSHIP COMBOS

So much for the idyllic marriage. I hope you find one; however, I'd like to point out another possibility to watch out for. This happens all over the world (including in the States and Canada), but I can only talk about Mexico in this book: A woman will move down, usually in a vulnerable state, and find herself attracted to a Latin man. So far, so good.

There is a subculture of Latin males (usually at beach resorts or other areas that attract lots of gringas) who prey on these women. These guys are young and very romantic. They sweep lonely gringas off their feet, women who would not fall for this at home. After the hook is set, they suggest that there could be a way for the two of them to be so much happier.

Watch out for the "if-only" amante (lover).

How's that? you ask. Simple, if only we started a little restaurant (or bought a fishing boat, or a boutique, or a hotel, etc.), then I could quit my job as a fisherman (or clerk, or bellboy, etc.), and we could spend more time together. Sounds dreamy, you say, the visions of being a foreign-business owner dancing in your head. Of course, you have all that money doing nothing back home, and this could be a perfect investment. Of course, you would put it in his name to avoid the complications of Mexican laws. Some men would even be willing to marry you, just to help you out.

Just say, "Whoa!"

Whoa! You may think I am being silly, that you are smarter than that. Yes, you probably are—under normal circumstances. Unfortunately, these guys are good (a lot smoother than I will ever be, that's for sure), and the romantic Mexican moon has powers that we don't understand. I have personally known several women who fell for these scams. What usually happens is that you do get the business going and one day find yourself spending all your time working while he is out "promoting" it.

Often he is "promoting" another business (and probably more) with a new gringa in town, or maybe just making a new friend. When I was a travel writer, part of my job was to revisit the same tourist hotels and restaurants every year. I can tell the stage of this kind of relationship by the atmosphere and quality of such hotels and restaurants. By the time she finally leaves, disgusted, I had taken the business out of my guidebooks.

Please don't get me wrong, or take this out of context. I also know couples who have run successful businesses and had great marriages. I am all for romance (not that I understand it), and it's no skin off my nose whom you date. Just take it easy and take a second look. Then have the second look take a second look. Ask around among other women and find out if this guy has a reputation for romancing women into business. It will be worth the effort.

If a deal is too good to be true and must be closed today, get suspicious. Just take your time, and I wish you every happiness in the world.

Yet Another Type of Scammer

One last thing. I'm not your papa and have no real stake in this issue, but a number of my women friends have asked me to include a paragraph about the following. There is yet another type of fellow who can turn out to be bad news. He is the older guy who hangs around with younger gringo groups. He will be a romantic sweet-talker and being with him will be great fun. Have fun, enjoy yourself, but don't expect it to come to more than that.

These guys are not looking for a lasting relationship. Why else do you think they are hanging around with twenty-year-olds? (And how, we poor older American and Canadian guys ask, does he do that? Latin charm, my friend—something we'll never have.) Accept them for what they are and don't get too involved. If they want to come to visit you in your home country, fine, but don't be surprised if they are also visiting a number of other women. Some of them would like to marry a gringa in order to get their papers to live in the United States.

CANDID ADVICE FOR MEN

Okay guys, your turn.

Just between us guys, let's be honest. The reason a lot of you want to live in Latin America is so you can meet and marry a Latina. There's nothing wrong with that. There are some Latinas who would love to marry a gringo, some for true love and some because we have reputations as good providers (if not as lovers). It's not that uncommon for a young Mexican woman to marry a sixty-plus-year-old gringo. While a social security check here is not much of a prize, in Mexico (for women in the under-middle-class), it's a good deal.

First of all, remember that not all Latinas are interested in you. Many of them are very happy with their own culture and men and don't want some ignorant, uncultured gringo coming along and bothering them.

Although these women may wear tight skirts and stockings, it doesn't mean they are loose. Many of them get their fashion sense from MTV and magazines that profile Hollywood and Mexican cinema stars. They're nice Catholic girls underneath, so use some class or you will risk offending their brothers. They all have brothers, none of whom has a sense of humor about his sister. If you find a woman you like and begin to court her, it will probably take longer than you think, at least in Mexico. If you read the story earlier in the book about how I used the word *casada*, married, for *cansado*, tired, you can get an idea of what could happen.

In that story, remember I mentioned that the mother and daughter left the table where we were having dinner after my linguistic mistake? I didn't say why: They didn't want to be around for the bloodshed. The *hermanos y tios*, brothers and uncles, were preparing to do me bodily harm for having misled their sister or niece. I barely escaped with my life, and only after I convinced them that I was not married, but just ignorant in Spanish, did they take my word for it and we all had drinks together. But for several weeks I knew that they had their eyes on me.

Even groupies are different.

As a final note on how Mexican girls differ from American girls, let me tell you about a famous Mexican rock star. His has one of the biggest bands in Mexico, with a huge following. When groupies get in to visit him in his hotel room, they're more likely to want to talk about music than, well, what you would expect from American or Canadian groupies. (He loves playing in the United States and Canada.) And you, my friend, aren't even a rock star. Enough said?

LOVE ME, LOVE MY FAMILY

Since I'm sure you didn't read the part of this chapter on women who marry Mexican men, I'm repeating some of the information, with slight twists for you guys. Marry a Mexican woman and you marry her family. That means that you'd better like children, grandchildren, and in-laws, because you will have plenty of each. Your esposa-to-be will always defer to your mother-in-law-to-be. Get used to it. Your mother-in-law will try to control you, too, but not directly. It'll be through your wife. Your father-in-law and his father will have a say in how you live, if you have a business, and how you conduct your business. Of course, the flip side of that is that you will have employment if they own businesses.

The extended family provides a warm, loving group to help you when you need it. It can ease your entry into social and business circles. It can also mean a meddlesome set of in-laws and a lot less alone time. Some love it. Some don't. Test the waters before you go swimming.

PARENTING

Mexican men have a different definition of parenting.

Men aren't expected to share the parenting fifty-fifty (though this is changing in the upper-middle-class circles). You won't have to do as much with the children as you would be expected to in a marriage in the United States or Canada. You will, however, be expected to provide the necessities damn well. If the two of you start a business, you may find that if you don't do a very good job, she will run it better than you. A lot of guys told me they moved to Mexico for the adventure and found themselves years later living a far more bourgeois life as shopkeepers and Babbitts than they would have back home. Think about it. Then all the best to you.

If you are younger, you may simply be interested in dating, whether Latinas or gringas, it doesn't matter. You'll find it easier, in general, to date gringas, but maybe not as easy as you think. First of all, there are many who are traveling with other women because they don't want to be bothered by guys. There are also a number of them who are only interested in dating Latin men. Then there are those who have "gone native" and will refuse to speak English. Rather than waste your time bothering them, move on to greener pastures.

TRAVELING TOGETHER

Many women will be receptive to traveling together, and after that, you'll simply have to work your charms. You'll find European women to be more interesting than American women, and easier to get to know. The Europeans tend to hang around ruins and take more budget accommodations, regardless of their income. They, of course, like the beaches, and are particularly attracted to the topless beaches. Your chances will be better if you speak some Spanish and at least appear as if you know what's going on. Be their protector.

It won't hurt to learn a few French, German, or Italian phrases. However, don't do as I did once and pretend to be Swedish (I have a weakness for Swedes). After all, there are only about 5 million Swedes. What were my chances of getting caught? Pretty darn good, my friend, pretty darn good. At least 2 million of them seem to visit Mexico. *"Jäg talar un lit Svenska"* won't get you far.

European Women

You'll meet Germans and French everywhere. The Italians tend to congregate on beaches, particularly along the Pacific Coast below Acapulco and Quintana Roo. Expect to meet a lot of Quebecois, or French-speaking Canadians from Quebec. They tend to keep to their own little groups, so you are probably better advised to not have great expectations about breaking into their cliques. Many of them are wonderful people, once you get to know them. Of course, if you speak French, they are more likely to think you are wonderful too.

After you've lived in a place for a while, there is a tendency to become arrogant and condescending to newcomers and tourists. Believe me, this does nothing but keep otherwise interesting people from getting to know you. Friendliness and helpfulness will get you where you want to be.

CANDID ADVICE FOR GAY MEN AND LESBIANS

GAY MEN

You'll find Mexico a giant contradiction. While the strong Catholic background and macho culture are disapproving of your lifestyles, you will also find a general "live-and-let-live" attitude. Some areas are, of course, more gay friendly than others (especially the larger beach resorts [small ones are not], San Miguel de Allende, Mexico City, Cuernavaca, and, surprisingly, Morelia). In general, as long as you are not too outrageous, you'll get along with and be accepted by the Mexicans. If you are flamboyant, you'll find life more difficult. There are fewer hate crimes in Mexico, so you will be physically much safer than you would be in the States or the Caribbean, but you will be treated as an outcast.

There is one exception. Those who take up with young Mexican boys are treated not only with scorn, but they are often physically attacked by the local citizenry and beaten by the constabulary. This is just as true in the "gay-friendly" towns as anywhere. In jail, they are beaten regularly. Even if the worst does not happen and you fall for a young man (not a boy), be careful. Just as there are men who prey on gringas, there are men who prey on *maricons*, homosexuals. Many gay men have told me about coming home and finding everything they owned gone. There was nothing they could do. Going to the police would have only put them at more risk. They chalked it up to a life lesson. Learn from them.

Just remember to act as straight as you can when you are dealing with the police. They are often really homophobic.

It's a matter of definition.

There's an interesting attitude toward what constitutes male homosexuality. Far more Mexican men than you'd suspect have had sexual experiences with other males. Mexican males do not consider themselves homosexuals just because they've had sex with another man. It's only a matter of convenience and not a lifestyle choice. Consequently, it is not all that uncommon for a man to have a quickie with another man, then go home to his wife or girlfriend and have sex.

LESBIANS

Lesbians have it better and worse than gay men. It's common for Latin women to be more affectionate in public than in the States, so gay women displaying affection will not be considered unusual. You can be more open here that in most places back home. Kissing in public (other than *besos*, kisses, on the cheek), however, will cause you problems. What drives many lesbians up the wall is the typical Latin machismo, which makes American and Canadian males seem positively liberated. My lesbian friends have told me that the women who are happiest in Latin America simply have learned to accept the attitudes and attention that come with machismo. After all, they're men, what do you expect? A pig can't change his stripes, to mix a metaphor. Those women who are the unhappiest are the ones who try to change the Latin men. Live and let live and enjoy your life.

Life in Mexico can be a mostly freeing, although occasionally confining, experience. It's up to you.

Since the last edition, there's been an explosion of gay/lesbian Internet sites about Mexico. Do a Google search and read the bulletin board comments from others with similar lifestyles to get a better understanding about what to expect.

Part Two

WHERE TO *Live* IN MEXICO

Mexico is a huge and diverse country. It encompasses climates as varied as deserts to tropical jungle to mile-high mountains, and areas with springlike weather all year long. If you are being transferred by your company, they probably did not pick a spot based on the lovely climate, but you could still get lucky. If you have more control over your destiny, then you will have to choose an area that appeals to you. I recommend that you visit several and stay for a few months in each before making up your mind.

The following thumbnail sketches are meant to give you an overview. You can only get to know a place by going there and hanging out for a while. Even if you buy one of those books that goes on for pages and pages on life in any one of these locales, you won't really know if it is for you until you get there. **What I have tried to do is to give you a snapshot of what the towns are really like, without the hype and hyperbole, from someone who has spent enough time in each and talked to enough locals to eliminate the chaff.** My opinions are just that. God made both heaven and hell; man usually manages to make his own without any help from a higher power.

There will be some people who will disagree with me, particularly boosters of some of the towns about which I am not particularly laudatory. I call them as I see them, and have tried to be as impartial as possible. Still, your heaven may be my hell, but, if you read carefully, you will see that I am not down on any one place. I've simply tried to state that some places may not be your cup of tea if you are cut from a different cloth. **Why beat your head against a wall trying to fit into a community because all the other books say it is a wonderful place to retire?**

Why not try to find a place where you will be happy? That's what life is about, being happy. We've all spent too much of our lives trying to fit into somebody else's mold. Now that you are moving away, go somewhere where you can be yourself.

When I took off to find a place to live in Mexico, I had advice from dozens of people about where I should go. I was so mixed up I thought that they knew more than I did about what was good for me, so I tried to like a few places that were obviously wrong for me. I investigated about a dozen towns before I found the one I settled in, and even then I didn't make the perfect choice. Had I had a book such as this one, I would have at least tried out a few others.

Housing costs caveat: Throughout the book, I have included a range of housing costs. These will, no doubt, change, probably going higher, but will give you a general idea of what to expect. The properties at the lower end of the scale are less plentiful than the ones at the higher end. I've excluded incredible bargains, as these are fleeting. I've also thrown out the multi-million-dollar luxury homes and condos. While the range is rather broad, it does give you an average high and low to look for when shopping.

Chapter 4
BAJA CALIFORNIA

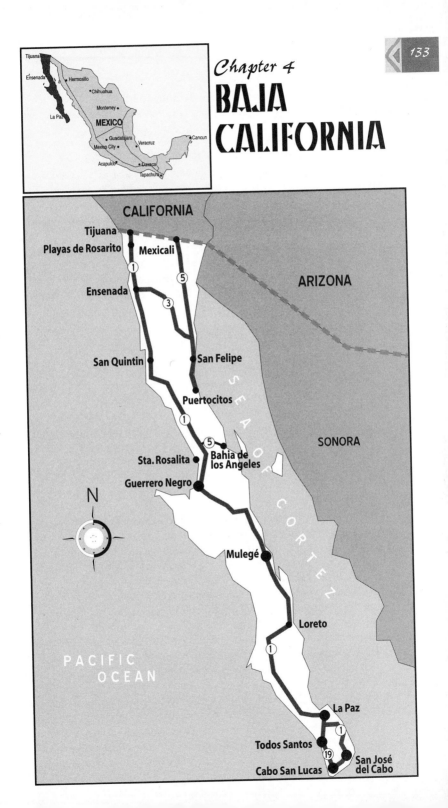

Mention "Mexico" in California, and people automatically think of Baja California. Mention "Baja" to gringos in other states or Canada, and they wistfully say that they hope to make it to Baja someday, as if it's the end of the Earth. **Baja is a land of contrasts, and very different from mainland Mexico.** With a unique personality and much American influence, the culture is a hybrid mixture of California, the United States, and Baja Mexico. There are few indigenous people (they were either killed or wiped out by disease). People in La Paz have told me that they didn't even lock their doors until about twenty years ago. Then an immigration of mainlanders occurred, who were seeking work during the building boom, and things changed.

There has always been some prejudice between Baja natives and mainland Mexicans. When it comes to the largesse of the federal government, Baja has generally gotten the short end of the stick. Baja has a lot to offer a variety of people, but, essentially, many of those who love the mainland do not care for Baja and vice versa.

Baja on a budget? Depends on how big a budget.

Baja is expensive. Cultural differences aside, Baja, in general, is far more expensive than anywhere on the mainland. On mainland Mexico, only Puerto Peñasco, Sonora (Rocky Point), Mexico City, Monterrey, Cozumel, and Cancún compare in terms of the cost of living. If you are on a shoestring budget, lace up that *zapato* and *correlé*, and run over to the mainland (especially Mazatlán, if you want to live in a beach town). There are some who live on comparatively small amounts of money in Baja, but, other than in San Felipe and Mulegé, it is a struggle. If you desire a lifestyle and weather that is similar to Southern California, lots of amenities and comforts, and can afford it, Baja might be your choice.

There are two states that make up the Baja Peninsula: Baja California Norte and Baja California Sur, which were free territories for many years. Due to their physical isolation from the rest of the country, and the proximity to California, in many ways Baja has more in common with California than with Mexico City. Politically, Baja has often defied the central government in Mexico City and gone its own way. Most of the foreign residents of the Baja are from the West Coast of the United States, with a few Canadians, mainly from British Columbia. Although Baja is still Mexico, it is more progressive than many mainland states, in general, and more English is spoken.

Baja is for nature lovers and fishermen. Baja is a land of stark contrasts and great natural beauty. Nature lovers adore it. Sea kayaking, whale watching, and windsurfing opportunities exist on both coasts (the Pacific and the Golfo de California, referred to as the Gulf of California in the rest of the chapter) in abundance. The wild, stark deserts appeal to many. Fishermen think they have died (although fishermen never die, they just keep on casting) and gone to heaven. **There are hot springs, mainly near the border and San Felipe.** Those desiring a partying lifestyle, complete with Hollywood stars, famous rock bands, rappers, etc., will love Cabo San Lucas. Those seeking colonial architecture (with a few exceptions, notably La Paz), native crafts, and an indigenous population will be sorely disappointed. There are still some very isolated spots on Baja where four-wheel-drive vehicles are a necessity. The main highway (Hwy. 1), which runs north to south from the border at Tijuana to Cabo San Lucas, is a good paved road. There is now a toll road (Hwy. 2) that cuts west to east to connect you to the mainland. Few people live along it, so your main highway is the north to south Hwy. 1. Near the population centers, it is four lanes; in many places, it has been amplified by toll roads; in the middle, it is a two-lane road, easily driven by all but the newer, wider-body RVs.

Foreigners who have settled here are a mixed breed. There are those in Los Cabos (which means both Cabo San Lucas and San José del Cabo) who seem to believe they have moved to California South, instead of Baja California Sur. There are those around San Felipe and south of there who are old-style desert rats who wanted to get away from their countrymen. Those who have settled in the north (Rosarito, Ensenada, and San Quintin) run the gamut from weekenders from California to retirees who don't want to be far from the border. In between there are people who fit neither category and chose Baja as a resting place because they love the land and the people. Every Baja town is different and could suit someone.

ROSARITO, BAJA CALIFORNIA (NORTE)

Ambiente: Think San Diego, though more laid-back. Most activity centers on the beach. On weekends, you will see as many gringos as Mexicans. Some estimates put the gringo population here at 25,000. It's located about an hour south of the border (although traffic delays can triple that drive time; they are reported on San Diego radio), so there are many who commute to jobs in San Diego and live here.

Climate: "Mediterranean." Think San Diego. Summers: 70s–80s. Winters: 60s (though sometimes 50s or upper 40s) to 70s.

Altitude: Sea level

Population: 85,000

Housing: Plenty of it and plenty pricey. Property near the beach is at the higher end of the scale. Property in town is at the lower end.

Homes (buy): $30,000–$250,000

Condos (buy): $50,000–$100,000

Rentals: $500–$1,500

RV space (sometimes with trailer): $20,000–$35,000

Medical Care: Adequate. For serious conditions, most people go to Tijuana or San Diego.

Area Code: 661

ENSENADA, BAJA CALIFORNIA (NORTE)

Ambiente: Think San Diego, though more laid-back and with less traffic. Most gringos settle around the beach Bahía de Todos Santos. It is a little more "Mexican" than Rosarito, and doesn't get as large an influx of weekenders. It is known as "The City of Science," due to the large research facilities here. I've found the people of Ensenada to be quite friendly and open.

Climate: "Mediterranean." Think San Diego. See above.

Altitude: Sea level

Population: 225,000 (officially, but it's probably closer to about 370,000) It is the third largest city in Baja, with about 15 percent of the state's population.

Housing: Good availability and quite pricey. Property near the beach is at the higher end of the scale. Property in town is at the lower end.

Homes (buy): $28,000–$225,000

Condos (buy): $45,000–$100,000

Rentals: $450–$1,400

RV space (sometimes with trailer): $18,000–$35,000

Medical Care: Quite good

Area Code: 646

PROS

It's only seventy-five miles south of San Diego, California. **With the highest ratio of scientists to the local population in Mexico, you are likely to meet some very interesting Mexicans.** There is an active port and fishing industry here, so the city has other sources of income than just tourism. This, to me, means that there will be a cultural activity that a gringo could enjoy, and a chance to meet Mexicans in social settings. The literacy rate is considered higher than in most border cities.

CONS

With an estimated gringo population of 36,000, settled mostly in the resort communities along the Pacific Ocean, this is not a cheap place to live. With so many gringos, it is tempting to stay in your gringo community and never interact with the locals.

IN-BETWEENS

You won't find much of a price difference between here and Rosarito, so it's a question of which community you prefer. With fewer weekenders it is less rowdy, but there is plenty of nightlife. The gringo community is well established and there is a preponderance of permanent residents.

LIVE BETTER South of the Border IN MEXICO

SAN QUINTIN, BAJA CALIFORNIA (NORTE)

Ambiente: Small town, artistic and nature-loving foreigners

Climate: Hotter than Ensenada and Rosarito in summer (90s–100s). "Mediterranean" (60s–80s) in winter. Desertlike with warm days and cool nights.

Altitude: Sea level, but there are plenty of volcanic bluffs, and nearby mountains rise to 7,000 feet.

Population: 35,000 (estimate)

Housing: Property near the beach is at the higher end of the scale. Property in town is at the lower end.

Homes (buy): $30,000–$200,000

Condos (buy): N/A

Rentals: $400–$1,000

RV space (sometimes with trailer): $15,000–$30,000

Medical Care: Barely adequate

Area Code: 616

This is the last town of any size in Baja Norte. While everywhere is subject to development and exploitation, in 2000, the National Ecology Institute killed a $700 million tourism and real estate development. For now, at least, this is still a small town with a historic past and a small, hardy breed of foreigners.

San Quintin is a unique spot in the Baja. Some of the houses in the Pedregal area, where most gringos buy, are built on volcanic rock. This was an English boomtown in the 1890s, and nearly abandoned by the 1900s, when the promises of a great wheat-growing region were defeated by a drought. There is a sunken seventeen-ton railroad locomotive in the mouth of the bay, a relic of this boom gone bust. Since it is a logical stop for anyone driving the length of the Baja, there are hotels and RV parks enough to make a visit comfortable. It's still something of an agricultural area.

PROS

This is far enough from the border to attract a different type of gringo. Those who settle here are looking to get away from *gringolandia* and are more likely to integrate themselves into the local population. There are artistic types, fishermen, and those who really want to get away from it all. Real estate, while still expensive by mainland standards, is less expensive than in other places (comparable to San Felipe). If you are a nature lover, you will find a lot to do—whale watching, fishing, and exploring the desert and even mountains and caves with pictographs.

CONS

Since it is far from a major population center, convenience items are harder to come by and pricier. Medical care is barely adequate.

IN-BETWEENS

This is a special place for special people. Try it out before you settle down here. The laid-back and quiet lifestyle can be perfect for some and hellish for others.

SAN FELIPE, BAJA CALIFORNIA

Ambiente: A mix of California, Arizona, and Mexico. Lots of U.S. influence. Those who live here are in all age ranges and far less likely to be the party-hearty crowd you'll find in Cabo, though weekends can be a pain with all the partying tourists.

Climate: Hot, hot, hot (mid- to upper 90s) summers. Mild winters (60s–70s).

Altitude: Sea level. There are some hills, if you consider 100 feet altitude.

Population: 6,100

Housing: Lots of availability, and it is inexpensive by Baja standards. Property near the beach is at the higher end of the scale. Property in town is at the lower end.

Homes (buy): $20,000–$150,000

Condos (buy): N/A

Rentals: $300–$900

RV space (sometimes with trailer): $15,000–$30,000

Medical Care: Adequate

Area Code: 686

PROS

San Felipe is close to the U.S. border, only 118 miles away. Living here can be dirt (sand, really) cheap in RV parks that are little more than spots on the sand without hookups, or expensive in classy condos or luxury houses. There are first-class RV parks with clubhouses and Jacuzzis that are as expensive as any in the United States, with real community feels. The town is small and pleasant. It was a fishing community, but today tourism is the main industry. There are plenty of hotels and restaurants in all price ranges except rock bottom. **Everything here is expensive, by mainland Mexico standards, but cheap for Baja.**

There is plenty of English spoken. The scenery is a stark desert. The Gulf of California is dramatic and the reason so many Americans settle here. There are hills in town that have serpentine streets and lots of houses. The winters are pleasant. **There is a hot spring nearby, in Puertocitos, and another on private land north of town.** The fishing is not as good as it used to be because of the degradation of the Gulf of California, which has been declared an ecological protection zone, about ten years too late. Communications are excellent.

CONS

The economy is dollar based, so you do not benefit from a good exchange

rate. On weekends, the place is full, often with rowdy people of all ages who come down to party. Then you will see more Americans than Mexicans. **It is hotter than Hades in the summer.** For me, it is too similar to California (and I am a recovering Californian and like California and Californians) and not enough like Mexico.

IN-BETWEENS

If you just want to get to warm winters, don't mind a lot of Americans, and can put up with the weekenders, this could be the place for you. It can be cheap, if you are willing to live basically in an RV.

PUERTOCITOS AND BEYOND

Ambiente: Haven for "don't-tread-on-me" escapees from civilization

Climate: Hot, hot, hot (mid- to upper 90s) summers. Mild winters (60s–70s).

Altitude: If you stand on top of a building

Population: 6,100

Housing: There is lots of availability, but prices are high because of all the Americans here. About 10–15 percent higher than San Felipe prices.

Medical Care: Primitive

Area Code: 664

PROS

The road is paved south to Puertocitos and a little beyond. **Puertocitos has a hot spring, though it didn't impress me.** My friend Carl Franz, author of *The People's Guide to Mexico* (required reading for anyone who wants to understand the Mexican culture), asked me not to reveal it. I intended to keep my promise, but when I got there, it was so obviously well-known by everyone in San Felipe, and such a disappointment to me, that I saw no harm in telling the world about it. It is also listed in every guidebook worth its salt. Finding it is a chore, and you have to pass many signs saying (in English) "No Trespassing."

There are scads of Americans living here on the hills overlooking the Gulf. They are a different lot than those in San Felipe—people who wanted to get away from development. **It looks a little like an old version of Sausalito, California, perhaps around the time of Jack Kerouac.**

As you drive south, you will find RVs and desert rats parked on isolated beaches. For those who want nothing more than the isolation of being in a magnificent natural setting, these little campos could be for you. **If you make it all the way to Bahía San Luís Gonzaga (four-wheel-drive recommended), you will find a tight-knit community of people who really wanted to get away from it all.** There's not much to the town, and "the" street is also a landing strip. Most of the residents are foreigners. If you are a self-sufficient type and a nature lover, you will love this area. It is still unspoiled (except for the horde of gringos who live here), and truly stupendous in its beauty.

CONS

If you are not a self-sufficient type and a nature lover, you will go out of your skull here. You've got to pack everything in, and what you have to buy is expensive. Communications are better than they were when I wrote the last edition of this book, but still iffy.

IN-BETWEENS

There aren't any. **You love it or hate it.**

MULEGÉ AND BAHÍA DE CONCEPCÍON, BAJA CALIFORNIA SUR

Ambiente: Laid-back, quiet, small town, very friendly, very accepting

Climate: Mild winters (70s–80s). Hot, relatively humid summers (upper 80s–upper 90s).

Altitude: There is not much, but some of the hills do offer a breeze.

Population: 6,100

Housing: Reasonable for the Baja. There are not a lot of choices, though there are new developments. Naturally, the prices are higher on the bay.

Homes (buy): $60,000–$150,000

Condos (buy): N/A

Rentals: $300–$500

RV space (sometimes with trailer): $5,000–$18,000

Medical Care: Adequate for a small town. For major emergencies, plan on being airlifted home or to Cabo.

Area Code: 615

PROS

If I were going to live in Baja, this would be the place. **Mulegé (not on the coast) is an oasis (literally) in the desert, with a river, trees, and even orchards.** It has a quiet, laid-back feel to it, and the Mexicans outnumber the gringos. There isn't a lot to do, and that is one of its attractions. There are some restaurants and hotels with some entertainment, but it ain't the Great White Way.

Bahía de Concepcíon is only a few miles south of Mulegé, and considered by some the most beautiful bay in Mexico. The waters border on crystal clear, and tropical fish abound. John Steinbeck, Zane Grey, Earl Stanley Gardner, and other famous and not-so-famous wordsmiths have called the bay a "natural paradise" with breathtaking beauty.

Mulegé has the fame of once having had a prison where the inmates were on the honor system. They could visit town during the day, but had to return to incarceration at night. If one strayed, they were all punished and they had to find the miscreant. It worked rather well. **Natural attractions beside the river and the beach are cave paintings in the Sierra de San Borjita, and paintings and petroglyphs of La Trinidad.** There are RV parks in town, and several hundred spaces at Bahía Concepcíon, as well as modest houses. **Housing is probably the most reasonable in Baja outside San Felipe, and not as plentiful.** Scuba diving is very good in the late summer and fall (August to November). Fishing is great, with yellowtail, rooster fish, and pargo close to shore near the estuary, and in the summer, offshore you can catch dorado, billfish, and yellowfin.

CONS
The quiet, simple lifestyle could get to you after a while. It is not for everyone. Manufactured goods are expensive. Communications are decent now and there is Internet service.

IN-BETWEENS
It's a love-it-or-leave-it place. Many people settle here "for the rest of their lives" and leave in a few years.

LA PAZ, BAJA CALIFORNIA SUR

Ambiente: Cultured, laid-back, old-style Baja

Climate: Moderately hot summers (80s to low 90s—cooler than Loreto) and mild winters (70s to low 80s)

Altitude: Sea level

Population: 300,000

Housing: Plentiful in all price ranges
Homes (buy): $120,000–$350,000
Condos (buy): $40,000–$150,000
Rentals: $350–$600
RV space (sometimes with trailer): $10,000–$20,000

Medical Care: Excellent

Area Code: 612

PROS
I've always liked this small city. It's the capital of Baja Sur and completely different from anywhere else in Baja. **La Paz was voted one of the best places to retire by** *Money Magazine* **in July 2003.** Among the virtues of La Paz are its sixteenth-century architecture and less of an emphasis on nightclubbing than in the Cabos. One thing that is a big plus for me (here I go with my prejudices again) is that you will not be besieged by time-share salesmen; at this writing, there are no time-shares in La Paz! It is large enough to offer many services and small enough to have a real sense of community. **There is an interesting mix of foreigners who live or visit here and they generally have good attitudes.** The constant influx of yachtsmen gives it a truly international flavor, besides there are great views of the bay.

The attitude of the residents is cordial and typifies all that is good about the Baja. Live and let live and genuine friendliness seem to permeate the atmosphere. For example, there are still many four-way stops instead of traffic lights. I have never seen anyone go out of turn or honk his horn. There are RV parks and housing that range from expensive to reasonable. The weather is beautiful, though warm in the summer. The fishing is great, with yellowtail caught from January to March, and marlin, pargo, rooster fish, sierra, and, my favorite, pompano, usually caught from April to November. Locals swear it is better here than in Mazatlán, but I have a soft spot for Mazatlán since I caught three marlin there one day. (I am the kind of fisherman who has never mastered the art of "catching.")

Scuba divers will find it more interesting than Cabo. Boaters will also appreciate the five different marinas, which are considerably less expensive than the one in Cabo San Lucas.

Housing is much less expensive than Cabo and has a lot more character. You generally get a larger house for the money, and quite likely one with charm. For those who like nightlife, there is enough variety here to satisfy almost everyone, though it does not have the glitz and glamour of Cabo. High-speed Internet access is fine, which is true in every city in Mexico today.

CONS
I really can't think of any.

IN-BETWEENS
In the winter, there are bullfights. (If we meet, ask me to tell you about my brief career as a clumsy bullfighter who tripped on his cape and nearly got gored. As they say in the TV commercials showing people doing adventurous things, "Don't try this at home [or in Mexico].") **Carnival (Mardi Gras) is a big deal here, and some say it is better than Mazatlán's. Another big event is the Fiesta de la Fundación de la Ciudad de la Paz, held May 3.**

LORETO, BAJA CALIFORNIA SUR

Ambiente: Upscale, planned development
Climate: Hot, hot, hot summers (90s–100s). Mild winters (70s–80s).
Altitude: It's at sea level, but is surrounded by the Sierra de la Giganta mountains.
Population: 12,000
Housing: Lots of condos and time-shares, pricey
   Homes (buy): $150,000–$450,000
   Condos (buy): $40,000–$150,000
   Rentals: $350–$600
   RV space (sometimes with trailer): $10,000–$60,000 (Note: There was a fire at the Tripui RV Park in 2004, so this may or may not be valid at press time.)

Medical Care: Adequate
Area Code: 613

PROS

If an ecologically aware "development" doesn't sound as if it's an oxymoron to you, then this could be your spot. But first, a little history: Location, location, location. This, I believe, is why Loreto is a town seeking its identity. Since it's 250 miles from Cabo and 700 miles from California, it's neither near nor far.

This is a beautiful place. **It is indeed an oasis, with an artesian aquifer, which helps it stay green much of the year.** This availability of water may be why the Jesuits built Baja's first mission there in 1697. It was also the capital of the Californias until a hurricane destroyed much of it in 1829, and the capital was later moved to La Paz. European immigrants settled and rebuilt the town in the 1850s, but it languished until World War II, when commercial fishermen started using it as a port.

This history lesson should give you an idea of why I think it is star-crossed. The fish population (similar to that in much of the Bay of California) was nearly destroyed by long-liners, so, in 1996, the government declared thirty miles offshore as a marine park. But since there has always been animosity between Baja and Mexico City, the government didn't do much patrolling, so the local residents took care of things themselves, to their credit. These people really respect their land and water and are among the most ecologically aware in the Baja.

Today, sportfishing is quite an industry, as well as some commercial fishing. You'll find the same species you can find in other spots in the Baja, including dorado (one of the few fish species I can claim to have caught), tuna, billfish, sea bass, and yellowtail. It's not unusual to glimpse dolphins or whales. So if you are a fisherman, or a nature lover, you will like this area.

Now on to the star-crossed part. **The Federal Tourism Promotional Fund, or FONATUR (the people who brought you Cancún and Huatulco), has tried to make this something of a socially conscious Cancún.** Their first project failed. Now they have Canadian investors and are building planned communities. The good news is that they promise to maintain open spaces, prohibit the building of high-rises, and make the whole thing have a European-village style. Despite the two planned golf courses (one has already been built), they promise to be guardians of the water supply and to use solar technology. It all sounds good. I wish them luck with this concept, and if the idea of an ecologically sound development appeals to you, then, by all means, check out Loreto.

The closest RV park is thirty miles south in Puerto Escondido.

CONS

I sometimes wonder if the place is star-crossed. There are always grand projects for it, but they never quite jell. One reason may be that the summer is ungodly hot. **Very few foreigners want to stay here in the summer.**

IN-BETWEENS

There is always the possibility that the development plans for the area will take off and it will turn into the ecological dream that is its vision.

TODOS SANTOS, BAJA CALIFORNIA SUR

Ambiente: Artistic enclave, small but upscale village

Climate: Moderately hot summers (80s–90s, 10–15 degrees cooler than Cabo) and mild winters (upper 50s–70s)

Altitude: It varies from sea level to a few hundred feet, as it is in the foothills of the Sierra de la Laguna.

Population: 4,400

Housing: Plentiful in all price ranges

Homes (buy): $70,000–$450,000 (and way, way up)

Condos (buy): N/A

Rentals: $600–$1,500

RV space (sometimes with trailer): $22,000–$60,000

Medical Care: Primitive

Area Code: 612

PROS

Only about an hour northwest of Cabo is a different world. **This is the artsy town of Baja.** It's still a village, and while it has developed a lot during the last few years, it's still not Cabo. Organic farming is big here, which says a lot. **There are art galleries, coffee shops, bed-and-breakfasts, and yet another of the "original" Hotel Californias immortalized by the rock band The Eagles.** (I'm not taking sides in this debate.) Without a doubt, there is a much gentler pace of life here than there is farther south. There is a certain chicness to this town, and dining can include fine restaurants with candlelight service. I've known writers who retired here because they like Baja but hate Cabo.

CONS

Some old-timers swear it has been "discovered" and "ruined." I guess it depends on when you personally "discovered" it. There's no doubt that it is a destination for day-trippers from Cabo, and anytime that happens, it changes the flavor of a village. Fortunately, since living here is not the same as living in Cabo, it attracts a different breed of gringo. I know some retirees who find it too "artsy" and others who say it is too "cute." Internet cafes exist, but there are no high-speed connections from your home.

IN-BETWEENS

If you like Santa Fe, you'll probably like Todos Santos. **It's still a fairly small town, which is either a benefit or a drawback, depending on your point of view.**

LIVE BETTER *South of the Border* IN MEXICO

CABO SAN LUCAS, BAJA CALIFORNIA SUR

Ambiente: Similar to being in Southern California. English is widely spoken. There are many foreigners and time-share salesmen. Party-hearty crowd.

Climate: Moderately hot summers (80s–90s — cooler than Loreto) and mild winters (60s–70s)

Altitude: 96 feet

Population: 45,000 (combined for Cabo and San José)

Housing: Plentiful in all price ranges

Homes (buy): $110,000–$750,000 (and way, way up)

Condos (buy): $80,000–$130,000

Rentals: $450–$1,500

RV space (sometimes with trailer): $22,000–$60,000

Medical Care: Very good

Area Code: 624

PROS

This is the end of the Baja, both literally and figuratively. **It is the most developed of the towns in the southern Baja and has the most to offer.** It is also the most popular for Americans to settle, less so for Canadians. The sea and the beaches are dramatic, and the sunsets are breathtaking. In fact, watching the sunsets is a favorite activity. **There are several RV parks, condominiums, houses, and apartments, and they are all expensive, roughly on par with Southern California.** One resident told me that her two-bedroom trailer cost $180,000, plus $450 a month for her space (up $100 from the last edition).

There are less-expensive RV parks, but the one above is typical of the really nice ones. Houses can easily run to more than half a million dollars, although I saw some two-bedroom houses for around $100,000. As is the case anywhere else, the key is location, location, location. High-speed Internet service is available.

There are lots of Californians here, particularly on weekends. Many have condos or time-shares and live here for extended periods of time. You will hear a lot of English and you don't really need to speak Spanish to get along quite well. **The fishing is superior. It is known as the marlin capital (a title disputed by Mazatlán) of the world, and there are also sailfish and swordfish.** Both the blue and the black marlin are caught here. Catch-and-release fishing has caught on here and you are allowed only one billfish per boat. **Scuba diving is very good. Snorkeling is also good.**

You can get English-language newspapers daily. Cabo has a lot to offer those who appreciate its charms. Locals are very proud of their world-class golf courses—six of them between Cabo and San José. There is an American consular agent and a dandy English-language newspaper, the *Gringo Gazette* (www.gringogazette.com).

CONS

Among the attractions of the place is the extensive nightlife. The world-famous discos feature world-famous bands and can be very loud. **The downtown area is too noisy at night for me to sleep.** On weekends, another of the charms is the thousands of foreigners who fly down, many of whom are there to party. **It is expensive as can be.** You sometimes get the feeling that everyone wants something from you, from the time-share hustlers to the vendors. **The charm of this formerly isolated oasis has been eradicated by the Americanization of it.** But gringos still flock in to live here. Perhaps it is the herd instinct.

IN-BETWEENS
You either love it or hate it.

SAN JOSÉ DEL CABO, BAJA CALIFORNIA SUR

Ambiente: It is more relaxed and less glitzy than Cabo.

Climate: Moderately hot summers (same as Cabo) and mild winters

Altitude: 96 feet

Population: 39,000

Housing: Plentiful in all price ranges

    Homes (buy): $70,000–$550,000 (and way, way up). The low end is in town.

    Condos (buy): $45,000–$100,000

    Rentals: $450–$1,500

    RV space (sometimes with trailer): $14,000–$25,000

Medical Care: Excellent

Area Code: 624

IN-BETWEENS

This is just northeast of Cabo San Lucas. **It has more charm, more of a "Mexican" feel, and is a lot quieter—but it has changed with the times.** The more people "discover" a place, the more they change its atmosphere. Most of the weekend jet-setters flock to CSL to party and disrupt life. (Okay, I have my prejudices, if you haven't figured that out by now. It's one of my dubious charms.[?]) In the last edition, I recommended this as being much less expensive than Cabo San Lucas. Things change.

    While the median housing prices in the town are less expensive than the same locations in Cabo, beach lots, houses, and RV spaces, while a little less expensive, are not a bargain. In the previous edition, I also said that it is much less Americanized. While this is still true, comparatively speaking, don't expect it to be an isolated oasis; there are plenty of gringos here. Thanks to large developers, there are expensive housing enclaves along the beaches that make it look little different from CSL, except in town.

    It has plenty of restaurants, and there are RV parks between the two towns. There is plenty of housing, in all varieties, and you can still find bargains here. Figure you can live here for about three-quarters of what you'd live for in Southern California (less if you rent). I have seen one-bedroom apartments for $500 to $600 a month. The last time I checked, San Diego and L.A. apartments started at $700 and went way up. My last place in North Hollywood was $575 when I moved in and is now $750. I still stand by my earlier statement: If I had to live in the Cabo "metroplex," I would choose San José.

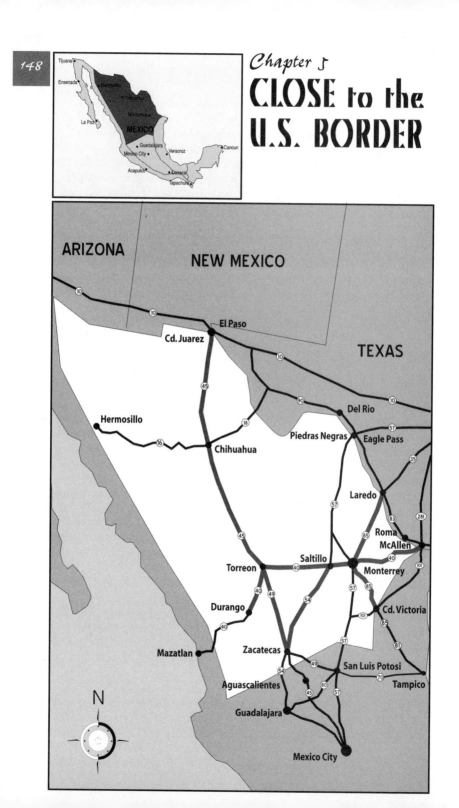

PUERTO PEÑASCO, SONORA

Ambiente: This is a small fishing port with lots and lots of Americans and weekend visitors from Arizona. English is widely spoken.

Climate: Mild winters (70s–80s), hot summers (90s–100s)

Altitude: Sea level

Population: 30,000

Housing: Real estate is very expensive, comparable to Baja. While less expensive than Cabo, and perhaps La Paz, real estate here is high by mainland Mexican standards. Average rentals run about $500 to $700 a month, though it is possible to find deals in the $400 range, but that is rare. An average home costs about $300,000, with a low-cost home being about $100,000.

Medical Care: Adequate. There is a hospital, but for major care most people go back to Arizona.

Area Code: 638

PROS

This is the closest beach to Arizona (sixty miles) and a lot of Zonies (Arizonans) live here. On weekends it is overwhelmed by tourists. They are a well-behaved bunch, for the most part, so the town does not lose its charm when they arrive. **You will be able to get along here without speaking Spanish, if that is what you want to do.**

Besides beaches and desert, nearby Mount Pinacate has nine major volcanic craters, and an estimated 400-plus volcanic craters overall. Mount Pinacate is dormant now, and accessible only by four-wheel-drive vehicles. The Pinacate Biosphere covers 600 square miles. The landscape is so forbidding that the Apollo astronauts trained for moonwalks here during the 1970s. The town used to be a drinking and gambling den during U.S. Prohibition times, as did many border-area towns in Mexico, but today the only gambling going on is in the real estate market.

You can't swing a dead Chihuahua without hitting someone in real estate. Prices have gone out of site, both for basic necessities and real estate. This town now "boasts" real estate prices higher than some parts of the Baja. There are two RV parks with annual rentals at about $2,000. Monthly rates are about $350 to $500. The views of the bay and the beaches are dramatic. **The atmosphere is laid-back, although there seems to be more hustle and bustle than there was when I wrote the last edition.** There is a development called La Choya where less-expensive houses can be found. There are condos, houses, and apartments for rent, as well as RV spaces. **Although I would not type this as a budgeteer's haven, you could find a place here without being a millionaire.** In the last edition, I quoted gringo residents who lived there on about $600 a month. It would be tough to do that now. Frankly, you have better have $1,200, or more, a month to eke out a living in this area. There are a few rentals in the $600 range, but most are higher. Many of those living on a budget have moved farther south, to San Carlos or Kino Bay. Las Conchas is a gated, pricey, exclusive community with guards and security patrols, etc. You could spend $250,000 to $1 million for the privilege of living there. New developments have gone in at Playa La Jolla and Costa Diamante. Even newer ones are planned for the beaches south of town.

The seafood (especially the shrimp) is great, but the fishing has gone downhill from its glory days. The industry has been star-crossed. Around 1955, it boomed—thanks to blue shrimp, a delicacy—then, during the 1960s, Japanese and Korean ships nearly destroyed the shrimp population. The government woke up and threw them out. Then the shrimp got a disease that nearly finished the job. During the 1990s, fishing made a comeback, and in 1994, the Mexican government declared the area around Puerto Peñasco and the Sea of Cortez a protected biosphere, killing the commercial fishing industry. Much of their fleet was sold to fishermen in Guaymas. From a high of 80 percent during the 1980s, the percentage of the economy brought in by fishing has dropped to around 50 percent. Tourism is now the most important industry.

The locals have a wonderfully acceptant attitude toward the gringos. Because it is a small town, you will soon know everyone. There is an English-language monthly newspaper, the *Rocky Point Times* (P.O. Box 887, Lukeville, AZ 85341; www.rptimes.com). It is well written and many people subscribe to it back home to keep up with the community.

CONS

Some may find the preponderance of Americans to be exactly what they wanted to get away from. The smallness of the community means that you will know most everyone's business before too long. The cost of living can be expensive. Summers are hot.

IN-BETWEENS

You don't even need a tourist permit or car permit to come here. You are close enough to the United States to bring down anything you need. Customs is sometimes lenient, sometimes not. I can't guarantee that you will be able to bring everything you want without paying some duty, but there seems to be no dearth of material possessions in the homes of the foreigners.

MONTERREY, NUEVO LEON

Ambiente: Can-do attitude, optimistic, bustling, big-city flavor

Climate: While winters are relatively mild for the most part (60s–70s days, 30s–40s nights), it often dips to below freezing. Summers are more often hot than not (90s to low 100s days, 60s–70s nights).

Altitude: 3,000 feet

Population: 1,111,000 (officially, though the metro area is estimated to be 3,500,000)

Housing: Reasonable for a big city close to the border. Similar to Mexico City and Guadalajara, Monterrey is spread out and housing should be considered by location, not on a citywide basis.

Homes (buy): $30,000–$750,000, depending on the area

Condos (buy): $90,000–$500,000, depending on the area

Rentals: In outlying areas, such as Villa de las Fuentes, $300–$500. In trendier areas, $600–$1,000 can be found, but $2,000 and up is common.

RV space: N/A

Medical Care: Excellent. Monterrey offers some of the best hospitals in the country, on par with U.S. hospitals.

Area Code: 81 (Only Monterrey and Guadalajara have two-digit area codes.)

PROS

"The Colossus of the North," as the third largest city in Mexico is known (also known by old-timers as "The Pittsburgh of Mexico"), is a bustling, modernistic metropolis. It is considered by consular officials working here as one of the safest cities in Latin America. You'll find a strong business climate, fast traffic, and more of an identification with Texas than Mexico City. Local residents often drive to McAllen or Laredo, Texas, to shop, or to South Padre Island, Texas, to vacation. Many *Regiomontaños*, as residents are proud to be identified, own condos on the island. It's unlikely you would choose this city as a retirement choice, but are more likely to be transferred here by an international company.

Housing in the Residential Areas

The municipality of San Pedro Garza Garcia has the highest income per capita of Mexico and Latin America. Houses and apartments are very similar to the ones you have in United States, roads are okay, and people drive similar to Americans. Most of the people in San Pedro Garza Garcia speak English as a second language. Rents are high, comparable to Mexico City.

The neighborhoods of San Geronimo and Cumbres in the municipality of Monterrey are as good as San Pedro Garza Garcia but at 30 percent less. You have great access, shopping, banks, safety, etc., but since it is not San Pedro, it is worth less. Similar to Beverly Hills and Hollywood, locations nearby might be cheaper but not in those zip codes.

San Nicolas de las Garza and Santa Catarina are south and north of the city, respectively, but both have great access. Although they are not as safe as the municipalities above, prices are very affordable.

Villa Guadalupe and Apodaca are also good neighborhoods.

Monterrey is one of the safest cities in all of Latin America.

Monterrey is an industrial city (steel, glass, breweries, manufacturing), so

many business people are transferred to work here. Monterrey can be called "Light Mexico" for foreigners, meaning that the culture, architecture, roads, safety, shopping, etc., is very similar to the United States. Monterrey is so safe that many ATMs are drive-through and open twenty-four hours. Women can drive late at night alone without fear, etc. There are flights to and from all of Mexico and some flights to the United States from their airport.

Monterrey is Yanqui friendly.

While the downtown area still has a somewhat colonial feel and buildings, it is dwarfed by the modern city that spreads for miles and miles. You'll find high-speed Internet service, trendy restaurants and coffee shops, and many people who speak English. The people here are quite friendly. Even if the government in Mexico City takes one of its nationalistic turns, *Regiomontaños* are likely to remain *Yanqui* friendly. You can live as well here as in any city in the States or Canada.

Regional Food

Topo Chico, the ubiquitous mineral water seen all over Mexico, is bottled near here. While it doesn't contain as many minerals as Peñafiel or others, it is far more than merely purified water. There is a decent variety of restaurants. The region produces lots of beef; a northern specialty is *carne seca* (dried beef, but not the same as jerky) and your breakfast is likely to be *machacado con huevo* (scrambled eggs with dried beef). Although my favorite food in the world, *cabrito al pastor* (young goat cooked over a mequite-fired open pit for hours), is more common here than anywhere else in Mexico, you can find most cuisines of the world here.

Want to start a fight? Follow Mikey's advice.
    Speaking of **cabrito,** *Monterrey is proud that they make the best in the world. The really good* **cabrito** *restaurants in Mexico City or Acapulco are owned by* **Regiomontaños.** *This may be heresy, but I believe that the best* **cabrito** *is found in Hidalgo del Parral (Pancho Villa's birthplace) or San Luis Potosí. Saltillo and Monterrey are next. But don't you dare mention that in this city unless you are spoiling for a fight. It would be similar to telling a New Yorker that his city is second in anything.*

Culture

Since it is such a big city, your choices in housing run the gamut from relatively inexpensive *casas* to mansions or high-rise condos. If you want big-city life for much less than you'd pay in the States or Canada, this is a fine city. There are art museums, fine arts, and good shopping for handcrafted products from all over Mexico. Leather goods, ironworks, and handblown glass are local specialties. When I was a young import-export impresario, I became the Whip King of New Orleans (don't ask, don't tell), importing whips from nearby Hualahuises. Though I can't swear that Monterrey is the velvet painting capital of the world, it seems that way. Monterrey kept me supplied with velvet Elvises, which made a nice living for me. (I never claimed to have any culture.)

Speaking of culture, Monterrey has a lot more than I do, from art museums to theaters and symphonic concerts. There are also traveling concerts by international stars, rock and otherwise. (No, the Monterey Pop Festival of sixties fame was not held here, as I grew up thinking. That was in Monterey, California, I found out about ten years too late.) **The area is known for "extreme sports," including mountain climbing, rock climbing, caving, rappelling, parachuting, and others.** International conventions are held at the modernistic Cintermex convention center. The Observatorio is quite a professional operation.

Escapes

It is less than three hours (depending on what part of the city you live in and the traffic) to McAllen, Texas. If you just want to escape for a few days, it's no great feat. In an hour you could drive west to Saltillo, a far more relaxed atmosphere. **Along the way, you could stop at an interesting cave with stalagtites and stalagmites called Garcia Caverns.** Supposedly, there are some hot springs in the mountains around Saltillo (forget the mere *balneario*, or swimming place, on the highway), but I haven't made it to them yet.

If you drive south from the city for less than an hour, you could go to Horsetail Falls (Cola de Caballo), which is interesting enough in itself. But if you drive behind the falls, you will climb several thousand feet through a pine forest. This spectacular road (one of the most interesting and little-known routes in Mexico) winds its way to Saltillo. Along the way, you could stay at an Alpine-like cottage.

If you kept heading south on the main four-lane highway instead of stopping at the falls, in a few hours you could be in the semitropical area of Ciudad Valles, where there are some hot springs. In a way it's similar to living in Los Angeles—pick the climate you want and you'll find it a short distance away.

Higher Education

Monterrey is famous for being the home of one of the best universities in Latin America, Tecnológico de Monterrey. It is affiliated with Harvard. It is an expensive school with branches all over Mexico. It offers an M.B.A. program in English.

Additional Resources

- U.S. business resource: American Chamber of Commerce, Río Manzanares 434 Oriente Col. Del Valle 66220, Garza García, N.L.; Phone: 01-52-818-114-2000; Fax: 01-52-818-114-2100; socios_mty@amcham.com.mx.

- Canadian business resource: Canadian Chamber of Commerce, Zaragoza, 1300 Sur, Edif. Kalos, Piso A2; Office: 201, 64000, Monterrey, N.L.; Phone: 01-52-818-343-1899; Fax: 01-52-818-343-1897; info@cancham.org.mx; www.cancham.org.mx.

- English-language schools for kids: The American School Foundation of Monterrey, Rio Missouri 555 Ote., Colonia Del Valle, Garza Garcia, N.L., 66220; Mailing Address: APDO 1762, 64000, Monterrey, N.L., Phone: 01-52-818-153-4400; Fax: 01-52-818-378-2535; www.asfm.edu.mx. Pan American School, Monterrey Campus, Hidalgo 656 Pte., Monterrey, N.L., 66400; Mailing Address: APDO 474, 64000, Monterrey, N.L.; Phone: 01-52-818-342-0778; Fax: 01-52-818-340-2749.

- Newcomer's club: Newcomer's Club of Monterrey(newcomersgroup@ yahoo.com; www.newcomersofmty.8m.com). Monthly meetings (subject to change) held on the second Tuesday of the month at 9:30 A.M. (unless it's on or near a holiday): Applebee's, Ave. Vasconcelos #158 Ote. L-1 Col., Jardines del Campestre.

- Jewish resource: Adat Israel, Canada 207, Monterrey, N.L. 64620, Progressive; Phone: 01-52-818-346-1728.

CONS

Traffic and Weather

Traffic, traffic, traffic. **I've lived in L.A. and would rather drive there than in Monterrey any day.** It's similar to Chicago in that it seems to be heavy and fast all day.

Weather, weather, weather. One of the coldest Christmases I remember (taking into account that I seldom wander north of the Mason-Dixon Line) was in Monterrey. While rare, occasionally it can snow. Although it has more altitude than the Rio Grande Valley of Texas (which has none to speak of), the summers can be uncomfortable (oh heck, they can be hotter than Hades).

Pollution

The overwhelming pollution of yesteryear from the factories (as I said earlier, Monterrey used to be called "The Pittsburgh of Mexico," not just because it was a steel city, but because it had such bad air pollution) has been cleaned up. **But, thanks to the millions of cars and the geography, air pollution is a reality.** It's not on the scale of Mexico City, but similar to Los Angeles, Houston (these two cities of mine often vie for the worst air in the USA—I swear my moving to them had nothing to do with it), and Chicago.

Living here can be expensive. Although it doesn't have a dollar-based economy as does Baja, prices are similar to U.S. prices in many areas. It is a noisy city, unless you settle in an outlying area. One thing to watch out for is drainage. When it rains, flooding can be a problem. Worse than that, years ago Hurricane Gilbert came ashore on the Gulf of Mexico coast, crossed the mountains, and flooded the city, killing many hundreds of people. (The official news put the death rate much lower, which is typical.)

IN-BETWEENS
If your company sent you here to work, you'll be able to work as hard as you like and not be considered unusual as you would in some cities in Mexico. The fast pace and modern atmosphere will make you feel right at home, yet the truly Mexican flavor of the city will remind you that you are still in Mexico.

SALTILLO, COAHUILA

Ambiente: Very Mexican feel, a slow pace for such a large city. It's like a small-town girl who moved to the big city and hasn't lost her charm. Water can be in short supply.

Climate: Much cooler than Monterrey. In winter, it often freezes (50s days, 30s nights). Summers are much milder than Monterrey or the Rio Grande Valley of Texas (70s–80s days, 50s–60s nights). Low humidity.

Altitude: 5,114 feet

Population: 563,000 (officially, though estimates are around a million)

Housing: Less expensive than nearby Monterrey

Homes (buy): $20,000–$250,000 ($90,000–$100,000 can get you a very nice house here.)

Condos (buy): N/A

Rentals: $250–$1,000 (executive homes could be higher). $400 here will get you more for your rental than most places in this book.

RV space: N/A

Medical Care: Adequate

Area Code: 844

PROS
When Texas was part of Mexico and Saltillo was the capital, well-to-do Texicans (including Sam Houston) used to escape the Texas heat by coming to Saltillo during the summer. When I was a kid, BAC (before air conditioning), my better-off friends used to escape the Rio Grande Valley heat and summer in Saltillo. Needless to say, you needn't transport your air conditioner with you when you move here. Heaters, however, should accompany you.

The surrounding mountains are both lovely to look at and a treasure to explore. There are Swiss-style chalets at their heads (see the mention of the drive on the back road between Saltillo and Monterrey) and apple orchards at their feet. Saltillo is one of my favorite places. **Despite its size, it still "feels" like an old Mexico town.** I fell in love with my first ex-wife here, but I like the town anyway. You're only an hour farther away from the States here than in Monterrey, but won't feel the need to escape the hustle and bustle as you would there. The *cabrito* here is even better than in Monterrey. The Holy Grail of *cabrito* in this part of Mexico, in my humble opinion, is the Restaurante Rey de Cabrito. It must have an acre under its roof and nothing on the menu but *cabrito*. I'd move here just to be able to eat goat (as opposed to crow or being an old goat) every day.

While many people seek to live in Mexico during the winter, you would probably choose Saltillo over many other places for the mild summers. High-speed Internet service is available. The people are friendly, though they still have some of that "mountain-people" reserve. Traffic is bearable. **It's not an especially noisy city, and there is plenty of life in the zócalo at night.**

There is a church with English services, which is probably your best bet to meet other expats. Call Damon Tripp at 01-52-844-418-1370. Services are at 10 A.M. Sundays. Damon was a hospital administrator (a gig I once had and understand his leaving it to live a sane life). He was in Austin and could be knocking down $200,000 or so doing that, but they decided (his wife, Delight, and three small kids they are homeschooling) they would like to be medical missionaries in Mexico, and there they are. They do many things, including building orphans' homes, this service, and making medical missionary trips around the country.

The bird museum is famous all over Mexico and the desert museum is quite a deal. Saltillo now has a Sam's, Wal-Mart, and H. E. B. food store.

CONS

It's still a big city. **There is no expatriate community to speak of.** It doesn't have the "high-brow culture" of Monterrey nor the "colonial culture" of cities in the interior. It is what it is. Some find it boring. **If you're moving to Mexico to experience the charm of Colonial Mexico, you'd be better served by heading farther south.**

There is a hospital, Hospital Christus Muguerza Saltillo, Carretera Saltillo-Monterrey, km 4.5 (Saltillo, Coah., 25204; Phone: 01-52-844-411-7000) and some English-speaking doctors, but for a serious situation, you might have to make the trip over the mountains to Monterrey to reach a world-class hospital.

The altitude may be hard on a lot of people, especially those with heart conditions.

Water can sometimes be in short supply, especially in times of drought. My experience is that the water pressure fluctuates a great deal, depending on your location.

IN-BETWEENS

Most gringos who live here work at a *maquiladora* (so-called twin plants with offices on both sides of the border that produce goods in Mexico solely for export), as well as the Chrysler, GM, Sunbeam, and other international plants that have changed this from a sleepy village to a big city. **Few have chosen to move here unless they married someone from Saltillo or have business here.** As you'd expect, there are a number of people here from Detroit, as well as Texans who just think that the lack of 100-degree weather makes this God's country.

It's close to the United States (well, Texas anyway). **It's a little high in the middle of a cost-of-living comparison. The weather is an attraction in the summer and a turnoff in the winter.** If you've always wanted a house with Saltillo tile, you're in the right place. Throw in the famous local serapes and blankets and you'll have a Saltillo house.

CHIHUAHUA, CHIHUAHUA

Ambiente: Similar to West Texas, New Mexico; Old West meets modern Mexico

Climate: Winters: mid-30s to low 50s nights, upper 50s to upper 60s days, but it drops to freezing often and snow happens. Summers: (Well, they can be beastly) mostly mid-60s nights, mid-90s to 100-plus days, but mostly just in the 90s. Hot.

Altitude: 4,600 feet

Population: 671,800 (official), 1,000,000 (estimate)

Housing: Good variety, inexpensive

Homes (buy): $20,000–$150,000. The average is about $40,000, but more in the less than $40,000 range than many towns. Of course, there are houses in the $200,000–$500,000 range as well.

Condos (buy): N/A

Rentals: $200–$600

RV space: N/A

Medical Care: Good hospitals, many doctors, and great dental care. El Paso, Texas, is close by.

Area Code: 614

Many businesspeople will be transferred here. It is also a city open to entrepreneurs. So if you're looking for something different from the typical retirement community, check out Chihuahua.

Much of the text was contributed by Margot Lindsay-Valdes, an American who married a Mexican physician and has lived in Chihuahua for many years. While I've peppered her comments with my own "Mexico" Mike asides, I think she did such a good writing job that it was a better service to my readers to digress from the format of the rest of the book. Thanks, Margot! She's graciously offered to help anyone seriously considering moving to Chihuahua (Margotlv@mail.com). She didn't mention it, but I hope she charges for more than perfunctory answers. She is an expert on everything there.

¡Chihuahua! I love Chihuahua. Although I started my MTV career here, I don't hold that against it. Juxtaposing that is the friendliness of the people. One morning around 2 A.M., one of the greatest loves of my life, Toby, and I came in from the Copper Canyon rail trip. The staff at our hotel, which used to be called the Villa Suites, took pity on us, since all the restaurants were closed, and shared their Christmas dinner with us! It could have happened anywhere in Mexico, but service such as that at a five-star hotel epitomizes Chihuahua to me. *Chihuahuaenses* are down-to-earth people. (A trick I learned to spell this city is to think verbally "Chi huah huah," similar to the military exclamation.)

It's got friendly people and a unique Wild West atmosphere. (It's really no wilder than anywhere else, but I feel like swaggering and talking about the long cattle drive I just finished. But that's my fantasy, probably not yours.) It's easy to navigate and still has an Old Mexico flavor, despite its modernization. For a big city, it doesn't seem as noisy as most. And the variety of scenery nearby makes it perfect for weekend trips. Within a few hours you can be in pine forests, snow, and really rugged mountains.

The Barranca del Cobre, or Copper Canyon, or Sierra Tarahumara, is something that no one should miss experiencing. The entire region comprises more than 200 gorges. When people refer to the Copper Canyon, they usually mean only one of six massive gorges in the area covering 25,000 square miles (64,000 square kilometers). You could put the Grand Canyon, Arizona, in it and have room left over. The train ride of 393 miles to Los Mochis on the Pacific Coast takes a good eight hours, though there are hotels along the way where you can stop for the night. The ride goes from sea level at Los Mochis to 8,000 feet. Oddly enough, not much copper was mined from these mountains. The name came from the copper-and-green colored lichen clinging to the walls of the canyons.

The native population of Tarahumara is a story unto themselves. A popular (and true) story about them is that they are renowned for running long distances. A promoter entered one in a marathon (26.2 miles) and the native didn't even place. When the promoter asked him why, the Tarahumara replied, "Too short, too short." These people can actually run down deer. There are a few hot springs south, east, and west, each with a different flavor (and mineral content). See my book *Spas and Hot Springs of Mexico.*—MM

Chihuahua City (as locals call it, to differentiate it from the state with the same name) is situated in the northern state of Chihuahua. The state of Chihuahua is the largest in Mexico. Because the city is only four hours from El Paso, Texas, the people here are, for the most part, bilingual, and look to the north for products and ideas. Unlike other Mexican cities in the south that were developed and planned centuries ago (though it was founded in 1709), Chihuahua City has been in the process of being developed during recent years. The city officials have taken great pains to keep the layout as practical and functional as possible. Because of this, the newer areas of the city resemble any city in the United States. Modern roads connect the entire city of Chihuahua, and four-lane freeways with tolls make traveling from city to city within Mexico easy and safe.

Recently, many American businesses have been pouring into the area, aware of the opportunities available to them. There are still many opportunities for new business, and, in turn, the housing market is booming right along to accommodate the influx of people moving north from other parts of Mexico. Land has more than doubled in price during the last few years, but not with the fevered pitch of the Mayan Riviera, and it continues to rise as the city continues to grow to the west.

Weather

Chihuahua's weather is usually sunny all year long, but it can be unpredictable at times. We don't get much rain because we are in the desert, so rain is a blessed event! The city places restrictions on watering in the hot summer, and you have to comply with the rules or you might find yourself fined. The city itself is situated in the Sierra Madre mountains, providing a magnificent view of red and brown majestic mountains all around. Sunsets are breathtaking here. The mountain shelters us from hurricanes, tornadoes, and other natural disasters, so unpredictable weather usually takes the form of heavy rain, occasional snows, and windstorms. The rainy season is usually in the summer, and the temperatures vary from the nineties to the hundreds.

We do not get the extreme temperatures of Phoenix, Arizona, to the north or Monterrey, Mexico, to the east. The winters can be very cold and it isn't unusual for it to snow. Usually the weather can be predicted by what's going on in the Pacific. When the Santa Ana winds blow in from California, Chihuahua usually gets them too. I would say the biggest problem are the dust storms. If a hurricane is brewing in the Pacific, that means rain for us, which explains our rainy season in the summer.

Chihuahua is a desert city, but there are palm trees everywhere. You will not find cacti as you see in Arizona. *Siccomoro,* sycamore, trees line the streets, and roses grow the way weeds do. Gardens are small but people are creative with what they have available to them.

Why do Americans come here?

Many Americans came here in the past because of the *maquilas,* twin plants, or *maquiladoras,* or other industries here. Over the years, the *maquilas* have grown and downsized, depending on the economic environment of the United States. Many companies have plants here, including Ford, Hallmark, Motorola, John Deere, Honeywell, and Zenith, to name a few. It is not unusual to have many families here from the United States, Canada, and Europe managing these companies from an engineering standpoint. Many families have come to live here for a two- to five-year period and, in the past, have been richly compensated. Depending on the openness of the family and their willingness to adapt to a new culture, many have left with memories of interesting experiences and new friends from Chihuahua who remain in touch for a lifetime.

The International Women's Group, or IWG, was formed by a group of wives and has been in existence since the 1970s. The group is a support system for families that are new to the area. They have social activities and perform charity work in the area. The various *maquilas* provide support to help those less fortunate in the community. For example, this group provides breakfast for more than 300 schoolchildren every month who would go to school without nourishment and without financial help. (If you would like to know more about this group, you can contact Margot at Margotlv@mail.com.)

Home Delivery!

In Chihuahua, it is possible to have everyone come to you. You see many motorbikes around bringing food, medicine, etc., to people's houses at no charge. This is great if it's in the middle of the night and you have a sick child in need of medicine. It's also nice to have all types of food delivered to your house.

Television and Movies

There are many movie theaters in Chihuahua, including Cineplex and Cinemark. Movies are inexpensive; a day movie costs $3 and a night movie costs $4. The movies are subtitled, so we often get them a couple of months after they are released in the United States. Children's movies are usually dubbed. The theaters have a Web site so you can check the times online. At the mall they have a VIP theater, in which the seats are leather and recline, and there are waiters who will serve you everything from cocktails to sushi. A VIP seat costs $5.

If you want to rent a movie, Blockbusters are everywhere, and their movies are also subtitled. Of course, DVDs are available everywhere and you can put them in the English mode.

You will notice here that everyone has a satellite dish. I have two dishes and get more than 1,000 channels. I can see almost every network from every city in the United States and channels from Spain and Italy. I also get pay-per-view for free and the entire set of premium channels. You can buy the dishes that give you all the channels without having to pay a fee for the service.

Transportation

Since many of the expats coming here are businesspeople, I've included this transportation information, which I don't usually do.—MM

Chihuahua has a small airport that has many flights. Before 9/11, there were more, and sometimes we have services to some cities and sometimes not. Continental has had two flights a day from Houston for four years and the flights are usually full. Aeromexico flies to Monterrey and then Atlanta, and there are other flights daily to Hermosillo and L.A.X. and Hermosillo and Phoenix. There are many flights to Mexico City and they are full. Charters run regularly to Las Vegas and various beaches in Mexico. Flights are not cheap; there isn't a lot of competition in Mexico so people here often drive to El Paso to fly on cheaper airlines, such as Southwest, etc.

The buses here are very nice; they are not Greyhound. They are Mercedes buses and they run continually everywhere. The buses charge by the level of service. A deluxe bus to Ciudad, Juaréz, costs about $30. There are bus attendants who serve drinks and snacks. The seats are similar to those on airplanes, and they show movies from TVs. It is a very safe, comfortable way to travel.

Education

There are many good schools in Chihuahua. There is a need for more schools with all the growth (those wishing to teach should go to Mark Farley's www.teach-english-mexico.com and sign up). Recently, a group of Canadians came down and opened an international school. There is also an American school that has been around for many years. Some names of excellent schools include Hamilton, Madison, Everest (boys), Alpes (girls), Espabi, and LaSalle. You can find all these schools in the phone book and many have Web sites.

The schools are divided into public (state) and private. All the schools require uniforms. Many schools are bilingual and many are Catholic. Montessori is very popular and there are often waiting lists to get kids into certain schools.

There are many language schools in the area, and even though the majority teach English, you will easily find teachers who will come to your house and give you private lessons for $5 to $10 an hour. Look in the phone book.

Hospitals, Medical Care, and Health Insurance

Although *Mexico Health and Travel Safety Guide* doesn't list Chihuahua in their book, Margot's observations seem accurate. I personally have been treated by doctors and dentists in Chihuahua and they always fixed me (as much as this mistreated body can be fixed) quickly and reasonably.—MM

Chihuahua has an excellent medical community. Three of the larger hospitals are Clinica del Parque, Clinica del Centro, and Cima. Many of the doctors were trained in the United States and Canada. In the phone book you will often find where the doctor was trained and if he speaks English. Pedro Leal is the owner of Clinica del Parque and his entire family is involved in the hospital. He was trained in Chicago and does heart transplants. He is very well-known by doctors in the United States and throughout Mexico. His children are all doctors. The hospital was recently remodeled and it is very nice.

This is right in line with my comments on health care in general.

A basic consultation and doctor's visit will run you about $20 to $30 here. A big difference in the approach to medicine is the time the doctors spend with you. It reminds me of the way doctors used to be in the States. They really care about you and get to know you. They are genuinely more interested in you than your money. I think this is due to the fact there isn't the problem with malpractice insurance. Health care is less expensive. I had two children here and a couple of surgeries and have been treated as royalty. My American friends always comment on this. Doctors are always accessible at all hours and come to your house when you cannot get to them.

Cima is a hospital brought here a couple of years ago from Baylor University in Texas. It looks the same as any hospital in the United States and is very modern. I find it to be very Americanized in its approach to medicine; if you go there, you will get a lot of tests done. They are very thorough. They are also expensive. Many people come to this hospital from the United States for plastic surgery, especially breast implants, liposuction, and tummy tucks. Most of the doctors I have encountered at Cima speak English.

Contrary to what many Americans think, you cannot just buy narcotics at the pharmacy. The government carefully controls medicines. Mexican doctors, in my opinion, do not prescribe things as freely as American doctors do. When I had a cesarean (obviously, this is Margot talking!), I was given an aspirin and that is it. The attitude is more holistic here. This was a shock to me at first; I am used to getting pain pills and codeine. You will not get such medicine so easily here.

A "temporary" filling I got after cracking a tooth on a popcorn kernel (popcorn sold from street vendors is one of my favorite addictions) lasted for six years.

There are many excellent dentists here and many Americans come down here for such things as dentures, bridges, and other procedures that are very expensive in the United States. Braces here are less expensive, $1,500 compared to the $5,000 you will pay in the States. The same as dentists everywhere, some charge more than others.

There is a dental school here. My husband is an orthodontist. He is American Board Certified and got his degree at Louisiana State University.

Health insurance can be purchased here or in El Paso. As I said before, El Paso and Chihuahua work together in many different areas and this is one of them. Aetna and Medlife are two companies here. I have used Aetna, which my company provided in the United States, for surgeries here and have had no trouble getting reimbursed. They even calculated the peso-to-dollar rate differences.

Safety, Crime, and Children—Chihuahua is a very safe place for kids and adults.

I find Chihuahua to be one of the safest places I have ever lived. I know as we get more things and people become aware of the haves and have-nots things will change. I think, at this moment, this is the safest place to raise my children. The downtown area of the city, with its nightclubs and bars, isn't such a great place to hang out on a weekend night, but I think that can be said about anywhere. I don't see the drug problems here that you have in the United States. I think this has to do with the cultural mentality of the people. Family is very important and so is religion. Children are taught more respect for adults from an early age. Everyone comes home to eat lunch together, families spend time with each other, older adults are taken care of and respected, and many mothers don't work. It is a different way of living.

Mail, Newspapers, and Magazines

The mail here isn't something I use. People pay their bills for lights, etc., at the OXXO (similar to a 7-Eleven), at the grocery store, or at the bank. There are even drive-through areas to pay your electricity bills. Its just something you get used to.

There is a Mail Boxes Etc. here; they bring my mail down to me, though I can get it in El Paso if I like. I find this a great service since I don't like to drive all the way to El Paso. They have a Web site and they notify customers when a package has arrived. I pay about $200 a year for these services, and if they have to bring something over the border, I pay a percentage on the price of the object. I get *USA Today, The New York Times,* and the El Paso paper delivered to my door for $75 every three months. I like this a lot, and the man who runs the service is very reliable.

Sanborn's and VIPS are two restaurant/pharmacies throughout Mexico that also are newsstands. You can usually get just about any magazine you want here, and they also sell books in English.

Theater, Events, and the Arts

Chihuahua has many cultural events within the city. There are museums and theaters downtown and around the city. Every year the *Nutcracker* comes to the Teatro de Héroes for a special performance.

Country Clubs and Health Clubs

Chihuahua has two country clubs with nineteen-hole golf courses. Memberships run from $16,000 up to join, but they are beautiful clubs. Campestre, the oldest club, even has a horse stable and will board horses. The newer club is called The San Francisco Club. Both clubs are very nice with every service you would expect at a club in the United States, but they cost two or three times as much there.

Shopping and Buying U.S. Things

We have two malls here, along with many strip malls. A new addition is Palacio del Sol that is on Periférico. A big department store here is Liverpool, which is similar to Dillards. It is all over Mexico City and has beautiful things, including a restaurant. J.C. Penney is also here, and they have a full-service beauty salon and spa. The mall is very large and has a child's play area called Moy. You can drop your child off here, for a minimal fee, to play on the rides and participate in many activities. The child cannot leave without you getting him or her.

Aladinos, Super Gelos, and Wal-Mart are major stores. You can get almost anything you want from the United States here in Chihuahua now. **You will pay more for American products and it is easy to find a comparable Mexican counterpart.** Kellogg's of Mexico, for example, makes the same cereals, they just use different packaging and names. It's just a matter of getting used to it all. Specific stores mentioned above, such as Aladinos, only sell American products with a high price.

Clothing can be expensive here, which is ironic since it is all made here! Wrangler, Champion, etc., all have factories in Mexico, but they are unable to sell the clothes here. Downtown there is a market called El Pasito, a great place to buy knockoffs. Suburbia is a store throughout Mexico that sells clothes and is comparable to Target.

One thing Margot forgot to mention is that Chihuahua is famous for its leather goods. In fact, I believe that you get the best deals and most variety here. There is a leather shop downtown that I visit every time I'm here, Todo es Piel. I once found a very light-green leather jacket like no other I'd seen in the world. Handmade boots, saddles, gloves, etc., are all bargains here.—MM

Final Thoughts

There is a big difference between the north and south of Mexico. The work ethic in the north is similar to the States and the pace is faster than in the south. If I were to retire, I would pick a beach or an area with a milder climate, but I would not hesitate to stay in Mexico. I think now is a good time to get your digs in since the country is changing so quickly.

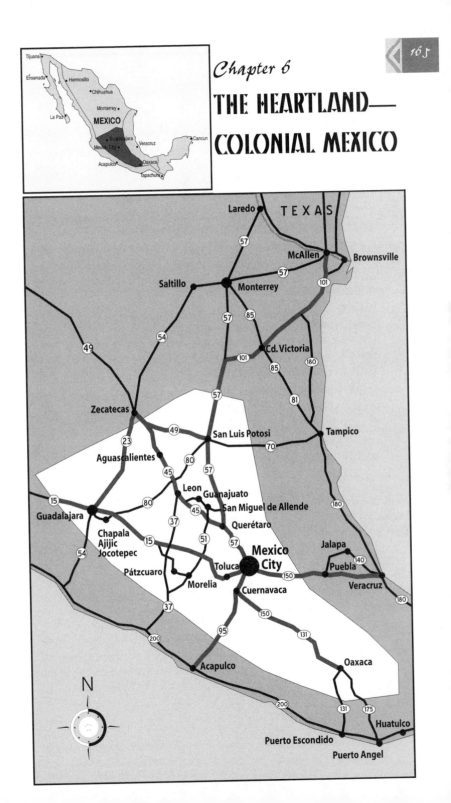

SAN MIGUEL DE ALLENDE, GUANAJUATO

Ambiente: Cultured, artistic. Gringos are very much in evidence.

Climate: Cool summers (70s to low 80s days, 50s nights), moderate winters (mostly 60s–70s days, 40s–50s nights, though it can get down to the upper 30s). You'll need sweaters and jackets. The rainy season is May to Oct.

Altitude: 5,903 feet

Population: 50,000 (official), 85,000 (estimate. Estimates of the foreign population run from 2,000–8,000 — take your pick. 3,000–4,000 is probably realistic.)

Housing: Surprisingly, not as expensive as you would think for renters. Buyers pay a premium to own here. There is price pressure from rich Mexico City residents and rich Americans and Canadians. There are some bargains, but not many. The least expensive housing is in the Guardiana area.

Homes (buy): $50,000–$250,000, with some nice ones in the $100,000–$150,000 range. The low-end ones are rare and generally fixer-uppers located in a nearby colonia (Guardiana, for instance). I keep hearing about $20,000–$30,000 houses, but have not seen one.

Condos (buy): N/A

Rentals: $450–$1,500. $600 here will get you a decent apartment. There are some in the $250–$450 range that will be out of town.

RV space: N/A

Medical Care: Adequate for minor to moderate medical situations. Good hospitals are located in Leon and Querétaro.

Area Code: 415

Thanks to Sherry McFarlane, a San Miguel resident, for help with this chapter. She does folk art tours of Mexico that are head and shoulders above anyone else's. Contact her at mexfolkart@hotmail.com

PROS

This is one of the two towns most people think of when talking about living in Mexico. The other is Lake Chapala. These two most popular expatriate communities are very different. Which one you choose, if these are your two choices, depends a lot on how well you mix with the local cultures. San Miguel attracts a younger crowd overall (though there are plenty of people in their sixties, seventies, eighties, and better here) and a rather artistic crowd (practically everyone seems to have been an art director of something). The majority of expats come from New York, Texas, New Mexico, or Canada.

It is not an artists' colony.

The expats range from very upscale retirees to bohemians who manage to eke out a living and can afford to live here. Please don't call it an artists' colony. It's not a colony; it is a Mexican town that appreciates art (the Instituto, as the local art school is called, has been encouraging and teaching artists for years). Don't expect it to be a place where mainly artists live. There are a lot of plain folks, retirees, and a smattering of artists and writers all living in harmony. During the last few years, there seem to be more writers gravitating here. I hope that doesn't ruin the property values.

Despite its being the location of my very brief bullfighting career, I still like this town. (While most people with diminished cranial capacity are content with "running with the bulls" during the annual Pamplonada festival, usually held the third Saturday of September, I had to get into an arena with a cape and test my manhood, which I very nearly lost. Nearly getting gored was the highlight of my MTV career, which probably says a lot. We were filming *Road Rules*, which is how I ended up—down really—in the bullring.)

This is a very pleasant town in the central highlands, the Bajio, of the country. Some people say this is the perfect climate (but several cities vie for that title). The weather is temperate most of the year. The summers are warm during the day (but not hot) and mildly cool at night. The winters are a little cooler during the day and cooler at night. You'll be able to wear a sweater or your leather jacket as often as you like. Even I don't need much more (and I will never live north of the Mason-Dixon Line again), and often only have my leather jacket on because it looks good, not because I am really that chilly.

Living History

The town was declared a national historical landmark and it is known for its colonial architecture. Because of its landmark statues, no modern-style buildings can be constructed downtown. The narrow, serpentine, cobblestone streets, which wind through centuries-old stone buildings, impart a colonial or nearly European (though not to the extent that Guanajuato does) feel to the center of town.

News and Library

There is a sizable foreign community (estimates vary greatly, but let's just say there are a lot) with a number of activities to get involved in. There is an English-language newspaper, *Atención* (Biblioteca Pública de San Miguel, #25 Insurgentes, 37700 San Miguel de Allende, Gto.). The last time I checked, U.S. or Canadian subscriptions cost $80 per year. It is a good paper, despite having run stories by me. Even if the price goes up, I'm sure that if you sent them a check for $80, they'd take care of you; if it goes up, they would probably let you know. New since the last edition is an English-language paper called *El Independiente* (Calzada de la Presa 53, 37700 San Miguel de Allende, Gto.), which focuses on travel, art, culture, and current events. It's a biweekly. An international subscription costs $45 per year.

There's a lending library with English-language books. You should make a contribution to the library if you are in the neighborhood.

If you are an equestrian, you'll love it here, and can join the riding clubs outside town.

There's an American consular agent, an active American Legion post, and a Canadian consulate. There are two hot springs, with waters of the same mineral content as Baden-Baden, Germany, which are reputed to retard aging. (See my book *Spas and Hot Springs of Mexico*, if you are a hot spring devotee, for springs throughout the whole country.)

Culture Galore

One of the most popular reasons for going to San Miguel is to study Spanish at the Instituto Allende (Calle Ancha de San Antonio, #20, 37700 San Miguel de Allende, Gto.; Phone: 01-52-415-152-0190; Fax: 01-52-415-152-4538; iallende@instituto-allende.edu.mx; www.instituto-allende.edu.mx). The Instituto is affiliated with the University of Guanajuato. It is an accredited school, offering B.V.A., M.F.A., or continuing education with a totally bilingual staff, and open year-round. Off-season discount rates apply from March through June and September through December. They also offer classes in many other subjects, in just about any area of artistic endeavor you can think of, such as painting, glassmaking, photography, and so on. It is a cultural hub of the town.

In addition to the language school information mentioned above, there are also many cultural and artistic activities connected to the Instituto. You can take courses in almost anything that interests you, either here or at people's homes. Writing, photography, painting, sculpting, massage, and a wide variety of "touchy-feely" courses or seminars (such as the course in miracles, Zen, meditation, and whatever happens to be hot in the New Age scene at the time, etc.) are offered all around town. Some of the instructors are quite good in their fields, with international reputations. Some are just sincere. Either way, you will not lack for a group that wants to help you develop your inner or artistic self.

A wide variety of restaurants is available, representing many countries. **Vegetarians are well fed here.** You can get *The New York Times* (Sunday edition). Adequate medical treatment is available for minor problems, but for major emergencies you will have to go to Leon or Mexico City. There is a fine golf course and country club.

San Miguel de Allende is a good singles' town.

If you are single of any age or lifestyle, you will have many opportunities to meet a partner, either among the foreign community or among the constant stream of travelers—mainly Texans, New Yorkers, Californians, Canadians, and Europeans—though every state in the union is represented. You can find inexpensive hotels and rooms for rent, and, after you've been there for a while, you could wrangle a house-sitting arrangement for other foreigners.

You can also spend a bloody fortune and live in luxury as you have only dreamed of, or live on the outskirts of town for $300 monthly rents; the choice is yours. **There is a good, honest realtor I can personally vouch for to assist you, Sr.** Abraham Cadena (Calle Ancha San Antonio #21; Mailing Address: APDO Postal #26, San Miguel de Allende, Gto.)

Additional Resources

- Additional English-language schools: The Warren Hardy School, San Rafael 6, San Miguel de Allende, Gto., 37700; Phone/Fax from 9 A.M.–noon, U.S. Central Time: 01-52-415-154-4017; Afternoons, U.S. Central Time: 01-52-415-152-4728; info@warrenhardy.com; www.warrenhardy.com. Habla Hispana Spanish School, Calzada de la Luz 25 San Miguel de Allende, Gto., 37700; Phone: 01-52-415-152-1535; Secondary Phone (try the primary first, please): 01-52-415-152-0713; U.S. address: Angelica Rodriguez, director, Habla Hispana Spanish School, 220 N. Zapata Hwy. #11A, Laredo, TX 78043; info@mexicospanish.com; www.mexicospanish.com. Centro Bilingüe de San Miguel, Sara Hernández Murillo, directora, Correo #46, Centro San Miguel de Allende, Gto., 37700; Phone/Fax: 01-52-415-152-5400; centrobilingue@yahoo.com; www.geocities.com/centrobilingue.
- Medical care: Many expats have good things to say about the Hospital de Fé and its doctors. It has a MedToGo rating of 3/5. (Hospital de Fé, Librmiento Dolores Hidalgo #43, Mesa del Malanquín [a few blocks from the bus station]; Phone: 01-52-415-152-2233 or 01-52-415-152-2320; Fax: 01-52-415-152-2329. Ask for the fax tone, *"Quisiera el tono del fax, por favor."* English, French, and German are spoken.)
- Jewish resource: Jewish Community of San Miguel de Allende, Villas del Parque 34, San Miguel de Allende, Gto., 37700, Jewish Renewal; Phone: 01-52-415-152-2659; Fax: 01-52-415-152-2659.

CONS

Buying real estate here can be expensive due to the desirability of this town. Well-to-do Mexicans, as well as well-heeled Americans and Canadians, want weekend houses here. Although you can rent houses and rooms reasonably, you have to be financially successful to buy something here.

IN-BETWEENS

San Miguel is more international in flavor than any of the other places mentioned in this book. It has the greatest mix of ages and lifestyles. It is also more liberal than any other place, besides Puerto Vallarta. There are more artists and writers and sculptors and photographers per square foot here than anywhere except Santa Fe, New Mexico. There is a local joke that half of the new residents were former directors of the Santa Fe Art Museum. Of course, many of these people are dilettantes, but so what? **If you are looking for the "artsy" lifestyle, you will find it here.**

You'll meet fellow scribblers or dabblers from all over the world. Once I was looking for a friend of mine and walked into another house. A familiar face asked if he could help me, and I told him who I was looking for. He politely directed me down the block. It was ... well, I'll never tell, but he sells a lot more books than I do. I was doing a radio show on one of the biggest syndicated shows out of New York City and the host had a house in San Miguel. The same as in Los Angeles, you're as likely to meet somebody famous as a nobody (such as me, for instance). Everyone mingles. With this diversity of expatriates comes a diversity of lifestyles.

The ages of the foreign residents are all over the place, from the twenties to the nineties. The foreign societies here tend to get involved in local projects and take an interest in the community they live in. The foreign residents tend to speak at least a little Spanish, and many of them speak it very well. The foreigners here seem to be genuinely interested in Mexico and are likely to have traveled to other parts of the country. There are few foreign businessmen, though some foreigners own farms in the area.

An excellent resource is *The Insider's Guide to San Miguel* by Archie Dean, a longtime resident. It lists everything from apartments (and costs) and utilities to watch repair. Archie updates it frequently, sells it only in San Miguel, and only does small press runs.

GUANAJUATO, GUANAJUATO

(No, I didn't mistype it. The name of the city and the state are the same.)

Ambiente: Very Spanish, cultured, conservative. Few gringos in residence.

Climate: Mild, cool summers (70s days, 50s nights), moderate winters (mostly 50s–60s days, 40s–50s nights, though it can get down to the 30s, with frost). You'll need sweaters and jackets.

Altitude: 6,471 feet

Population: 85,000

Housing: Plentiful and reasonable

Homes (buy): $26,000–$90,000, with lots of nice ones in the $60,000–$70,000 range
Condos (buy): N/A
Rentals: $200–$1,500. $500 here will get you a very nice apartment.
RV space: N/A

Medical Care: Adequate. For long-term care, Leon is very close.

Area Code: 473

PROS

Guanajuato is for those who seek a truly unique (an often overused word, but, in this case, applicable) environment. Guanajuato is a traditional Colonial

Mexican city with strong European roots. **There is no place like it in Mexico, perhaps the world.** It's hard to put a number on the foreigners living here, but there are nowhere near as many as in San Miguel. Some estimate that there are at least 1,000, probably more. Of these, about half are Europeans.

"Unique" sums up this small city. Only an hour's drive from San Miguel de Allende, it is another world. It has been called the most European of Mexico's cities. The atmosphere here is more conservative than in San Miguel. **There is a tremendous amount of culture here.** (Even so, they let me visit occasionally, if I promise not to stay too long.)

It is built in a dramatic setting. The houses are built on hills and each one seems to overlook the next. A local joke is that if you want to know what's happening with your neighbors, just lean out your window. Meandering through the middle of the town is a series of subterranean streets that form a mazelike expressway. It's an old mining town and its riches are based mostly on silver. **The city center is a car-free zone, which makes life more pleasant and getting around a bit more of a challenge.** If you are not up to walking, then you will find this a very challenging city. The physically challenged would find it impractical to live here. In the town square, the zócalo, there are band concerts at night, a collection of sidewalk cafes, and a lot of people to watch. There are often groups that meet in front of the cathedral to begin a *callejonada*, or a singing, drinking stroll through the city's labyrinthine streets. It begins with the troubadours (dressed in period costumes) telling ribald stories on the church steps. After a sufficient crowd has gathered and everyone is properly lubricated from the wine *botas*, they begin serenading and wandering. You shouldn't miss it.

Living, in general, is considerably less expensive than in San Miguel— about 30 percent less overall. The middle-class and higher-end places offer more for less. While you can rent a very basic apartment for $200 to $250, if you can bump that up to $350 to $400, you'd get a much nicer place than you would in San Miguel.

Similar to its sister city, a place in the old section of town will be very romantic and charming, and most likely have ancient plumbing. If you choose one of the suburbs, such as Marfil, for instance, you will find more spacious and modern quarters. However, since everything is built "Mediterranean-style" (houses atop each other), they will be noisy until about 10 P.M. After that, your neighbors will settle down and it can actually get quiet.

This was once called "The Beverly Hills of Guanajuato." It was where the wealthy of the city built their spacious mansions and lovely parks. Then when silver took a downturn and a series of floods made it less desirable, those mansions were abandoned. Today the area is again a lovely place to live and has regained some of its bygone grandeur. There are other, more modern developments as well. In fact, if you choose a suburb to the north of town, you'll find less "Mediterranean-style" construction.

There are a lot of cultural and art happenings here, many of which are associated with the university. The crowd is either young or young at heart.

For more information about Guanajuato, two good Web sites are www.guanajuato-travel.com.mx and www.guanajuato.gob.mx. The director of tourism for the state, Desmond O'Shaughnessy Doyle, director general of promotion, Guanajuato State Tourism Office, has graciously offered to accept e-mails directly from readers of this book (desmond@guanajuato.gob.mx).

Additional Resources

- Medical care: Médica Integral Guanajuatense, Plaza de la Paz #20, Zona Centro (near Basílica and the Tourist Center), Phone: 01-52-473-732-2305; Fax: 01-52-473-732-6985. They have a 2/5 MedToGo rating.
- Language schools:There are several language schools in Guanajuato. For a site with links to many of them in San Miguel de Allende, Guanajuato, and other towns in Mexico, see www.spanishamigos.com/mexicoguanajuato.html. The Universidad de Guanajuato (Departamento de Servicios al Estudiante, Lascurain de Retana #5, 36000 Guanajuato, Gto.; Phone: 01-52-473-732-0006; info@quijote.ugto.mx; www.ugto.mx/english/index.htm) offers courses and can arrange for you to stay with a family. They also offer for-credit courses and are affiliated with about a dozen universities in the United States. There is also the Instituto Miguel de Cervantes (Cerro del Erizo 100, Valenciana, Guanajuato, Gto.; Phone: 01-52-473-732-8069, Fax: 01-52-473-732-8017; info@spanish-immersion.com; www.spanish-immersion.com). The Academia Falcon (Paseo de la Presa 80, Guanajuato, Gto., 36000; Phone/Fax: 01-52-473-731-0745; infalcon@academiafalcon.com; www.academiafalcon.com) is associated with the University of Arizona and offers credits for bilingual educators.

CONS

There is not nearly as much English spoken here as in San Miguel. For some, this is a plus. **On weekends it becomes very crowded, with thousands of people from Mexico City crowding in to escape.** It is nearly impossible to find a hotel during these times, and the streets are even more crowded with cars. The foreign community is small. **The close quarters everyone lives in could get to you after a while.** The winding and steep streets can be difficult for some people.

IN-BETWEENS

This is a fine choice for someone who wants to get away from other Americans and Canadians. It has a very artistic feel to it, so you probably could write or paint a masterpiece here. **The old-world charm gives you a sense of the permanency of place and a feeling of the impermanence of man.** It is not for everyone, but it could be an ideal place for someone who is self-sufficient and artistic.

GUADALAJARA, JALISCO

Ambiente: Cultured, sophisticated, big-city feel, a goodly number of foreigners

Climate: Perfect year-round, though some think it's a little hot in the summer (60s–80s summers, 50s–70s winters)

Altitude: 5,092 feet

Population: 1,646,183 (official count in 2000). The metro area is estimated to be from 3,677,531–6,000,000 (I'd vote for the latter) and growing.

Housing: Many choices, from moderate to expensive

Homes (buy): $40,000–$150,000, with lots of nice ones in the $70,000–$90,000 range (but not in the gated communities listed for businesspeople, where houses begin at $250,000 and go way up)

Condos (buy): $60,000–$150,000

Rentals: $250–$900. $900 here will get you a nice rental house or very nice apartment.

RV space: N/A

Medical Care: Excellent

Area Code: 33 (Only Guadalajara and Monterrey have two-digit area codes.)

This is the place most people think of when they think of retiring to Mexico. They really mean Lake Chapala, about forty-five minutes south, but everyone has heard of Mexico's second largest city. I am indebted to Martin and Gretta Parker and Shirley Kasparek, expatriates in Chapala, for assistance with this chapter.

There are about 100,000 foreigners in the entire state of Jalisco. Retirees in the state of Jalisco are mostly centered in Lake Chapala and Puerto Vallarta. Those working for international corporations comprise the bulk of foreign residents in the city of Guadalajara.

Guadalajara for American and Canadian Businesspeople

This is the second largest city in the country. Since the majority of foreign residents of Guadalajara are businesspeople working for international corporations, this first section is devoted to those being transferred here. While some gringos do move to Guadalajara just because they want to, or to retire, they are more likely to move an hour south to the Chapala area.

You'll find doing business here a little different from Mexico City. While it is certainly not laid-back, *Tapatios* (as people from Guadalajara call themselves) live at a little slower pace. They are very progressive and excellent businesspeople, but they don't seem to exhibit the hustle and bustle that is more common in Mexico City. However, many *Chilangos* (a generally, though not always nonderogatory term for people from Mexico City—use it only if your host does) moved here after the devastating earthquake in the 1980s, so this is changing.

Business resources: A good source of business information is the American Chamber of Commerce, Av. Moctezuma 442, Col. Jardines del Sol, 45050 Zapopan, Jal.; Phone: 01-52-33-634-6606; Fax: 01-52-33-634-7374; direccion_dgl@amcham.com.mex; amcham.com.mx. Canadians will find information relating to doing business in Mexico from the Canadian Chamber of Commerce, Circunvalación Agustín Yañez 2567 E, Guadalajara, Jal., 84150; Phone: 01-52-33-630-5005; Fax: 01-52-33-630-5055; cancham@ prodigy.net.mx.

While a suit and tie are still preferred, dressing a little more casually is often acceptable. Consider the difference between Mexico City and Guadalajara similar to the differences between New York City and Chicago.

Housing within the City

You'd probably like to have an idea of the different neighborhoods that will be suggested to you by your personnel department or Mexican counterparts. If your company is sending you there and needs to lease space, there's even a Web site devoted to such things: www.cpamericas.com.

Providencia: Providencia has the feel of an old, established community. I've found that the people are friendly and not as "exclusive" as in some of the other neighborhoods. It is also the least expensive of the lot—least expensive is relative. Living here will cost around $1,200 a month and up.

Country Club: To me, this is a too-exclusive area, but if you like golf, what else could you ask for? As the name suggests, this is centered on the Country Club of Guadalajara. It is a very nice section with old trees and houses that vary from simply quite nice to mansions. Look at spending about $1,700 a month here.

Colinas de San Janier and Lomas del Valle: If a walled-in, very exclusive area appeals to you, this is your choice. Even the condos are walled. Low-end rent here starts around $2,700 and go up.

Housing in the Suburbs

Club de Golf Santa Ana: This is quite an exclusive country club community, located on the southwest side of town. Count on paying around $2,100, or more, for rent.

Ciudad Bugambilias: This area has a nice suburban Mexico feel. It's pretty, with flowers (*bugambilias*, what else, predominating) all over. It will give you great views (the clubhouse is atop a big hill) and costs about $1,700 a month.

Rancho Contento: I like this area. It's walled in and feels as if you have entered another world. It has real character. It has the feel of a village, with its cobblestone streets that wind all around. You can count on getting lost a few times. Living here entitles you to use the nine-hole golf course and other facilities. It's a bargain (of sorts) at $1,500, and up.

PROS

The climate is practically perfect, a perpetual spring. The city offers cultural attractions from symphonies to plays to museums to picturesque markets. Public transportation is excellent. There are enough activities by the foreign community so that you will not feel alone. My favorite hot spring (Rio Caliente) is about an hour and a half to the northwest. (See my book *Spas and Hot Springs of Mexico* if you are a hot spring devotee and looking for springs throughout the whole country.)

Guadalajara is an international city.

Because it is a big city, you can buy a wide variety of products—from food to furniture, from all over Mexico—at reasonable prices. There are also many imported goods. It has several fine golf courses and country clubs. There are some RV parks here that have a real sense of community, and many of the residents have returned here year after year. It is easy to drive to from the Arizona border or Texas border (easily only two days away from Texas and three days away from Arizona).

The cuisine here is truly international, with many different countries represented. You can spend as much or as little as you want when eating out. There is an English-language newspaper, the *Guadalajara Reporter* (Duque de Rivas #254, 44140 Guadalajara, Jal.; www.guadalajarareporter.com) that serves Guadalajara and the Chapala areas as well as Puerto Vallarta. You can subscribe to the print version of the paper from the United States if you want to get an idea of what is going on in the area. Since subscription costs change, you'll have to go to their Web site to get the current rate.

There are both American and Canadian consuls, an American Legion post (see bibliography for addresses and phone numbers), and a synagogue (Juan Palomar y Amaas #651, Fracc. Monraz, 44670 Guadalajara, Jal.; Phone: 01-52-33-641-6779 or 01-52-33-641-6463). They also have kosher products from Tecnologia Narciso, Monterrey, and import delicatessen foods from Mexico City. High-speed Internet service is available.

Additional Resources

Medical care is on par with the United States.

- Medical care: **Medical care is top-notch and there is a wide variety of hospitals and doctors to choose from.** *Mexico Health and Safety Travel Guide* (MedToGo) says, "We evaluated what we believe to be Guadalajara's top three hospitals and found them as a whole to be as well equipped as the majority of medical facilities in the U.S. Unlike many destinations in Mexico, travelers with potentially serious medical conditions should feel as safe in Guadalajara as they would in any other city in the industrialized world."

Following are the top hospitals according to the authors of the excellent guide to Mexican hospitals, *Mexico Health and Safety Travel Guide: The traveler's guide to Mexico's best hospitals and English-speaking doctors*, available from www.mexicomike.com and www.medtogo.com/?agentcode=mexmike. Hospitál San Javier is in the northern part of the city (Avenida Pablo Casals #640, Co. Parados Providencia, Guadalajara, Jal.; Phone: 01-52-33-642-6623), Hospital Bernadette is in the central part of the city (Hidalgo #930, Col. Centro, Guadalajara, Jal.; Phone: 01-52-33-825-4365), and Hospital Ángeles del Carmen (Tarascos #3435, Fracc. Col. Monraz, Guadalajara, Jal.).

- Language schools: There are several language schools here. The Mexican–North American Cultural Institute of Jalisco is a wonderful place that can help you learn Spanish and about the culture of the area (Enrique Diáz de Leon #300, Guadalajara, Jal.; Phone: 01-52-33-625-5838 or 01-52-33-625-4101). You can also take classes at the university. The Instituto Cultural (Enrique Diáz de Leon [Tolsa], 300, 44170 Guadalajara, Jal.; Phone: 01-52-33-825-4101 or 01-52-33-825-5838) is a member of the Association of U.S.–Mexican Binational Centers and is also a good place to go.

- English-language school for kids: The American School Foundation of Guadalajara, Colomos, APDO 6-280, Col. Providencia, 44640 Guadalajara, Jal.; Phone: 01-52-33-648-0299; Fax: 01-52-33-817-3356; asfg@asfg.mx; www.asfg.mx.

CONS

This is a huge city. It now has pollution problems, though not as severe as Mexico City. Driving is challenging, to say the least. Even I am challenged there. **Traffic jams and rush hour traffic are facts of life.** The cost of living is reasonable, but if you want to rent or buy a house in the foreign community, the cost will be high. Outside these gringo enclaves, prices are only a little bit higher than they would be in a smaller city. The idea of living in a big city solely because the weather is nice just doesn't appeal to me. Unless I had a business or artistic reason to be here, I would move instead to the Lake Chapala area.

IN-BETWEENS

There is a diverse group of foreigners living here. There are embassy personnel from around the world and executives and employees of international corporations. Because it is a business city, it is easier to get things done here than in a smaller town or a "retirement" community. *The Wall Street Journal* and *The New York Times* are available.

There are stockbrokers, FedEx, DHL, excellent telephone and fax services, and the opportunity to dress up for events. It is an excellent place to conduct business since there are convention centers, and the major hotels can put your clients up in the style they are used to anywhere in the world; they know how to cater to business travelers. There is an international airport with direct flights to the United States and good connections to the rest of the world. It is a very sophisticated city.

The Mexican businesspeople who live here speak English quite well. The foreign businesspeople here have mostly learned to speak Spanish out of respect for their Mexican colleagues. The foreign retirees are a mixed lot. Some of them have chosen to integrate themselves into the community and speak Spanish. Because it is possible to live here and never speak a lick of Spanish, many of the old-timers have chosen this option. Some have told me that the retirees living here tend to be on more of a budget than those in the lakeside communities.

If you are a younger person thinking of living here, you will not have much foreign company to socialize with, except for those working for foreign corporations. If you want to study Spanish or art, it is a fine place. **If you want to live the life of an artist, and would like to meet Mexican artists, my vote would be to hang out here for a couple of months to absorb the culture and then move on.**

CHAPALA AND AJIJIC, JALISCO

Ambiente: An American-Canadian colony

Climate: A little cooler than Guadalajara. Perfect. Rainy season is from June to Sept.

Altitude: 4,922 feet

Population: 50,000 (estimate. However, that does not include the 40,000–50,000 gringos living here in the winter. About 8,000 stay year-round.)

Housing: Available, but tends to be pricey. With the population surging in winter with "snow-birds," the inexpensive places are gone quickly.

Homes (buy): $85,000–$250,000. Most houses now selling are in the $95,000–$150,000 range.

Condos (buy): N/A

Rentals: $500–$1,000. $1,000 here will get you a decent house, but not a mansion.

RV space: N/A

Medical Care: Very good, and Guadalajara is only twenty-six miles away.

Area Code: 376

Lake Chapala and Ajijic are distinctly different places. Ajijic is a little more upscale (also more expensive to live in) and has a different sense of community than Chapala, though these distinctions will only be apparent after spending some time in the area. For the purposes of this book, we can consider them one and not be too out of line. These medium-sized towns are about an hour away from Guadalajara, yet worlds apart. Although there are more younger (age forty to fifty) gringos here than when the last book was written, it is still true that the majority of the gringo population is fifty-five and older.

Mexico's largest lake, which had been receding for years, is now back to its 1990 levels. This has fueled an increase in tourism, especially on weekends, when many from Guadalajara stream into town. Thus these small towns are crowded on weekends: Getting a table at a restaurant is harder and parking is a nightmare. The historic Nido Hotel, located on the town square, has finally closed after years of decline. There are now several bed-and-breakfast facilities. Eating out is actually more expensive than in many parts of the United States. Ah, progress! Chapala and Ajijic are the places most prospective retirees mean when they say "Guadalajara." They've been promoted as retirement communities for decades and have quite an active collection of gringos living in them. There are so many American and Canadian organizations that you could spend all of your time involved in them.

The Lake Chapala Society (16 de Septiembre #16-A, Chapala, Jal.; www.lakechapalasociety.org) is quite a deal, with around 3,000 members from thirty-one nationalities. They have an English-language lending library, social events, charity projects, a talking book library, a videotape library, and more. They also publish a nifty directory of their members. You should join them while you are here. A single membership costs about $35 and a couple can join for about $45 a year; it is a good investment.

While bridge and other social pursuits are the norms, there are also charitable causes to get involved in. These groups will help local schools, clinics, or other community projects. You will never feel alone here, and many people feel that it offers many of the conveniences of a retirement community in the United States. There is also a fine golf course and country club.

There is now a small smog problem. Parking is at a premium. The lifestyle is relaxed. There is an adequate variety of restaurants but it is not a gourmet's delight. Food costs are reasonable to high. The American Legion has a strong post here. Nearby Jocotepec has a hot spring. (See my book *Spas and Hot Springs of Mexico* if you are a hot spring devotee looking for springs throughout the whole country.)

PROS

There are approximately 40,000 to 50,000 gringos in the Lake Chapala and Ajijic area. Though this fluctuates, some say it is equally divided among Americans and Canadians, and others swear the ratio is two to one of Canadians to Americans. Obviously, it is one of the most popular retirement destinations in Mexico, since (according to the U.S. embassy) there are only about 1 million or so American gringos in the whole country. There are probably somewhat fewer Canadians.

Medical Care

Medical care is adequate for most situations, but for major surgery or emergencies, you will have to go to Guadalajara. A lot of people who do not have medical insurance use IMSS. Also, the Maskaras Clinic in Riberas de Pilar has a yearly medical services plan for a set price. The Ajijic Clinic has a small hospital on its premises, and both locations have various specialists who visit on a weekly basis.

MedToGo mentions Clínica Ajijic with a 2.5/5 rating (Caretera Ote. #33 [corner of Javier Mina], Ajijic, Chapala, Jal.; Phone: 01-52-376-760-0662; Fax: 01-52-376-766-0500).

Internet and Telephone Service

There are good Internet connections (both dial-up and high-speed) here and a group that runs a dandy home page (www.mexconnect.com). They can provide you with a tremendous amount of information about living in the area or Mexico in general. Internet service providers are lagunanet.mx and Prodigy, which is the Telmex provider. Their prices are comparable and run about $20 for dial-up and $40 for broadband. Most people use callback services for international calls. There are several services available. A call from Guadalajara runs about $0.11 a minute and $0.17 from the lakeside area.

CONS

The housing market, particularly for higher-end houses, is booming, and has been for the past several years. While those are quite high, there is still some middle-class housing that is not out of reach. Any place with a large foreign population will have higher costs than places where the competition for housing is not so fierce; you are paying for the convenience of having a lot of English spoken and the companionship of your countrymen. You can avoid these costs by living farther away, down the lake. Even today, I have talked to people who are paying between $300 and $400 for decent apartments, though the average is closer to $500 to $600.

The famous PAL trailer park has closed.

IN-BETWEENS

It is easy to live here and never interface with the Mexican culture because of all the other foreigners to talk to and the activities of the American Society and other groups. Many of the residents have chosen to isolate themselves this way. Their contact with Mexicans is limited to their maids and shopkeepers. They often do not travel throughout the country and know very little outside their area. This is, of course, not a blanket description of all the residents of the area. Many of them came here because they love Mexico and wanted to live in Mexico. Still, there are enough people who are living here only because the weather is great and the costs are lower than for a comparable lifestyle back home to make it worth noting. Most of the foreigners here are retirees in their sixties and beyond. Many of them have been living here, or coming back here, for years and years.

A businessman is unlikely to be transferred here, though if you are willing to commute to Guadalajara, you might find it a pleasant place to live. The drive isn't as bad as the one you might take if you lived in a suburb of Chicago, Houston, Los Angeles, or Seattle. If you are younger, you will not find much companionship. If you are an artist or writer, you might possibly want to check it out.

The area attracted D. H. Lawrence and a host of others throughout the years, and wherever you have wealthy retirees, you have people interested in promoting the arts. The trap I see is that you could get so involved with doing things in the society that you forget why you came here in the first place. **The lifestyle of the foreigners here tends to be conservative.** Ajijic is a little more upscale, according to local residents. They say that Chapala-ites tend to be more on a fixed income and watch their pennies. Chapala does have more hotels, and the possibility of checking it out for an extended time without making a commitment is greater.

JOCOTEPEC, JALISCO

Ambiente: Very Mexican

Climate: A little cooler than Guadalajara. Perfect. Rainy season: June to Sept.

Altitude: 4,922 feet

Population: 2,500

Housing: Adequate. At the time of the last edition, this area was considerably less expensive than Chapala. Not anymore. Take the housing costs of Chapala and deduct maybe 10 percent.

Medical Care: It's close enough to Chapala and Guadalajara so as not to worry.

Area Code: 387

PROS

The farther you travel along Lake Chapala, the closer you get to "old" Mexico. **Jocotepec (and the other communities along the lake) have a different character, more Mexican in flavor.** The area is growing and there are more amenities here now than there were at the time of the last edition. Its days of being a cheaper retreat are gone. You can stay here and feel a bit more isolated from the social hustle and bustle of Chapala, yet be close enough to drive over and take part in whatever activity pleases you. The physical distance is minuscule, but the "feeling" of distance is enormous. There is a hot spring.

CONS

You have farther to drive for medical care. The distance from the social happenings may be a bother. The accommodations tend to be plainer. Restaurants tend to be Mexican cuisine. There is no golf course.

IN-BETWEENS

Jocotepec and the other communities along Lake Chapala might be more suited to those who want to immerse themselves in Mexico and are willing to learn some Spanish. **There are fewer locals who speak English, though this is rapidly becoming less and less so, thanks to the encroaching development.** Artists and writers might find the area more conducive to creating. You will find no foreign businessmen here. A younger person will have no foreign social life, though you could find it somewhat easier to integrate with the locals.

CUERNAVACA, MORELOS

Ambiente: Cultured, a good mix of Mexicans and foreigners

Climate: It's not called "The City of Eternal Spring" for nothing. The weather is darn near perfect for most tastes. Late Nov. to late May is the dry season, when it rarely rains. From June to Sept. it rains gently (though sometimes heavily) every day for a couple of hours. Winters: upper 50s to low 80s. Summers (before rains): mid-60s to upper or mid-90s. Once it starts raining again, it cools off to mid-60s to mid-80s.

Altitude: 5,058 feet

Population: 400,000 in the city. The metro area is estimated to be about 1,000,000.

Housing: All price ranges

> Homes (buy): $80,000–$250,000, with some nice ones in the $100,000–$150,000 range. There is price pressure on houses from rich Mexico City residents who want a weekend home, foreign businessmen, and well-to-do expats. I've heard of houses in the $60,000 range, but they are scarce.
>
> Condos (buy): N/A
>
> Rentals: $500–$2,000. An interesting situation is a room rental at a *temascal* spa for $200 to $300 a month (www.cuernavacainfo.com/temazcal.html).
>
> RV space: N/A

Medical Care: Good. The Hospital Clínica Londres has a 4/5 rating by MedToGo. There are excellent hospitals in Mexico City.

Area Code: 777

PROS

God must have been trying to make the perfect climate when He created Cuernavaca. It never gets too hot or too cold. The rains in the rainy season fall from June to September, mainly at night. This nurtures some of the most beautiful gardens and golf courses in the world. Indeed, Cuernavaca is famous for its gardens, in particular the Borda Gardens. For those who need a moist climate in order to breathe, such as someone who has had an operation on his larynx, this is the ideal location. Although it is a metro area of about a million people, there is a peace and tranquility here that make you forget that. It's estimated that there are about 5,000 foreigners here, 2,000 from the United States, about the same number of Canadians, and the rest from Europe.

Cuernavaca is a golfer's heaven.

This city is cosmopolitan enough to satisfy any taste. There are restaurants of almost all nationalities here. The zócalo, or main square, is alive day and night with activity. In the evenings, there are often free band concerts. The sidewalk cafes are great places to sit and watch the world go by, or to meet new and old acquaintances. There are seven golf courses in the neighborhood.

There is plenty of housing, ranging from simple Mexican-style apartments, to exclusive communities, to new developments specifically built for foreigners, to rentals in all price ranges, to simple dwellings. **There are hot springs nearby and two spas in town.** There is an archeological site in the city, Pirámide de Teopanzolco. Medical care is very good, with hospitals (though only one, Hospital Cliníca Londres, Calle Cuauhtémoc #305, [at the corner of 5 de Mayo], Col. Lomas de la Selva, Cuernavaca, Mor.; Phone: 01-52-777-311-2482; with a 4/5 rating by MedToGo) and doctors aplenty, many of whom speak English.

This is a spa haven.

There are two spas in the city, Hosteria las Quintas (which is my favorite in Mexico, and is a member of the exclusive Top 25 Destination Spas in North America) **and the Misión del Sol, which has a New Age spiritual ambiance including a Zen meditation center** (www.spagetaway.com). Speaking of spirituality, there must be a lot of it in the neighborhood. The old Barbara Hutton estate (now the Camino Real Sumiya) has a Zen meditation garden and a prayer temple. Misión del Sol spa and resort qualifies as a spiritual retreat. Within driving distance are several hot springs. (See my book *Spas and Hot Springs of Mexico* for more details or the Web site above.) Many artists and writers have found the intellectual climate here to be stimulating. The foreign population doesn't overwhelm the city. You really feel as if you are in old Colonial Mexico; the art and architecture give you an appreciation for the history of the country.

The Museo de Cuauhnahuac, in the Cortés Palace, has a Diego Rivera mural and a comprehensive history of Mexico through the colonial period. The Museo Casa Robert Brady exhibits more than 1,200 works of art from pre-Hispanic to colonial to modern eras. Works of Rufino Tamayo and Frida Kahlo are on display. Handicrafts from all over the world are also exhibited. A unique museum for those who are interested in herbs is the Muséo de la Herbolaría, which was established to preserve and promote traditional folk medicine. Communications are excellent and Internet access is available.

There is a local foreign resident library, the Guild House (Tuxtla Gutierrez #111). They also have activities for foreigners and information about other foreign societies, such as the Center for Creative Arts, the American Legion, the Navy League, and the American Benevolent Society. The Newcomer's Club can help you acclimate and get to know other expats (Admon de Correos, APDO 376-3, Cuernavaca, Mor., 62250; Phone: 01-52-777-315-2272; Justandiemx@aol.com).

Additional Resources

▪Language schools: In my opinion, the language schools here are better than those in San Miguel de Allende, perhaps because the atmosphere here is different and you are forced to use your fledgling language skills. Living with a family is offered at a very reasonable fee, but is not mandatory.

Chac Mool USA and Canada (1303 Candelero Ct., Placerville, CA 95667; Phone: 888-397-8363; In Mexico: Privada de la Pradera #108, Col. Pradera, Cuernavaca, Mor. 62170; Phone: 01-52-777-317-1163; www.chac-mool.com) is one. Contact Sherry Howell in California. She is quite knowledgeable about the area and helpful. They offer the more progressive "natural approach" to learning Spanish, with less emphasis on teaching grammar (the more traditional style) and more on conversing through use. Another is the Center for Bilingual Multicultural Studies, which offers more of a university atmosphere, with younger students (San Jeronimo #304; Mailing address: APDO Postal #1520, 62000 Cuernavaca, Mor.; Phone: 01-52-777-317-1087).

- Newcomer's club: Newcomer's Club of Cuernavaca, Minerva 1, Colonia Delicias, Phone: 01-52-777-380-0702 or 01-52-777-326-0251; jburalif@yahoo.com; www.clickoncuernavaca.com/newcomers/Newcomers.htm.
- Jewish resource: Cuernavaca Synagogue, Madero 404, Col. B.C.S.; No phone.
- The Web site cuernavacainfo.com has information on a variety of interesting places in the city.

CONS
There aren't many. Some may find this city too big for them. Others may consider the weekend intrusion of thousands of people from Mexico City a nuisance. **If you are looking for a place to get away from it all, this isn't it.** It is not for those truly on a strict budget, though lower-cost housing is available, as in any city—but you will have to look hard for it.

IN-BETWEENS
This has been a popular retirement community for decades. Some people commute to Mexico City to work, and a few companies transfer their people here. It is also popular with U.S. students who have exchange classes with the university here.

MEXICO CITY, OR MEXICO, D.F., AND TOLUCA, MEXICO

Ambiente: World-class city. You can find almost anything you need or want. Sophisticated, cultured, business oriented. To me, it's rather similar to a combination of New York and Paris.

Climate: Winters: 70s to mid-30s, with rare nights below freezing. (Houses have no heat, so bring sweaters.) Summers: upper 70s to low 50s. (Mar. and Apr. are actually the warmest months.)

Altitude: 7,349 feet

Population: 21,234,000 (estimate for the metro area. The population of the city itself is a mere 8,682,000.)

Housing: Ranges from almost reasonable to very expensive

Mexico City is huge and cannot be considered with blanket values for housing. Low-cost housing exists, but it is hard to find. Also consider Toluca, forty miles away, which is less expensive. Below are some of the more popular areas.

Medical Care: Excellent, with world-class hospitals

Area Code: 555 (Note: All numbers in Mexico City now have ten digits. A number that used to be 525-XXXX is now 555-525-XXXX.)

Many thanks to Jesus Garcia of Cetra Relocations (www.cetra.com.mx) for his help in updating this chapter.

Mexico City is a city of neighborhoods.

Housing in the Northwest: The Northwest includes Santa Fe, Polanco, Lomas de Chapultepec, Vista Hermosa, Contadero, and Bosques de las Lomas. It is close to great shopping malls and supermarkets, is safe, trendy, and near to most business headquarters. Rents go from $1,500 for a two-bedroom apartment up to $10,000 for a four-bedroom house. Mid-range prices are $2,000 to $2,500 per month for a three-bedroom house or apartment.

North: The north includes Satélite, Jardines de Satélite, San Mateo, and Lomas del Bosque. It is cheaper than most residential areas in Mexico City, but commute time can be painful. This area is safe, but not as safe as the Northwest, since it is closer to the industrial area. Mid-range prices can be found, $1,200 to $1,750.

West and South: Napoles, Valle, San Ángel, San Jerónimo, Condesa, Altavista and Coyoacan, Tepepan, Jardines de la Montaña, and Paseos del Bosque make up this region. It is not as safe and trendy as the Northwest, but it has its charm. It is an expensive area, and traffic gets annoying due to small roads. Very colonial. Rents go from $1,500 for a two-bedroom apartment up to $10,000 for a four-bedroom house. Mid-range prices are $2,000 to $2,500 per month for a three-bedroom house or apartment.

The Colonial Area (Downtown): While I have known people who've lived downtown, and very cheaply, the general consensus is that you are trading safety for economy. This area might be cheaper, but I won't recommend it due to safety issues. For nearly the same prices you'd pay downtown for an apartment you can find one in Coyoacan, Valle, Napoles, etc.

Inexpensive Rents

Alternative living solutions: For students, writers, painters, etc., there is a different option, called *pensiónes*, which are small, one-bedroom apartments attached to houses. Imagine a widow or an old couple that owns a big house. They might rent out two, three, or four bedrooms in their house for approximately $150 to $300 per month.

It may take you a few months to find a place anyway. A journalist friend of mine spent two months finding a place she could afford (she worked on *The News*—not noted for its high pay). She had to commute an hour to work and take a cab at night. If you are looking for an apartment and speak a little Spanish, get a publication called *Segundomano*, Secondhand. It comes out on Tuesdays and Fridays and is full of classifieds (that's all it has) and is the number one way to find an apartment in Mexico City. If you are looking for a dog, cat, pen pal, or other things, they are in there too. You may find your place in the English-language papers, but many of the choice places do not advertise in any paper, English or Spanish. Another alternative is to put an ad in both English and Spanish newspapers.

Less-expensive short-term living for businesspeople: Another option for businesspeople (or anyone) not willing to pay $150 to $200 a night for a hotel are the apartment hotels, or temporary accommodations, that go from $55 per night for a one-bedroom apartment to $200 per night for a three-bedroom modern apartment. Take a look at www.kingsplaza.com.mx. All these apartment hotels can be rented through Cetra Relocations at special rates, due to the volume they manage (www.cetra.com.mx).

Consider Toluca.

Toluca—an alternative to living in Mexico City: If you're going to be stationed here, you might consider living in Toluca, forty miles (sixty-five kilometers), or about an hour, west by way of an excellent toll road. Locals will swear it's only thirty minutes, but I've included some time to get out of Mexico City to be realistic. This could be an excellent choice, especially if your business is on the west side of the city, or even downtown. Don't even consider it if your business is on the eastern or northeastern side of Mexico City, as it would be an awful drive.

Toluca has a mere 1.5 million souls, housing costs about half what it does in Mexico City, and it is closer to more places to explore on weekends. You're within an hour or so of hot springs, mountain streams with trout, and alpine-like getaways. Pollution isn't as bad and neither is crime. There are even housing developments halfway between the two cities. The only drawback is that you have to climb up a mountain (well, your car does anyway) to get there. Toluca itself is the highest city in Mexico, at 8,793 feet (2,680 meters), and there is a snowcapped volcano, Nevado de Toluca, with two crater lakes at more than 12,000 feet, visible from the city. But the toll road is always in excellent shape, and it is a pleasant drive through forests. I've even seen a restaurant advertising *cabrito al pastor* on the road, but never stopped, as I was always doing this trek too early in the day.

While traffic is nowhere near as intense in Toluca as in Mexico City, it is still pretty congested. The only difference is that people drive faster in Toluca. My experience is that cops are about the same. It's considerably chillier (frost is not uncommon in winter) than Mexico City, so wear warm clothing.

PROS

I like Mexico City. It is one of the world's greatest cities and is truly international. Although you may not be able to find everything here that you can find in New York, you can certainly find a lot more than you would expect. **It is a businessman's town, with excellent communications, daily copies of** *The New York Times, The Wall Street Journal,* **and the best local newspapers in Mexico.** This is still a newspaper town, and the papers compete with each other for scoops and readership. Some of them are national in scope, including *En Directo, Excelsior, La Journada,* and *El Universal.* There is also a national English-language daily. There were two at the time of the last edition, and there may be again. Someone is always trying to compete with the Mexico City *News* (www.thenewsmexico.com).

If you are journalist, this is the place to be. If you are a freelancer, I've found that opportunities to write stories, particularly about outlying areas, are easier to sell to the Mexico City bureaus than to the Stateside bureaus. Heck, the Associated Press even ran a hard news story of mine just because I was the only guy in a flood area and I'd made friends with the bureau chief. There are Mexico bureaus of the Associated Press, including the *Los Angeles Times, New Orleans Times-Picayune, Dallas Morning News, San Antonio Express-News, San Jose (California) Mercury News,* and *The New York Times,* and many more in the city.

You'll meet people from all over the world here. Meeting them is not as difficult for tourists as it would be in a large U.S. city. As a resident, it's not as easy to meet others as in a smaller town, such as San Miguel de Allende, for instance. Your best bet is to ally yourself with some of the English-language expatriate organizations. There are cultural events and trendy restaurants.

Shorts can be worn by both men and women, but most Mexicans wear slacks or jeans.

A Little Lexicology
Chilangos *is the local slang for people who live in Mexico City.* **Chilango** *was originally (and depending on the tone used when it's said, still is) a derogatory term, but many people who live in Mexico City use it to describe themselves, so I don't think it still carries the sting it used to. Still, I wouldn't call someone that to his face unless he had already used the word in conversation in reference to himself, and then only if I knew him pretty well. Mexico City is to Mexico what New York City is to the United States. Many people from outside New York say, "He's a New Yorker," in such a way that you know how they feel about New Yorkers. It's the same with* **Chilango** *when said by someone from elsewhere in the Republic.*

An older term, **Chapulin,** *literally "grasshopper," is occasionally used by an older person. It originally referred specifically to a person living in Mexico City of European extraction, but that nuance was lost as it gained popularity.*

Throughout Mexico (and on road signs), "Mexico" is used to refer

*to Mexico City. More popular, especially among residents, is to refer to
the city as D.F. (pronounced "day ef fay"). A few people will still use*
La Capital. *Whatever term a resident uses, it will always be said with
pride, as people are very proud of their city. Similar to New Yorkers or
Parisians, they consider anywhere else in their country provincial.*

There are bargains.

**Although housing is expensive here, food, gasoline, and entertainment
can be quite reasonable.** (Gasoline costs less here and on the borders than in
the interior.) By the same token, you can pay New York prices at the trendier
eateries and clubs. Theater and classical music venues are still inexpensive and
are world class.

The international airport has flights to all of Mexico, the United States,
Canada, Europe, and Asia, as well as to Central and South America. If you're
just coming in to do business and fly out the next day, consider one of the
hotels by the airport. When getting to town, take only the approved taxis. You
buy tickets from a kiosk in the airport.

Food and Culture

The cuisine is truly international, with many nations represented. **Vegetarians have several choices here. There are even kosher restaurants.** For us
cabrito lovers, there are two decent choices. For the adventurous, there are
restaurants specializing in Aztec cuisine.

Artistic types will find a lot to do here. This is the art capital of
Mexico.**There is more art, culture, and history here than you can absorb in
two lifetimes.** There are classes and seminars on all of the above all the time,
so that if you wanted to study in Mexico and absorb the many facets of
Mexican culture, this would be a fine place to do it.

A Little Archeological Gossip

There is quite a variety of live theater here, including some plays in
English. The National Museum of Anthropology is one of the great museums
of the world. (An interesting side note is that the anthropology museum in
Jalapa was actually bigger, until the Mexico City officials heard about it. They
added to the Mexico City museum to make sure that they were the biggest.
Size, apparently, does matter.)

There is a jai alai fronton, and, of course, a bullfight ring. There is both
an American and a Canadian consulate (see pages 262–264 in the appendix
for locations).

The best source for information about the city and the country is the
slick book *Travellers Guide to Mexico*, published in Mexico City. You will find it
in all the best hotels and at bookstores. Buy a copy if you want to know more

about the culture or about doing business in Mexico, or if you intend to do any upscale traveling to the main tourist spots.

Transportation

Public transportation varies from excellent to adequate. Buses are cheap and ever present. In times of peak traffic, however, you're better served by taking the Metro. The Metro (subway) system is top-notch. While I still love the Metro, it is incredibly crowded and a shopping mall for pickpockets. You cannot bring on much more than a briefcase, although I once saw two incredibly beautiful Swedish girls (let me have my fantasy, they were blond and tall) sweet-talk a guard into letting them on with their backpacks. Taxis are cheap. Because robberies in unregulated (gypsy) cabs are still an issue, take only cabs from cabstands, or have someone call one for you. An alternative to buses or taxis are *combis*, which are similar to minivans and have limited routes. Alas, while they are safer than unregulated taxis, there are also safety issues with them.

Best Medical Care

If you need medical care here, you couldn't be in a better spot. Medical doctors will charge higher fees here (they have to pay rent too), but their prices are still a bargain compared to physicians' fees in the United States.

Mexico Health and Safety Travel Guide lists three world-class hospitals (a 5/5 rating, the highest, in their book) in the city, as well as several physicians in a variety of specialties. The top-rated hospitals are: The American British Cowdray Hospital (Sur 136 #116, Colonia Las Américas, Mexico City, D.F.; Phone: 01-52-555-230-8000 or 01-52-555-230-8080), Hospital Ángeles de Pedregal (Camino Santa Teresa #1055, Mexico City, D.F.; Phone: 01-52-555-652-2011, 01-52-555-652-3011, 01-52-555-652-1188; Emergency Phone: 01-52-555-568-1540, 555-652-6987), and Hospital Médica Sur (Puente de Piedra #160, Colonia Toriello Guerra, Tlapan, D.F.; Phone: 01-52-555-424-7200; Emergency Phone: 01-52-555-666-7059).

For Businessman

If you are a businessman, you will have to spend some time here sooner or later. As the center of government and financial power for the country, it is the place to conduct business. Try to pace yourself. The altitude is high and the air is difficult to breathe. Take dark suits and leave your white shirts at home. Not only will you blend in better, but a white shirt will be gray by the end of the day. Winters are downright chilly. Bring a sweater or wool suit. Topcoats are probably gilding the lily, but if you are cold natured, you could sometimes need one. Summers are hot. Short sleeves are gaining acceptance, but for first meetings you should still wear long sleeves underneath your suit.

Mexico City is a happening place and things get done here, so it is actually possible for a businessman to fly in, get some work done, and fly out the same day (but be sure to read my comments on social customs for doing business on pages 85–89).

Save money on temporary housing.

If you are going to be here a week or so, consider one of the suite hotels instead of a regular hotel. The regular hotels are as expensive as sin. A good source for them is Cetra Relocations (www.cetra.com.mx), or contact my good friend Jesus Garcia directly (from outside Mexico Phone: 011-52-555-261-4390; Fax: 011-52-555-261-4310; jesus.garcia@cetra.com.mx). If you are being transferred here, you definitely should contact them, as they can take care of everything from getting you out of your house at home to setting up a new one in Mexico. I've seen a lot of these services, and while there are some good ones, I feel Cetra is the best. They'll help you (especially Jesus) with more than the move—they help with the transition for you and your family.

Business hotels know how to treat foreign executives. High-speed Internet connections, concierge services, business centers, and suites are the norm. Now that limos and expensive foreign cars are permitted in Mexico, you should ask your company to ferry you to your hotel in the company limo. Tell 'em "Mexico" Mike said it was okay.

Additional Resources

- English-language schools: The American School (Bondojito No. 215, Colonia Las Americas Mexico, Mexico City, D.F. 01120; Phone: 01-52-555-227-4900; Fax: 01-52-555-273-4357; www.asf.edu.mx/enghtm/sections/mission/index.html), The Westhill Institute (Domingo Garcia Ramos 56, Prados de la Montana I, Santa Fe Cuajimalpa, Mexico City, D.F. 05610; Phone: 01-52-555-292-4222; Fax: 01-52-555-292-4223; www.westhill.edu.mx), and Greengates (British) (Av. Circunvalación Poiente 102, Balcones de San Mateo, Cd. de Mexico 53200; Phone: 01-52-555-373-0088; Fax: 01-52-555-373-0765; sarav@greengates.edu.mx; Web site: www.greengates.edu.mx).
- U.S. business resources: A good way to keep up-to-date with the business climate in Mexico is through the Web site www.mexicobusiness.com. This is a very accurate, frequently updated source of what's happening in the business world throughout Mexico. Good resources are Camara Nal., Comercio Cd. de Mexico (Mexico City Chamber of Commerce) (Paseo de la Reforma 42 Col., Centro, 06600, Cd. de Mexico, D.F.; Phone: 01-52-555-592-2346, 01-52-555-592-2665, or 01-52-555-592-2630) and American Chamber of Commerce (Mex. A.C., Lucerna 78 Piso 5 Col. Juarez, 6600, Cd. de Mexico, D.F.; Phone: 01-52-555-566-6895, 01-52-555-566-6406, 01-52-555-566-6663 or 01-52-555-703-3908/2911; amchammx@amcham.com.mx; www.amcham.com.mx).
- Canadian businesses resources: Camara de Comercio del Canada (Canadian Chamber of Commerce) (Manuel Avila Camacho 1, Cpl. Polanco, Chapul-

tepec, 11560, Cd. De Mexico, D.F.; Phone: 01-52-555-580-2873; www.cancham. com.mx) and Camara de Comercio del Canada en Mexico (A Cantu 11 P-7, Col. Anzures, 11570, Cd. de Mexico, D.F.; Phone: 01-52-555-545-3997; www.embamexcan.com/).

Additionally, several states have a chamber of commerce office or a trade mission: Arizona: Depto. Comercio del Estatda de Arizona, Av. Paseo del la Reforma, 10 Deso 700 Col. Centro, Edif. Torre CAB, 06030, Cd. de Mexico, D.F.; Phone: 01-52-555-546-5870; California: Mexico, D.F. 164 P-1, Col. Juarez, 06600, Cd. de Mexico, D.F.; Phone: 01-52-555-747-8262; Illinois: Av. Paseo del la Reforma 265, Col. Cuahutémoc, 06500, Cd. de Mexico, D.F.; Phone: 01-52-555-514-7548; Oficina del Estado de Texas, Paseo de la Reforma, 325 Col. Cuauhtémoc, 06500, Cd. de Mexico, D.F.; Phone: 01-52-555-514-2371; U.S. Export Development Office/U.S. Trade Center, 31 Liverpool, 06600, Cd. de Mexico, D.F.; Phone: 01-52-555-591-0155.

- Newcomer's clubs: Wives of foreign businessmen have associations and support groups that aren't found in many other locations. The Newcomer's Club and the American Society of Mexico will help new arrivals feel at home. They can be of particular help to the wives of executives transferred here (Hours: Monday, Wednesday, and Friday from 9 A.M. to 12:30 P.M.; Phone/Fax: 01-52-555-520-6912; Newcomers@newcomers.org.mx; www.newcomers.org.mx).

The Union Church is a center for expatriate activity (Paseo de la Reforma 1870, Colonia Lomas de Chapultepec, Mexico City, D.F.; Phone: 01-52-555-520-6912).

- Jewish resources: There are kosher restaurants and butchers and a strong Jewish (mainly Ashkenazi) community. Most Jews in Mexico live in Mexico City, an estimated 37,500. Guadalajara and Monterrey are neck and neck, with about 500 or so people each. The Mexican census has a space for "Israelites," which includes Protestant sects and those who profess their roots to be Jewish. Two of these groups are Casa de Dios and Eglisia de Dios. These sects are not recognized by the rabbinates of either Israel or Mexico. You'll often see a Star of David over a shop sign; it doesn't mean that the owner is Jewish, as more than one shop owner has confided in me, "It attracts business, and I just think it looks good."

While many Jews came over from Spain during the colonial period and stayed (most converted to Catholicism), another group emigrated from Europe before World War II; the ones who were refused admittance to the United States ended up in Cuba or Mexico.

I once traveled with a girlfriend who was Jewish and a vegetarian. She ordered bean soup once as the only safe food in a little restaurant. It contained pork fat. "Gee, if I had to eat something forbidden, why couldn't it have been a lobster?" she said.

CONS

There is just such energy here that you can get sucked into it. I find myself

LIVE BETTER *South of the Border* IN MEXICO

more creative when I'm here, but after a while the adrenaline and energy of 22 million souls begins to wear thin.

You always seem to be in a crowd. After a while, this get to you. This could be why so many residents flock to Cuernavaca for the weekend.

Cost of Living

Mexico City can be one of the most expensive places in the world in terms of real estate. Rent can be comparable to New York City, though there are still bargains you won't (at least I never did) find in the Big Apple.

Buying a place here should only be done if you are absolutely sure that this is where you want to be. **It is expensive.** For short stays of a few weeks or months, check out the fine suite hotels that have living rooms and kitchen facilities (see the note about them in the business section above). **The traffic is horrible.** Because of the intense traffic, allow an extra hour to get to important business meetings.

Contact Lens Woes

The pollution is indeed as terrible as you have heard. Pollution is still the number one complaint by visitors and residents. It is worst from December to April, when the thermal inversions can trap the pollution in the valley. Places such as Bosques do not feel the impact as much as downtown, but it is still there. Contact lens wearers will find it uncomfortable after the second day; bring a spare set of glasses.

Police

The traffic police, although they have improved (in terms of corruption), are once again asking for *mordidas,* "little bites," or bribes. Unless you absolutely have to, don't rent a car here. While corruption is certainly not unique to Mexico (there's plenty in the States, just on a grander scale), it is a reality. When you consider that a beat cop makes about about $400 a month, a few "tips" are considered just part of making a living wage. Whether you choose to pay them or go through official channels is up to you.

One new thing about traffic cops is that they are now arresting people for driving while intoxicated, so be careful when you've had a few. Even better, take a taxi home.

Crime

Not so very many years ago, crime here was not as bad as it was in major U.S. cities, but that has changed. Due to the seemingly constantly increasing unemployment rate and inflation, crime (against Mexicans as well as foreigners) is a reality. Be very careful. Take only official taxis from taxi stands, or have your hotel concierge call one for you. Don't be afraid, just don't be stupid. As for walking the streets and looking at a map, I have had so many locals help me and warn me to be careful that I am not really afraid to do it. I figure that a crook is going to realize you are a tourist anyway, so why be both paranoid and lost?

Be safe.

Car theft and carjackings are real. Just as in the United States, there are people who will point guns at you and take your vehicle. Let them have it. Car theft is a legitimate problem. If you do plan to have your own vehicle here, invest in a Club and an alarm system before you go. How much good this will do is questionable. Alarms are ignored by passersby. The Club can be broken in half by thieves with a can of Freon. Old-fashioned kill switches, but not in obvious locations, are probably more effective. Parking only in guarded parking lots helps, but it isn't a guarantee. Whatever you do, don't leave your purse or other valuables in plain sight in your car—whether it is parked or even while driving (see below). One scam is that one of the boys who tries to wash your window or sell you something at a traffic light will put a piece of chewing gum or other mark on your car, if he sees you have something to steal. His compadre at the next light will look for the mark, break a window, and grab and run. Daylight assaults are not unheard of, so try not to look too much like a tourist—overall, that sounds like silly advice; you're a tourist and you will look like one. What I mean is not to carry expensive cameras or wear Hawaiian shirts. As far as those writers who advise you not to wear tennis shoes, forget them. Wear what's comfortable and just try not to stand out. Mainly, keep an eye on your surroundings. Pickpockets abound, especially in crowds, which is just about everywhere.

Kidnapping: Yep, it happens. Will it happen to you? It's unlikely. Kidnappers don't waste their time with the average person, Mexican or gringo. However, if you are an executive with a foreign company, this is something to consider. You are a target. Many international companies give their executives kidnap and terrorism training now. It's a good idea. Many international companies provide their executives with cars and drivers who are alert to the dangers of kidnapping.

If you are a highly visible corporate executive, the possibility of kidnapping exists. This is only true for very high-level persons and should not be a worry for mid-level business travelers. I mention this partly to reassure some people who may be afraid to travel here, and to be honest about a problem that could affect a small number of foreigners.

Some very rich Mexicans and foreigners have been the targets of kidnappers (the same as in other places in the world, including the United States). They have taken precautions, such as hiring personal security personnel. If you have this high a visibility, your company has probably already given you a kidnapping seminar. You should follow their advice. They may be a little paranoid, but that is their business. Your personnel office should be able to direct you to reputable companies. If they are unaware of any, have them contact their counterparts in Mexico City and/or the U.S. embassy or the Canadian chancery in Mexico City. The rest of us are not worth the effort.

Terrorism

You have about as much to worry about from international terrorists in Mexico as you do in Des Moines. While the media may report on terrorists crossing the border to the States from Mexico, that's just the point: They're coming here. A good friend of mine was in Mexico on 9/11, and while she had a hard time getting back home, there was no likelihood of anything happening to her in Mexico. Unlike Paris, Madrid, or other international capitals, (in my opinion) terrorists may use Mexico as a stopping point on the way to the United States, but don't target it for their criminal acts. This, of course, could change, and I'd pay attention to my country's consular offices for updates.

Too much partying can get you into trouble.

Now, a word of warning for those who like to party late and/or visit ladies of the evening. You are perfectly safe in the Zona Rosa until midnight or so. After that, there are crooks who prey on staggering drunks of all nationalities. At some clubs, it is not unheard of for a hooker or bartender to slip you a Mickey (as opposed to a Mikey, who is never slipped to anyone).

Even if you take a hooker to your room, she could slip you one before she slips out of her slip. **Be wary of any drink (including mineral water) that you do not uncap yourself.** If you're going to stay out late and stumble home, try to do so with a buddy. Just as anywhere else, use caution.

Take a cab from a cabstand, even if you only have a few blocks to go. If you visit the houses of ill repute, find out from a local which ones have a "good" repute. You used to be safe in all of them, but not anymore. The good ones do not want trouble and try to keep their employees in line. You may be at risk, however, when you leave—so again, try to go with a buddy.

I have friends who spend a lot of time in places such as this and have never had any problems, but I think they are just lucky. Sometimes the areas of town are not the greatest, and no matter how well policed the bordello is, their wall of safety ends at their property line.

IN-BETWEENS

Don't expect life here to be laid-back.

Living here can be both invigorating and stressful. The opportunities for conducting business abound, but you may find yourself living the same lifestyle you did back home in terms of how much you work. Is that what you want? If so, come on down. Otherwise, choose Guadalajara or Monterrey, where life, while not slow, proceeds at a more realistic pace. Some people live in Cuernavaca and commute to the city to conduct business.

If you want to study the culture of Mexico, past and present, this is the best place to be. If you want to live a big-city lifestyle for a lot less than you could in Washington, D.C., Paris, New York, Toronto, Chicago, Montreal, or Los Angeles, you can do it here.

Just having lived in Mexico City could add a dimension to your life (or is that dementia?) that you won't find anywhere else in the world. **There's something about living in a world capital that is unlike living anywhere else.** But it takes its toll. Be prepared to pay it.

MORELIA, MICHOACÁN

Ambiente: Cultured, old-colonial charm in a big city

Climate: Cool summers (70s days, 50s nights), moderate winters (mostly 50s–60s days, 40s–50s nights, though it can get down to the 30s). You'll need sweaters and jackets.

Altitude: 6,400 feet

Population: 550,000 (officially, but estimates are closer to 750,000)

Housing: Adequate in all price ranges
Homes (buy): $25,000–$90,000
Condos (buy): N/A
Rentals: $250–$600
RV space: N/A

Medical Care: Good. MedToGo didn't review it, but there are hospitals.

Area Code: 443 (Be careful when dialing since nearby Pátzcuaro is 434.)

PROS

It will cost less to live here than in many other places. The colonial architecture is a treat for those who appreciate such things. Pink stone is popular and the styles include baroque and neoclassical. There are more than 200 historic buildings, and the city is rich in Mexican history. If you are a hot springs lover, you'll find several within the area that are developed, with hotels and restaurants, *balnearios,* and, if a government survey is to be believed, there are several hundred, both developed and undeveloped, throughout the state.

The weather is very nice and pretty constant all year, though it can get a little chilly (jacket weather) during the winter. It never gets too hot. **It is a very cultured, conservative city, and there are plays, concerts, and various activities at the university.** You could attend the university to take language courses. Hint: If you sign up in town, the course will cost about $50; if you sign up through a U.S. university, you will pay several hundred dollars. I met a middle-aged guy here who was living on about $150 a month, including renting a room in a house and going to school. At the time of publication, that figure has gone up a bit, to about $180 a month. However, remember that this is for only a room in a family's house, but it does include maid service and at least one meal a day.

The zoo, modeled after the San Diego Zoo, is excellent. **Nearby are some very interesting towns (Pátzcuaro, Villa Escalante, Santa Clara del Cobre, and more) noted for crafts and natural beauty.** You will not be overwhelmed by other gringos living here. There are a lot of cultural activities, including plays and concerts and other highbrow events. **The atmosphere is very Spanish and you truly get the feeling of living in colonial Mexico.** There is an RV park and there are plenty more in nearby Pátzcuaro. In fact, that might be a better choice. There is a golf course.

CONS

The conservative atmosphere will not appeal to everyone. If your lifestyle is at all nonconservative, then you had best skip this city. There is a strong social society here. Although you will be able to make friends here as well as in any conservative town, you will have a long way to go to be part of the social scene that makes the newspapers, if that is important to you.

IN-BETWEENS

Because Morelia is halfway between Mexico City and Guadalajara, both by the toll road and the old road, getting here by car is easy. There are no direct flights from the United States but many from Mexico City. **If you simply want a place to be and observe as a third party, rather than be assimilated into either a Mexican or expatriate community, this could be your place.**

PÁTZCUARO, MICHOACÁN

Ambiente: Very conservative, small-town mentality. Few gringos in residence.

Climate: Cool summers (70s days, 50s nights), moderate winters (mostly 50s–60s days, 40s–50s nights, though it can get down to the 30s). You'll need sweaters and jackets.

Altitude: 6,977 feet

Population: 65,000 (estimated)

Housing: Adequate in all price ranges
Homes (buy): $20,000–$90,000
Condos (buy): N/A
Rentals: $200–$500
RV space (sometimes with trailer): $10,000–$15,000

Medical Care: It's barely adequate, but there is good care in Morelia.

Area Code: 434 (Be careful when dialing as nearby Morelia is 443.)

PROS

Pátzcuaro is famous for the fishermen who ply the lake with picturesque butterfly nets. Quiet, situated on a placid lake, and surrounded by piney woods with trout fishing streams all around just about sums it up. **Prices are inexpensive.** There are several RV parks to choose from, one of which is right on the lake. The weather in the summer is very nice, and in the winter it is only mildly chilly. There is good trout fishing all around. There are a few "in" places where you can hear traditional music. The food is decent, especially the local delicacy: whitefish from the lake.

If you are interested in crafts, you could learn a lot from the Indians, who are famous for their wood carving and their lacquerware. The masks from here are superb. There is a real atmosphere of old backwater Mexico. **If you want to get away from it all, you can do it here.**

Century 21 has a new development in nearby Cupatitzio with new construction of 1,700-square-feet two- to four-bedroom houses, starting at $96,000 (higher than the average prices for older homes, but in a different category). This indicates to me that more foreigners are discovering the area.

CONS

See the last sentence of the above paragraph. There are very few foreigners here, though there are quite a few tourists, Mexican and international, especially on weekends. **The small-town atmosphere can get to you after a while.** Frankly, many would say it is a boring place to live. The lake is contaminated; the degree of which depends on whom you are talking to, so I wouldn't eat too many of the whitefish.

IN-BETWEENS

There aren't any. **You either love this place or hate it.**

Chapter 7
THE PACIFIC COAST

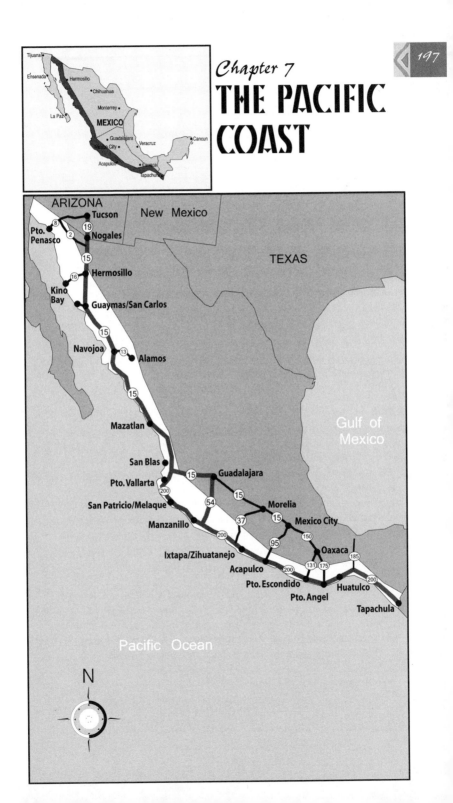

KINO BAY (BAHÍA KINO), SONORA

Ambiente: Quiet, good fishing, small town

Climate: Mild winters (50s nights, 70s days), hot summers (80s nights, upper 90s to 100s days)

Altitude: Sea level

Population: 6,000 (estimate)

Housing: Inexpensive but limited availability

Homes (buy): $50,000–$350,000 (less expensive in Kino Viejo). Beachfront homes basically start at $200,000.

Condos (buy): N/A

Rentals: $500–$750 (darn few of them)

RV space (buy): N/A

RV space (sometimes with trailer): $2,000 for six months at Kino Bay RV Park (www.mexonline.com/kinobayrv.htm)

Medical Care: There are a few doctors and a clinic, but you'll have to go to Hermosillo for a hospital.

Area Code: 662

PROS

Some call this "The Jewel of the Sea of Cortez." Sixty percent of the homes are owned by Americans and Canadians. **Kino Bay is a small fishing community (although, frankly, it is changing into a retirement town) on the Gulf of California, only seventy-three miles west of the state capital of Hermosillo and 235 miles from the Arizona border.** It is the closest seaside village to the Arizona border, except for Puerto Peñasco, farther north and west. It has the look and feel of Arizona by the sea. **It is quiet and laid-back, except on weekends. Housing is reasonable, less than San Carlos.**

RV Heaven

Trailer Life Magazine called it an "RV heaven." *RV Today* TV show has featured it. There are more than 600 RV spaces here, versus about 450 in San Carlos. Unlike many areas, the RV market is growing here. The Kino Bay RV Park, run by I. Fausto Garcia, is probably the nicest. He would be glad to help you with questions about the area and your RV (kinobay@usa.net; www.kinobayrv.com). His six-month rate is $2,000, but you can leave your trailer there for a whole year for $2,250.

You can get a ten-year permit for your travel trailer or boat and leave it (good only in the state of Sonora). You get this next door to where you get the "Sonora Only" car permit, which is only good for 180 days.

General Information

You can park your vehicle and do most of your getting around on foot. Fishing is great, especially for rock bass, corvina, mackerel, and many more. There are two boat storage facilities where you can safely leave your boat year-round. New since the last edition, there is a gas station at the north end with both gasoline and diesel.

The town is proud of the fact that they can deliver potable water out of the tap to the community.

Also new since the last edition, there is now a development called Kino Bay Estates, with prices from $45,000 to $175,000 for lots only (www.kinobayestates.com). While I don't usually give lot prices, housing here is so limited that this is worth mentioning.

The beach is beautiful, but the surrounding desert is barren. Winters are comfortable. **There is great seafood and the fishing is good.** The Seri Indians have a store in Kino Viejo where you can buy their handiwork, most notably carvings of ironwood. If you are adventurous, you can drive (with a four-wheel-drive vehicle) to some of their villages north of town and buy directly from them.

Unlike in many towns in this book, there aren't a lot of realtors, so I'll be glad to mention one: Kino Bay Real Estate (www.kinobayrealestate.com.mx).

CONS

This is a really small community, especially in summer, for good reason: It is beastly hot in the summer. There is little to do. On weekends it fills up with wealthy people from Hermosillo. They are nice people, but when you get a lot of tourists in one place things change. You could get bored here. Medical care is limited, but you are not that far (sixty-three miles) from Hermosillo, a modern city of 700,000 with hospitals, notably the CIMA hospital, which is highly recommended. You are only a few hours from the Arizona border. In order to buy anything except the basics, you'll have to run up to Hermosillo, where there are Wal-Marts and a Costco.

IN-BETWEENS

Many people here speak English. **It is a really quiet place.** The crowd in the summer is mostly RVers, and they tend to be older. Communications are adequate, but I wouldn't count on high-speed Internet service. You'll be lucky to get dial-up and that is not always dependable. Conducting business, even one based in Arizona, would be difficult.

SAN CARLOS, SONORA

Ambiente: Gringolandia, good fishing

Climate: Perfect winters (70s), warm to hot summers (90s)

Altitude: 26 feet

Population: 3,500

Housing: Moderately expensive. The RV parks are often full.

    Homes (buy): $70,000–$500,000 ($150,000–$200,000 common)

    Condos (buy): $30,000–$130,000

    Rentals: $500–$900

    RV space (sometimes with trailer): $20,000–$40,000

Medical Care: Barely adequate. For anything other than minor care, go to Hermosillo where Hospital Cima has a 5/5 rating in *Mexico Health and Travel Guide.*

Area Code: 622

PROS

This is a beautiful place, no doubt about it. That and the fact that it is only a few hours (250 miles via an excellent, if expensive, toll road) from Arizona are why it is so popular with *Norteamericanos.* **Housing is sufficient but on the pricey side.** Pricey is relative. I know people who have moved to Guaymas from Puerto Peñasco, for example, because they could no longer afford to live there, yet still wanted to be close to home. Someone moving from Cabo San Lucas in the Baja would think that prices are in monopoly money. It's similar to what happens in the States: Someone who moves from California to Oregon thinks everything is a bargain. Those moving the other way are appalled at how expensive things are.

Besides houses, there are condominiums and several RV parks, which are often full. Some of the RV parks have plenty of amenities, including clubhouses and social activities. You can buy a space in an RV park and "own" it. It will include a *casita* and sometimes even a sort of house. Often you can find a lot with a trailer that has retired from the road and will never move again.

Local Contacts for Real Estate, Apartments, and Consulting

For an apartment while checking out the area, see www.villa-vacation.com, properties #253 and #7888. Type the number in the box under the world map. These are owned by friends of mine: Don Downen, his wife, Pilar Valdez, and Kim Toles. They can also help you with relocation information and help in starting a business in San Carlos. That Web site is www.prodigyweb.net.mx/bigdon.

For real estate in general, or legal or business consulting, contact Kimberley Reid, www.consultantsintlmexico.com.

Sonora Bay Estates is an upscale development where the movies *Catch-22, Lucky Lady,* and *Zorro* were filmed (www.mexonline.com/c21marina.htm).

With so many Americans and Mexicans owning weekend houses or living here more or less full-time (though mainly in the winter), prices are stable and seem to be constantly going up.

There are plenty of restaurants, laundries, and other amenities to keep you from feeling as if you left everything behind to come here. Sonora is a progressive, well-to-do state. Many middle-class-and-above Mexicans also own property here. They flock here on the weekends, as do Arizonans.

The weather is pleasant, except in the summer, and even then it isn't too bad. The Gulf of California keeps things fairly moderate, though most people (at least most not from Arizona or Texas) will find it too hot. After all, you are on the edge of the desert. At least you can't complain about the humidity.

The deep-sea fishing is excellent. There is a golf course. The whole town is rather amiable. Living here is pleasant. Communications are quite good. There is Internet access. Medical care is pretty good for such a small place, and there is an ocean rescue squad who (with the help of volunteers) monitors the ship-to-shore radios. U.S. papers are available. Yachtsmen love the place and it has one of the largest marinas in Mexico. There is also an international airport with flights back to Arizona.

With its stark, dramatic setting, a nearby ocean (gulf really, but who's picky?), and generally pleasant *ambiente*, some people think of this as paradise.

CONS
It's hard to find anything bad to say about San Carlos. It is close enough to the United States to be accessible and far enough into Mexico to be worth the trip. It is a small town, though, and this could get to some people. The foreign community dominates the town, so English is widely spoken. You could live here and never learn a lick of Spanish. It is costly, and even the RV parks are higher than in other places farther south. **If you are on a tight budget, you might have to really hunt for somewhere to live, but it can be found.** Some rentals can be had for $400 a month. You might be able to snag or arrange a house- (or trailer-) sitting deal with someone who only comes down in the winter. You'll still have to pay rent, but you will have some power in negotiating.

IN-BETWEENS
You could isolate yourself and write a novel, or get involved with the large gringo community. There are more expatriates nearer to sixty than forty. You could conduct a business here, even one in Arizona, if you telecommuted: It's only a 250-mile drive on a beautiful four-lane toll road. English is commonly spoken. Some say that the area where *Catch-22* and other movies were shot on the outskirts of town looks a little similar to Italy.

GUAYMAS, SONORA

Ambiente: Not much. It's a commercial port city.

Climate: Hot summers, mild winters

Altitude: 26 feet

Population: 102,000

Housing: Less expensive than San Carlos. More choices.

Homes (buy): $50,000–$125,000
Condos (buy): N/A
Rentals: $300–$600
RV space (sometimes with trailer): $14,000–$30,000
Medical Care: Adequate
Area Code: 622

PROS

Guaymas is a seaport and naval station. This makes it a fair-sized town with some of the amenities that you'd find in a larger city. **Because it is more of a Mexican community than San Carlos, housing costs are lower.** There is more available and it is approximately 20 to 30 percent cheaper. Of course, you don't have the ocean views, but you don't have to pay for them. There is a hospital. There are RV parks; one of them is quite nice, the rest are good enough. If you cannot afford to live in San Carlos, you might consider Guaymas.

CONS

It is not very pretty. There is almost no beach. You will hear a lot more Spanish than English, which is a plus for those who want to live in a more Mexican town and really learn Spanish and understand the culture.

IN-BETWEENS

You get more of a feel of living in a Mexican community. **If you make the effort, you can learn more about Mexican society by living here.** Although there are some discos, that's about the extent of the nightlife. You probably will not be intellectually stimulated here.

ALAMOS, SONORA

Ambiente: Laid-back, artistic, colonial
Climate: Mild winters (60s–70s), hot summers (90s–100s)
Altitude: 1,245 feet
Population: 6,000 (official, which is probably about right)
Housing: Limited. It varies from cheap to elegant.
    Homes (buy): $15,000–$50,000 (fixer-uppers). On Historic Register or Grand Haciendas: $200,000–$1,200,000.
    Rentals: $350–$3,500. Very few and at a premium.
    RV space (sometimes with trailer): There are a few and prices vary tremendously.
Medical Care: Adequate for a small town
Area Code: 647

Thanks to Annette Hinman de Gaxiola (Patterson) of Alamos Rentals and Home Sales, www.alamosrentals.com.

PROS

With 360 days of sunshine, leave your SAD behind.

This is one of my favorite places, a unique jewel in Mexico's crown. (Gosh, did I say that? Sorry, it's my poetic nature sneaking out.) It's an old mining town that is rich in history and architecture. In fact, it has been declared a national monument by the Mexican government. As such, no new buildings can be erected in the old town, and all buildings must maintain their old colonial look. Residents claim that they get sunshine 360 days a year, so if you are affected by SAD (seasonal affective disorder), you probably could not do better than choosing here to live. However, that ubiquitous sunshine is pretty darn hot during the summer. It rains here, sometimes heavily, in July and August, which at least cools things off.

Stepping into Alamos feels as though you are stepping back in time. The feeling here is truly laid-back, sleepy even. There is a respectable gringo community (for a town of its size) and they are such an interesting lot that you'll find their stories fascinating. Many of them speak Spanish and are involved in community projects. They have assimilated into the culture without eradicating it.

Besides the usual assortment of Americans who have chosen to live in Mexico, there are a few of the Hollywood set who prefer a place to get away from it all rather than experience the glamour and glitz of Acapulco or Puerto Vallarta. Usually when Hollywood moves in, there goes the neighborhood, but these seem to be real people.

The weather is not quite as hot here as in the surrounding desert and there are trees. In the winter it has an ideal, dry climate. The foreigners here are of all ages. The annual music festival attracts world-renowned musicians of all types. The social life can be quite active, so there's little chance you will feel lonely here. They have three annual music festivals. The classical music festival is always held the last week in January and runs for nine to ten days. The Master Folk Art Festival is in March, as is the annual Wine and Guitar Festival. The town is booming! The cost of living is a little bit higher than in a larger town, but you are close enough to the border or to Hermosillo to run up to Sam's for those things that Alamos doesn't offer.

Housing prices vary from relatively reasonable to very expensive. You should count on finding an old historic place, and if you want to save some money, get one outside the city limits. There are still RV parks here—four, at last count.

CONS

The weather is not suited to everyone's taste. Summer is still quite warm. Ah heck, it is not hotter than hell, not as bad as San Blas, but it's not too far behind. It is a small community and you will know everyone and everyone's business in short order. There is a feeling of isolation to the town, and it is rather similar to Santa Fe, New Mexico, in that it could be too cute for some people's taste. I mean, everyone's house seems to be decorated *sooo* artistically, and you're likely to find copies of *Architectural Digest* lying around. The town is periodically written up in sophisticated magazines from Arizona appealing to a quite wealthy crowd. While not everyone who settles here has a million bucks in their socks, it seems that most do.

IN-BETWEENS

There is plenty of English spoken here. The foreign community is diverse—from artistic types who are barely making it to millionaires who live lavishly. Outside San Miguel de Allende and Oaxaca, you won't find a more interesting group. They are concerned about the community and seem to be a part of it. You won't find many Ugly Americans here. It would be a great setting in which to write a great novel or paint a masterpiece. Conducting business might be a challenge.

MAZATLÁN, SINALOA

Ambiente: Sun, surf, sand. Party-hearty in the Golden Zone, but surprising culture in the centro.

Climate: Winters: upper 50s–low 80s. Summers: upper 70s–low 90s. Humid.

Altitude: Sea level, but the El Faro lighthouse atop the Cerro de Creston is second only to Gibraltar in height (for lighthouses): 515 feet.

Population: 600,000 (It's the second most populous coastal city, after Acapulco. Estimates put it at nearly 700,000, including outlying areas.)

Housing: Inexpensive to moderately expensive. From simple homes to gated communities and condos.

Homes (buy): $30,000–$350,000 (The Golden Zone is the high end. Everything is less expensive in Mazatlán proper, El Centro, or Olas Altas. $150,000 will buy a nice home.)

Condos (buy): $50,000–$95,000

Rentals: $150–$2,000 ($400 a month in the old section will get you a nice two-bedroom house.)

RV space: $300–$400 a month

Medical Care: Excellent

Area Code: 669

> It's not that I spend so much less here than in (Chapala, San Miguel de Allende, Tucson, Vallarta, etc.). It's that I live so much better.
> —Typical comment by Mazatlán expats

"Cabo Bob" (also known as Linton Robinson), a Mazatlán expat for years, helped update this chapter. If you need help relocating, starting a business, or with just about anything on the West Coast of Mexico or Baja, he's your guy.

His charges for services are, like him, quite reasonable and will save you several times what you pay him (mazhelp@mexipost.com; www.mazliving.com).

Think of Mazatlán not as one city, but two (or possibly three) different towns. Mazatlán has a long history of foreign communities and was, in many ways, built by Europeans, Chinese, and North Americans as much as by the Spanish or Mexicans. These days most foreigners live in the Golden Zone, or Zona Dorada, although a growing number live in the downtown area—variously called Old Mazatlán, El Centro, Centro Historico, or Olas Altas. Though only minutes apart along the sweeping seaside walk called the Malecón, these are two very different communities, and few people would be equally happy in both.

Neighborhoods

The Golden Zone: The Golden Zone, at the north end of the huge sweep of beach from the old river port to the marina, was built completely for tourism. It is a strip of hotels, shops, restaurants of every quality, bars, hucksters, and exclusive residential neighborhoods. Top-end rents are much higher there (you see apartments for $3,500 in the paper every day) but a humbler two-bedroom might actually run about the same $300 to $400 a month as downtown.

The cost of living is much higher there: Restaurants think nothing of asking $20 for a meal or $2.50 for a beer, whereas the downtown standard is less than $10 a meal and around $1 for a beer. Groceries might be considered cheaper, since many of the big supermarkets are located in the north end. Common wisdom has it that you pay about 40 percent more in the Zone. If you want to (and can afford to) live the high life, with golf courses, penthouses, and limousines, you can do it here.

El Centro, or Centro Historico: The downtown, especially the historic center around Olas Altas beach, the central market, and cultural haunts of the Plaza Machado, is extremely different. Increasingly, foreigners are buying up and restoring abandoned 200-year-old buildings, and the growing atmosphere there is more relaxed, more cultural, more European. Almost everybody who sees the cafes and art school of the Plaza Machado thinks of squares in Paris or Rome.

The feel is not so much Vacationland as Urban-landia. Very few apartments are more than $400 a month; there are still a few around for less than $150. Three-bedroom houses renting for less than $500 are not uncommon. There are no mega hotels but lots of bed-and-breakfasts and furnished studios. The area is booming and filling up with foreigners (the same mix of Americans and western Canadians as in the Golden Zone) but it will be years before there are no opportunities to move there and create a fine old-Mexican home. There is one supermarket, and buses to Wal-Mart and such, but most downtowners enjoy shopping in the big old open market and picking up quick necessities in little mom-and-pop groceries.

The "Other" Mazatlán: There is a third Mazatlán, the "neither/nor" between and around the Golden Zone and downtown. Living Mexican style, in the *barrios* and *colonias*, is a way of life many find rewarding, and is certainly the cheapest way to go. It's not uncommon to run into Americans who occupy nice two-bedroom apartments for less than $100 a month. It's possible to live in Mazatlán on $500 to $600 a month. There are foreigners living modern "local" lives in small towns outside Mazatlán on less than that. (There are also people who pay $3,500 a month for mansions on the golf course and brag about the deal they are getting.)

Cultural

For those with cultural taste, that low cost of good living can be dramatic. Mazatlán has a very vital cultural community and music scene. In addition to many live music venues, where music from country to *"banda"* to great jazz is played and nobody ever heard of cover charges, there is an opera house, Angela Peralta Theater.

The story about the theater is fascinating. It was built in the early 1870s (then called the Rubio Theater). In 1883, the famous opera singer Angela Peralta, known as "The Nightingale of Mexico," arrived in town for a performance. A huge crowd met her and enthusiastically carried her to her hotel. She was so touched that she gave her adoring fans a performance from the balcony of her hotel. It was her last. Her ship was infected with yellow fever and she died before she could ever perform in the theater. The Rubio was renamed in her honor. Then the theater suffered its own tragedies. It was used as a movie theater, vaudeville stage, a boxing ring, and, lastly—a parking garage! Some good comes from every bad event, so when a hurricane hit Mazatlán in 1975, the inside was destroyed and the building was in ruins until restoration began in 1987. The beautiful theater reopened in 1992.

There are symphony concerts, a music conservatory, an internationally respected contemporary dance troupe, a ballet program, and a repertory jazz big band. Art lessons are dirt cheap and, especially during the big festivals from October to Christmas, there are cheap and even free events almost daily in the theaters and square. You can see an orchestra for less than $12, the *Nutcracker* for less than $20, or the national Cuban dance ensemble (which I saw in Cuba—don't miss it) for $15.

This is in addition to live jazz and blues in cafes, R&B by the sea, and rock of various stripes nightly, all for the price of a beer (which can run as low as seven pesos in places). So the cost of living in the Land of Maz is not just a matter of beer budget—it also takes in champagne tastes.

Working

Working opens up a whole legal can of worms. There are no-hassle incomes that can be had immediately, such as time-share sales and selling one's own artwork. There are people who work off the books, but if you are visible you can risk getting fined or even deported. Most foreigners elect to get their resident FM-3 card, pay for worker status, and pay taxes.

The economy is not all that healthy, though this can be advantageous to foreigners with outside income. The foreign population is growing: There is no employment for foreigners but there are business opportunities, and sometimes American know-how is as valuable as capital. Mazatlán has no mini-storage, employment agency, booking agents, wholesale jobbers, messenger service, rental agency, Thai restaurant, English-speaking wedding service, and other things you notice when you have been here a while.

Foreigners wanting to do business in Mazatlán have two extremely helpful avenues for reducing the tendency for official paperwork in Mexico to drive one insane. One is CAE (01-52-669-982-2111, extension 1392 when recording answers; no Web site). The other is Mazatlán Helping Hand (Help'n'Hand; helpnhand.mazatlan.com). Lee Newman is a longtime resident and construction pro who helps people do everything from move in to hire workers to get drivers' licences. To learn more about this company, see the article at www.pacificpearl.com/archive/2003/September/feature1.htm.

My favorite part of the city is Cerro de la Neveria, also known as Ice Box Hill. I swear it was featured in a science fiction story once (Heinlein?), but have never found the reference, so if you do, please let me know. For a lone hill, it had a colorful past: From the 1500s to the 1600s, its practical use was as a lookout for pirate ships. Much later, it got its nickname because the tunnels within it were used to store ice shipped from San Francisco, California.

Bombs Away!

During the Mexican Revolution, the hill was used as a lookout once again. In 1914, General Venustiano Carranza sent a biplane to bomb it with a bomb of nails and dynamite wrapped in leather. (I have ways of knowing if the details of the rest of the story are true, or fanciful, but as the reporter at the end of the movie *The Man Who Shot Liberty Valence* said, "Son, this is the West. When the legend becomes fact, print the legend.")

The pilot apparently flew past the hill. The bombardier, overcome with airsickness, lost his grip on the bomb, which fell into the street below. Two people were killed and several were injured. Thus, Mazatlán secured the dubious distinction of being the second city in the world to be bombed from an airplane. (Tripoli was the first.)

PROS

Mazatlán is the least expensive beach town in Mexico, and among the least expensive cities overall. This city, with about 5,000 gringos (equally divided among Canadians and Americans) is still a bargain. For years Mazatlán was the cheapest Mexican destination, but now the standard of living is starting to close the gap with other cities. But it's still very cheap, certainly among the cheapest of the beach resort cities. Most residents unhesitatingly rate it at about a three on the economic scale, giving Cabo, Cancún, or Mexico City tens.

It is on the beach and the scenery is spectacular, from the islands in the middle of the bay to the cliffs along the Malecón, or waterfront drive. The city itself is interesting enough, with a feel of old Mexico—once you leave the Golden Zone, that is.

Internet service is getting better all the time. Dial-up phone service is available at about U.S. rates. It's slow, but it works. Usually. Most foreigners use Prodigy or cable access. High-speed digital service is available in the entire area and tends to cost around $50 a month (the same as elsewhere in Mexico). There are cybercafes everywhere: They tend to be decently fast and extremely cheap by U.S. standards—enough to be a workable solution for a lot of people. Downtown rates tend to run around a dollar an hour. In the Golden Zone, triple that cost.

Even Mikey caught fish here.

The fishing is among the best in Mexico, and Mazatlán is known as the billfish capital of the world. You can angle for marlin, sailfish, dorado, and many more. Catch-and-release has caught on, but you have to let the captain of your boat know that's your desire or it won't happen. The fishing is so good (and at about half the prices of its competitor, Cabo) that even poor little Mikey caught three sailfish one day.

There is adequate housing in all price ranges. You could rent or buy anything from a simple Mexican house in a Mexican community, to a condo on the beach, to a luxurious villa in a gated community with a golf course. There are several RV parks, some with really nice facilities. If you want nightlife, there is plenty of it, mostly discos. There are bullfights. There is an English-language newspaper, the *Pacific Pearl* (P.O. Box 345, Mazatlán, Sin.).

Medical Care

The medical care is first-rate. *Mexico Health and Safety Travel Guide* states "Travelers to Mazatlán can rest easy, knowing that there is very capable medical care available in more than one location. Hospital Sharp is a modern facility with excellent physicians and cutting-edge technology equal to that found in the U.S. Clínica del Mar is a step down from Sharp, but is also a good hospital. The only services that Sharp does not provide are cardiac catheterization and cardiac surgery." The Sharp hospital was built in partnership (but not affiliated) with the hospital of the same name in San Diego, California. I've been there. I recommend it. Sharp: (4/5 rating with MedToGo) Av. Rafael Buelna (corner of Av. Dr. Jesús Kumate), Fracc. Las Cruces, Mazatlán, Sin.; Phone: 01-52-669-986-5678, 01-52-669-986-5679, Emergency Phone: 01-52-669-986-7911.; Fax: 01-52-669-986-5678, ext. 108. Clinica del Mar: (3/5 rating with MedToGo) Corner of Av. Revolucíon and General Cabanillas, Col. López Mateos,

Mazatlán, Sin.; Phone: 01-52-669-983-1777; Fax: 01-52-669-986-7254.

Plastic Surgery

Many foreigners are flocking to Mazatlán for plastic surgery. It may be partly my fault. One time, I was visiting the city and a doctor who had heard I was in town tracked me down (okay, maybe I am a little famous, but it won't go to my head) and he and his wife treated me as royalty. It seems that we had met on the beach years ago and I'd given him some advice on how to expand his plastic surgery practice to attract foreigners and, apparently, helped him design his brochure (which featured a well-endowed young lady—go figure). I swear I don't remember doing this, but it does sound like me. Because of my kindness, his practice had increased dramatically. Alas, I have long since lost his card, but there can't be many plastic surgeons in the city. If you find a surgeon, ask him if he knows "Mexico" Mike, and ask him to get back in touch (so to speak) with me.

The Carnaval, though it doesn't rival that of Veracruz or New Orleans (though it is bigger than Galveston's), is a growing event. **The shrimp here are among the best in Mexico and you can buy them really cheap at the local market, or you can buy fresh fish from the fishermen on the beach.** If you have culinary cravings, there are world-class chefs here. You can buy nearly any kind of consumer goods that you desire.

The Huichol Indians come to town occasionally and you can buy crafts directly from them. If you do, you will probably give them a better deal than they get from the local shops, some of which exploit them.

One of the most interesting soft drinks in Mexico, Toni-Col (bottled in El Rosario, Sinaloa), is sold here (and now in many other cities in the Republic from Baja to Mexico City and Guadalajara). It began in 1946 when the founder started out washing bottles at another factory. It's rather similar to vanilla cola. Thank God there are still independent bottlers around. Buy several cases and enjoy! Bring some back for me!

If the beach begins to bore you, you are only an hour's drive from the mountains. There you could buy all the wooden furniture you need for your castle.

There is an American consular officer here and an American Legion post.

CONS

If you do not get away from the Gold Zone, you will never experience the culture of the place. There are a lot of tourists. Much of the foreign community consists of time-share or real estate salespeople. **After a while, you get a feeling that everyone is trying to make a buck from you, and the materialism and hedonism of the place might affect you adversely.** During Carnaval and spring break there are lots of rowdy teenage and college kids. Although I considered living here once, it is not very conducive to writing.

Electricity bills run very high in Mazatlán, as they do in most of Mexico,

with its federal utilities and lack of hydropower. Cooking with bottled propane is quite cheap (a *very* smart thing for an immigrant to bring here would be a gas refrigerator). Light bills are inconsistent and unpredictable—many foreigners figure out it's cheaper to pay $100 more for an old high-ceilinged, shaded building with ceiling fans than to air-condition a newer place in the hot months.

Telephone service is not the nightmare it was in the past when everybody just got cellulars and said to hell with it (although cell phones are probably more common in Mazatlán than in American cities). You can get service quickly and it's pretty good.

Canadians and Americans have to get used to paying by the minute for local calls, but it's a dream compared to the past. Although this is true anywhere in Mexico, Mazatlán seems to have cornered the market on "legacy" phone and electric bills haunting new house owners and renters. Check the previous phone bill status of any place you rent or buy. Incredibly, billing follows the address here, not the individual. It's not at all uncommon for people here to get a home and then find out they can't get service unless they pay off a $700 bill the previous owner skipped out on. Check this out thoroughly with the phone company ahead of time. The other utilities are the same way—you can get presented with a two-year light bill your first week in your new digs. It's not a bad idea to get a little guidance on these matters. (Cabo Bob?)

IN-BETWEENS

Lots of people here speak English. **You will not be alone here, unless you want to be.** Besides the foreign community, there is a constant stream of tourists who stay for a week to a month. You are not far from the United States by direct flights or by a nine-hour drive on the toll road.

Weather

I placed the weather here, because it is both a pro and a con, depending on when you are here. **There are two climates in Mazatlán, both humid.** November to July is warm, sunny, and blissful (though there can be cold snaps where swimming is brisk and blankets are welcome). Late October, April, and May are wonderful months of perfect temperatures and water conditions.

The summer is extremely hot, wet, and sticky. September is the worst. One resident says, "The heat in August and September is intolerable—but here I am." The longer you live here, the more bearable the heat, and foreigners learn the wisdom of Mexican ways, such as midday siestas, walking on the shady side of the street, and chilling their bedrooms. Summer is also the rainy season, and if there are big storms, that's when they come. Summer storms are big, wild, and very electrical, but pass quickly. It's been several decades since a hurricane hit Mazatlán, and it seems to be less liable for really destructive weather than the Baja or areas to the south.

A Little History

Mazatlán is no stranger to foreigners. In 1847, U.S. troops invaded during the Mexican-American War. In 1864, the French occupied the city. During the American Civil War, a group of Confederate soldiers took the city over. Lastly, the British navy took over in 1871. The story goes that all this attention by the riffraff led to the tradition of bars on the windows and iron fences with sharp spikes that can be seen on many houses. Although Mazatlán had Indian artifacts dating back 10,000 years, the present city got its first permanent structures in the 1820s. It was a sleepy village until the 1960s, when tourist development took off. I mention this because local residents had become defensive about what most people think of as its lack of history. So if you want to make friends with the nice folks who live here, let them know you're up on their history.

SAN BLAS, NAYARIT

Ambiente: Funky. 1960's-style hippies are still here. There are lots of backpackers.

Climate: Winters: low 80s days, mid-60s nights. Summers: devilish. Mid- to upper 90s days, mid- to upper 70s nights, but it feels hotter. I swear it feels as though it's 100 degrees here in summer. The nights are still hot to me. Humid.

Altitude: Sea level

Population: 4,000 (estimate)

Housing: Limited choices. Mostly overpriced.

   Homes (buy): $20,000–$65,000, with many in the $30,000 category

   Condos (buy): N/A

   Rentals: $150–$600

   RV space: $250–$350 a month

Medical Care: Inadequate, except at naval hospitals for emergencies

Area Code: 323

Fans of San Blas have taken me to task for my lack of positive comments about their favorite place. Okay, the birders are very nice people and are not cheap. Fishing is good. The town is quiet. That's about as positive as I can get, folks.

PROS

   Think cheap in all ways.

Thanks, no doubt, to some hyperbolic travel writers, many people have heard of San Blas. There is a small foreign community here, mostly in the winter. **It is a laid-back fishing village.** Housing is cheap. There are RV parks, practically deserted in summer. There is a hot spring nearby. The fishing is good. The seafood is good. Food is cheap. The people who gravitate to this place are cheap. Locals still promenade around the square at night. **This is cheaper than many other places on the Pacific Coast.** The best birding in Mexico is around here. **If you are a bohemian, you could be happy here.**

CONS

The very idea of high-priced real estate here makes me wonder if lunacy isn't a local epidemic. The beach is ugly. **Additionally, it is populated with *jejénes*, also known as sand flies, or no-see-ums.** Local lore has it that Avon Skin-So-Soft is a good repellent, though scientific studies dispute this. These bugs can make an outing a miserable experience. Fortunately, they mostly come out at dusk. Because this is a really small town with few expatriates, you could easily get bored here. There is no culture. The tourists it attracts are mostly backpacker types and they are cheap. Communications are iffy. You could get dial-up service here, but I sure as heck would not depend on it. **Summers are very hot and humid; the Devil really does summer here.** There are not a lot of choices in places to live, and what there is is basic. **Forget luxury here.** The RV parks are basic. Unless you really want to get away from it all, and are on a very tight budget, I can't imagine why you would want to live here.

IN-BETWEENS

Little English is spoken. If you are a bohemian or a birder, you will dig the place. If you are not, you will hate it. There are no in-betweens here. **Love it or leave it.**

PUERTO VALLARTA, JALISCO

Ambiente: Sophisticated, charming

Climate: Winters: 70s days, 60s nights. Summers: upper 90s days, 80s nights. 80–90 percent humidity.

Altitude: The nearby Sierra Cuale mountain range has all you could want.

Population: 152,000 (officially), 350,000 (estimate)

Housing: Plenty of choices. Much more expensive than Mazatlán. Not quite Cabo prices, but getting there.

> Homes (buy): $40,000–$500,000 and way, way up. Bucerias, ten miles north of the airport, is somewhat less expensive than the city. Farther north, Rincon de Guayabitos and La Peñita are considerably less expensive. To the south, Melaque and San Patricio are more reasonable.

> Condos (buy): $100,000–$300,000

> Rentals: $400–$1,200 (The low end is scarce.)

> RV space (sometimes with trailer): $400–$600 a month. There are four RV parks and one in Bucerias, but they don't seem to have gotten into the lot sales as they have in Baja.

Medical Care: **Good**

Area Code: **Puerto Vallarta and Nuevo Vallarta: 322**

PROS

Vallarta, as the locals call it, still has a romantic feel to it, despite all the high-rise development. The cost of romance, however, has gone up since the last edition. It's an artistic place, in the sense that Santa Fe is artistic. There are several art galleries selling high-end offerings; I don't believe there are many starving artists here. Since the last edition, there is a now a library with English-language books and magazines. That's always a sign that the foreign community has grown.

Puerto Vallarta attracts a different kind of crowd.

This city on the Pacific Ocean was immortalized (or was that immoralized?) by Richard Burton and Elizabeth Taylor when they filmed *Night of the Iguana* there. BI (before *Iguana*) it was a tucked-away backwater place. AI (after *Iguana*) it became a chic place for the Hollywood crowd. It still attracts a chic crowd, though not the way it used to. **There is a sizable expat community here, with a character completely different from Chapala or San Miguel.** The bay is said to be one of the largest in the world, so there's a good chance you can get a house with a view.

There are younger residents.

The average foreign resident is younger than in Chapala. You'll find many Canadians and West Coasters. While there are certainly people from every economic and social background, you won't find many who are pinching their pennies living here. Vallarta is not cheap. This interesting mix of expatriates seems to include youngish couples who have sold businesses in the States or Canada, some financially successful artists, and a few writers who somehow eke out a living. This may be just Mikey's imaginings, but it seemed to me that there were more divorcées living on alimony here than in other places in Mexico. San Miguel is probably second. There is also a contingent of older retirees who have lived here for many years and wouldn't think of living anywhere else. There are two golf courses.

The temperature is nearly perfect in the winter, though somewhat humid. It can be beastly hot and humid in the summer. There are several cafes that come and go and provide a gathering place for the foreign community while they are around. John Huston, the Hollywood director, loved Vallarta, and there is a statue of him in town. There are art galleries by the score and a very literate crowd, both foreigners and Mexicans. The scenery is majestic, with low mountains covered with dense tropical vegetation meeting the sea (locals call it a jungle, but that is a stretch).

Houses with views are common.

The blue Pacific rolls on endlessly, and if you can afford an ocean-view house or condo, do it. Because the town is built on several hills, you can actually find real houses with good views of the ocean. The cobblestone streets add charm. Housing prices are all over the board. You can spend a fortune on a luxury villa; a fair amount for a condo in town; or a small fortune for a house in Nuevo Vallarta, with a golf course and gated community. You can rent a place in town inexpensively or pay through the nose for an ocean view. **The town is large enough and there is enough choice to make finding some sort of abode relatively easy.** The water supply has been officially declared potable by the secretary of health, though many residents still use purified water, because of the old pipes running to their houses. Ask locally.

There is plenty of nightlife, from discos to jazz clubs. There are both a U.S. and Canadian consulate.

There are good communications with the outside world. High-speed Internet service is available. Besides *USA Today*, you can get *The New York Times* Sunday edition and the *Vancouver Sun*. There's a local English-language paper, *Vallarta Today*, and a weekly supplement to the Guadalajara English-language paper, the *Colony Reporter*.

Medical Care

Mexico Health and Safety Travel Guide says the care here is good. They list two hospitals that passed their inspection: AmeriMed-Puerto Vallarta (3.5/5 rating) (Plaza Neptuno, Building D-1, Marina Vallarta, Puerto Vallarta, Jal.; Phone: 01-52-322-221-0023; Fax: 01-52-322-221-0026) and Hospital San Javier Marina (4.5/5 rating) (Blvd. Francisco Median Ascencio #2760, Zona Hotelera Norte, Puerto Vallarta, Jal. Phone: 01-52-322-226-1011 through 19; Fax: 01-52-322-226-1010).

CONS

It's expensive.

Although an *AARP Magazine* article put Vallarta on par with Chapala in expenses, I disagree. **Unless you luck into a deal, it is more expensive to live here.** Some would say that they are paying for the quality of life here. That's up to you. If you can afford it, it's a good place, but if you are on a budget, head north or south. **With 3 million tourists coming here a year, it's inevitable that there's a "tourist" mentality, which means a lot of partying and a feeling of impermanence.** If you're thinking about living in Punta Mita and Sayulita to save money, don't. You can pay more there than in Vallarta itself. Bucerias is your only option that is relatively close to the city.

The beaches near town are not very good for swimming. The beach itself is rocky. The summers are awful. It may not be hell, but the Devil must have a summer condo there. The cobblestone streets are rough on your car's suspension. There is always the chance of a hurricane or earthquake, though the former is pretty unlikely. Vallarta is usually spared, but it was hit hard a few years ago. There are no guarantees. With earthquakes, you never know. There is so much English spoken that it is easy to avoid learning Spanish.

IN-BETWEENS

The foreign community is quite tight-knit. **There are plenty of opportunities to get involved in the social scene.** There are several worthwhile charity projects to which you could donate your time.

MELAQUE, SAN PATRICIO, BUCERIAS, RINCON DE GUAYABITOS, JALISCO

Ambiente: These are small seaside fishing villages, but are not "sleepy" during the tourist season.

Climate: Winters: low 80s days, mid-60s nights. Summers: low to mid-90s days, mid-70s nights. Humid.

Altitude: All are at sea level, with mountains on the other side of town.

Population: Estimates vary wildly, probably less than 2,000 each

Housing: Has gotten more upscale since the last edition, but is still fairly reasonable. Lots of RV spaces and choices.

    Homes (buy): $25,000–$250,000

    Condos (buy): $25,000–$100,000

    Rentals: $200–$600

    RV space (sometimes with trailer): $10,000–$15,000

Medical Care: Inadequate, except at naval hospitals for emergencies

Area Code: Melaque/San Patricio: 315, Bucerias: 329, Rincon de Guayabitos: 327

PROS

I've bundled these beach communities southeast and northeast of Vallarta together because, while they are all different, they are also somewhat similar in that they are small towns, quieter, and places to escape to. They don't offer the same services as Vallarta, but are attractive to those who want to get away from the madding crowd.

The ones to the north, Bucerias, Rincon de Guayabitos, and La Peñita, are more residential and upscale in nature, and, frankly, more expensive and more gringoized. I consider the northern towns "Vallarta light."

The ones to the south, Melaque and San Patricio, are my favorites. They're more established Mexican fishing villages (though their northern sister could also be called such, but I just got the feeling that they are more participatory in the land boom of catering to foreign residents), have fewer gringos, and are less developed. **You'll have to visit each one to determine which *ambiente* appeals to you.** They are all less expensive than Vallarta, though none of them has the luxury or sophistication of their big sister. They are still all small towns and offer the peace and quite that are missing from Vallarta itself. Each has pros and cons, and each has limited but gradually increasing services, but lots in the way of natural beauty.

If you want to get away from it all, but not too far away, these towns might be for you. In any of them you are never too far from a beautiful beach with golden-white sand, palm trees, and a riot of tropical vegetation. Housing prices have jumped since the last edition, but, in comparison to Vallarta, are "reasonable," and RV parks are plentiful. Yachtsmen frequently anchor in their harbors and spend some time ashore, so you have an interesting mix of people. While you can spend a quarter to a half million dollars for a nice villa, you can still find older, smaller properties in the $30,000 to $45,000 range. Some condos sell for as little as $25,000, but watch the fees!

CONS

These are really small towns. There are not large foreign communities. There are few activities other than fishing and sunning, so you may get bored. **Medical care is minimal.** Communications are not always reliable. I wouldn't count on high-speed Internet service, and wouldn't be too dependant on dial-up service. The summers are still beastly—but way better than San Blas. And they just "feel" cooler than Vallarta, perhaps because there is less concrete and congestion.

IN-BETWEENS

If you are an artist or writer and want to create, these places could be ideal. If you need to socialize with other gringos, you will have enough company during the winter, but otherwise you will be pretty lonely. If you want to learn Spanish, you will have plenty of opportunities to practice, as not much English is spoken (more so in the south than the north).

MANZANILLO, COLIMA

Ambiente: Varied — there are artists, writers, and retired businesspeople here.

Climate: Winters: upper 60s–low 70s. Summers: mid-80s to mid-90s. Humid summers. Occasionally there are tropical storms or even hurricanes.

Altitude: A whopping ten feet. But a couple of hours away is the Nevado de Colima, an active volcano that last erupted in 1991. Now there's some altitude — 13,448 feet!

Population: 105,000

Housing: From simple apartments to middle-class condos near the beach to gated communities
Homes (buy): $35,000–$150,000 and up. You can buy a nice home here for around $80,000–$90,000 that would cost nearly twice as much in Vallarta.
Condos (buy): $50,000–$170,000

Rentals: $300–$900

RV space: $300–$500 a month

Medical Care: Good

Area Code: 314

PROS

You get more for your money here than in Vallarta, but it is for a very different crowd.

Those who choose Manzanillo are more likely to speak Spanish and more likely to prefer a Mexican environment than a gringo enclave.

Manzanillo has a very Mexican *ambiente.* That is probably its draw to those who love it, and there are plenty of foreigners who love it. The city is an important port and has industry enough to keep it from being dependent on the tourist trade to survive. The port, fishing, and mining industries are the backbone of the place. **Housing is reasonable for a beach community, and you have a choice of RV parks, condos, or houses that range from the luxurious, including gated communities, to the simple middle-class Mexican neighborhoods.**

Although it is a small city, Manzanillo still feels as if it's a small town. It's close enough to Guadalajara to make a trip there for culture or material acquisition a viable alternative. It is pretty, with nice beaches. The weather is marvelous in winter. The fishing is top-notch, with dorado, marlin, sailfish, and more. There are even supposed to be some coral reefs offshore, but I have not seen them. There is a golf course. The seafood is excellent. Communications are excellent. **There are adequate medical facilities and a hospital.**

CONS

On weekends Manzanillo gets crowded with *Tapatios,* or people from Guadalajara. Someone from New Orleans could live here in summer, but most of us would find it sweltering, similar to Vallarta. **There is little culture.**

IN-BETWEENS

The foreign community is small enough that it doesn't overwhelm the town. **Manzanillo maintains a very Mexican flavor and there generally is not a lot of English spoken.**

IXTAPA AND ZIHUATANEJO, TRONCONES, GUERRERO

Ambiente: These are very different towns with very different feels. See paragraph below.

Climate: Winters: low 70s to mid-80s. Summers: mid-80s to mid-90s. It rains daily during hurricane season (May 15 to Sept. 30). Subject to hurricanes.

Altitude: Sea level, with hills ringing the city

Population: Zihautanejo: 59,000 (official), Ixtapa: 5,100 (official). Just for fun, the United Nations claims there are 250,000 souls in the area, but I think that is rather optimistic. I'd opt for the INEGI (Instituto Nacionál de Estadística Geografía e Informática) figures noted above.

Housing: Not as many choices as some other towns. On the pricey side.

Homes (buy): $60,000–$500,000 (most homes will be in Zihuatanejo)

Condos (buy): $70,000–$300,000 (mostly Ixtapa)

Rentals: $700–$1,500

RV space: Rentals only (www.zihuatanejo-rentals.com/bungalowsmexica.htm)

Medical Care: Adequate. *Mexico Health and Safety Guide* doesn't recommend any hospitals here. Go to Acapulco for serious situations.

Area Code: 755

Ixtapa is another of those planned communities developed by FONATUR. It's not really a town but a resort administered by FONATUR with high-rise hotels and potable water. It is expensive and doesn't feel like a town. If I had to describe it in one word, it would be sterile, sterile, sterile. Okay, that was three words, all true (in my humble opinion). In Ixtapa, you'll pay Cabo prices.

Zihuatanejo, however, is a legitimate Mexican town, with lots of character, soul, and history. The downtown still has narrow streets, not quite cobblestone, but paved with stones. There are hills all around, and there is just a comfortable feel to the place. It sort of reminds me of Sausalito, California. In Zihua, as the locals call it, prices will be somewhat more reasonable but still up there.

Troncones is thirty miles northwest of Ixtapa and an ecological preserve. About 700 people call this village home. While not completely undeveloped, it offers some residential property and is pretty much unspoiled. It is much more expensive.

PROS

Zihua attracts an eclectic mix of people, characters even, who add variety to living here. There are Internet cafes with high-speed connections, coffee shops, and a real feel of community. The weather is wonderful, at least in winter. The fishing is good. The scenery is spectacular. Communications are adequate. La Ropa beach may be one of the loveliest beaches on the Pacific. **There is a golf course and scuba diving is said to be very good.** Great fishing.

Zihua Rob's Web site and discussion board is a good place to go to get an understanding of the community (www.zihuatanejo.net). For a different view of living there and a whole lot of fun, facts, and off-the-wall information, check out www.zihuatanejo-rentals.com. It's written by local expats and covers darn near everything you want to know, and lots that you didn't know you wanted to know. I really like this town, but it's not for everyone. Visit and decide for yourself.

CONS

These places are not for everyone. Even in Zihua, there are a lot of tourists. In Ixtapa, you are overwhelmed with them. **You are far, far away from everything.** Hurricanes pass by but don't hit these towns directly. You'll still get a lot of rain.

IN-BETWEENS

There are only about 100 expats living here. You'll soon (for better or worse) know everyone. There are die-hard fans of the area. They like its uniqueness. It's possible to get away into the hills and discover an entirely different landscape and world.

ACAPULCO, GUERRERO

Ambiente: Big-city glitz, discos, beaches, sensual, tropical, noisy

Climate: Winters are divine (70s–80s). Summers are devilish (upper 80s and 90s, with occasional days near 100), with rain and 90–100 percent humidity. It rains daily throughout hurricane season (May 15 to Sept. 30). Subject to hurricanes.

Altitude: Sea level, with hills ringing the city

Population: 620,656 (official, estimated is 1,200,000)

Housing: A wide choice, from super luxury to super simple
   Homes (buy): $20,000–$500,000, depending on area
   Condos (buy): $120,000–$300,000
   Rentals: $250–$800
   RV space: N/A

Medical Care: Very good

Area Code: 744

PROS

Ah, Acapulco! **The very name conjures up images of steamy sensuality, beautiful people, and beautiful beaches.** All of these are realities. The place is a veritable cornucopia of pleasures of the senses. The beaches, some long and sweeping, some tiny and private, have lured tourists from all over the world for many years.

Acapulco is truly tropical with palm trees, coconut groves, and mangoes, and flowers of every imaginable color screaming for your attention. The winter weather is heavenly. That means temperatures in the seventies and low eighties during the day and sixties at night. It is very cosmopolitan, with world-class shopping, Wal-Marts, and the occasional *tienda* sandwiched in between.

African Roots

Acapulco was once the haven for jet-setters and the Hollywood crowd, until the development of Cancún. Since then, it has been more of a Mexican resort with a steady European clientele. People of color will find that there is a tremendous lack of prejudice, as *Acapulcaños* are themselves dark skinned and there is more African heritage to this area of the country than any other except Veracruz state. Farther down the Pacific Coast are some of the poorest villages in Mexico, receiving little government aid. The poorer villages are the ones with people with the darkest skin. Interestingly, these people do not consider themselves descendants of slaves (which is likely). They are unaware of their heritage and simply call themselves "Mexicans." While racial prejudice is not as pronounced in Mexico, it exists. As a gringo tourist or resident, you are unlikely to experience it.

Potable Water?

Acapulco has undergone a tremendous building boom in the last ten years. They even have a purified water system—although many locals scoff at this. During the rainy season water from the slums on the hills runs down and is collected. Whether this is truly purified is a matter of debate. Most people still depend on bottled water for daily use.

The yacht crowd likes it, the rich and famous like it, the Duke (John Wayne) liked it, Stallone likes it, and Arnold the Incredible (Schwarzenegger) likes it. Many movies have been shot here and more will be. It has the only jai alai fronton on the mainland, besides Mexico City. That was one of the reasons I first went there, in the 1980s. A current guidebook listed the fronton as an attraction. It was then in the Caleta section. After hours of searching, a Mexican shop owner said simply, *"se fue."* That meant it was gone. I love the Mexican language. Sometimes it is simplicity itself; other times you need a road map to follow the sentence construction. Today the fronton is in the Gold Zone.

The city is large enough that it offers an incredible diversity of housing, ranging from the very, very rich suburbs to downright hovels that would be cheap enough for anyone's budget. U.S. newspapers are readily available—the same day they are printed. Communications are basically good, although there still may be problems (though less than a few years ago) when it rains. As in all big cities in Mexico, there are good high-speed Internet connections. There are RV parks, from one across from the beach on the busy Costera, the main drag, to inexpensive ones way out in the country, to one right on the beach in quiet Pie de la Cuesta, an hour away. The nightlife is superb, if modern music à la disco is your bag. The annual music festival attracts musicians from around the world.

There is an American consular agent, a Canadian consulate, a small English-language newspaper, and an American Legion post.

LIVE BETTER *South of the Border* IN MEXICO

Variety Is Key

You can choose your lifestyle here, from the Gold Zone, where most of the high-rise hotels are, to the old section around the zócalo, which has a real flavor of seaport Mexico, to the exclusive subdivisions out by Las Brisas, or the Princess Marquesa with its world-class golf course. There are several beaches, each with a different flavor and clientele.

There's an international airport with flights from around the world. There are enough French and German tourists that you could hang out with a European crowd if you wanted.

The food is outstanding. The variety of restaurants is overwhelming—from five-star gourmet palaces to funky *palapas* serving inexpensive seafood. There is scuba diving, though the Pacific cannot compete with the clear waters of the Yucatan. Medical care is adequate and there are hospitals here. Sounds great, huh? Then why don't more foreigners live here?

CONS

The summer is beastly. It is hot and humid with temperatures in the nineties, which feels a lot hotter. It rains every day. **The traffic is fast and noisy; it goes all night.** Even in the high-rise Gold Zone hotels I have a hard time sleeping. There is air pollution.

There is a sense of impermanence to this place, due to the transient nature of tourism. Acapulco is a big city. The foreign community is tiny. If you are rich enough to hang out with the Las Brisas crowd, you will find plenty of friends. If you are not, you will not. The water is beautiful. However, even though the city has installed a sewage treatment facility, the runoffs from the slums above the city still make some parts of the beaches questionable.

IN-BETWEENS

You can speak English or Spanish or French here and someone will always understand you. **You can party all night if you want.** The discos don't really get rocking until after midnight. Then you could lie on the beach and recuperate. You could write a great book here, but the temptations of the flesh would make it hard. You sense that a Graham Greene–like ghost haunts the older section. **It is a very libertine town.** There are clubs and social organizations for you. Its size makes lots of things available, but getting around is a pain. The smallness of the foreign community could force you to assimilate yourself into the Mexican society, which is a plus to many people.

PIE DE LA CUESTA, GUERRERO

Ambiente: Laid-back, funky beach town
Climate: See Acapulco weather above
Altitude: Sea level

Population: 4,000 (estimated)
Housing: Primitive, limited
Medical Care: Primitive
Area Code: 744

PROS

Only about an hour away, this small beach and fishing village is almost like something out of a South Seas novel. James Michener would approve. It is quiet and serene, and although there has been some building in the last few years, it is still a haven from the noise and activity of Acapulco; you are far removed from its hustle and bustle. Housing is reasonable, but as development comes, it is no longer the bargain that it used to be. Because there are not a lot of choices, and the area is becoming more popular, rents could even be more expensive than in Acapulco. There is a first-class RV park and a couple of very nice inexpensive ones on the beach. The food is great.

CONS

You had better like isolation. This is a small village with few full-time foreign residents. The very things that attracted you to this locale wear thin after a while. **Medical care is rudimentary.** If you get really sick, you will have to go to Acapulco.

I don't want to give the village a bad rap, as so many guidebooks have done, because the ocean is a changeable thing. The beach is stupendous, the sunsets are legendary, and the swimming is, *at times,* dangerous. The waves are larger than Acapulco's and the undertow can be fierce. Ask the locals what the situation is like before you jump in. I swam there and enjoyed it, and there are other times when I won't put my big toe in the water.

IN-BETWEENS

You could write a great novel here. If you are truly independent and self-sufficient, you might find it to be a perfect place. Little English is spoken so you will be forced to learn some Spanish. It's a unique place and not for everyone. There is little, if any, full-time foreign community. Those who settle here truly want to get away from the madding crowd.

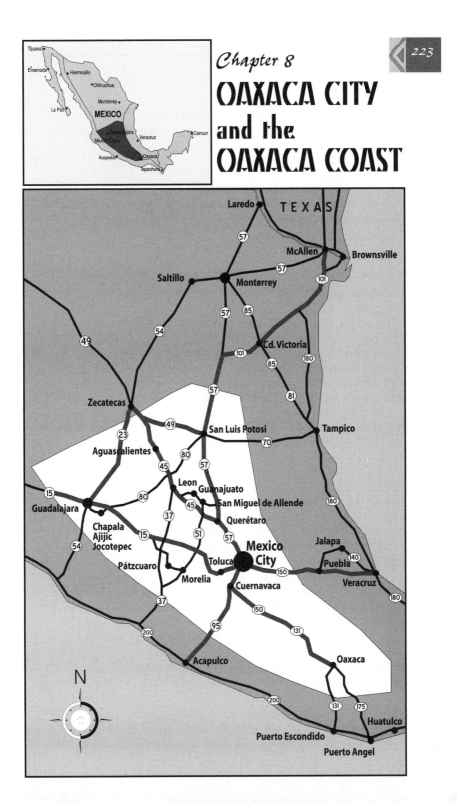

Chapter 8

OAXACA CITY
and the
OAXACA COAST

OAXACA, OAXACA

Ambiente: Conservative, old-world, international, Indian, cultured

Climate: Mild year-round. Summers: 50s to mid-80s. Winters: 50s–70s. Take a jacket for evenings.

Altitude: 5,069 feet

Population: 400,000

Housing: A little scarce. It's less expensive than many places, but a lot more costly now than at the time of the last edition.

Homes (buy): $30,000–$120,000

Condos (buy): N/A

Rentals: $450–$1,000 (centro. Outside the centro or in a suburb: $300–$600.)

RV space: N/A

Medical Care: Adequate

Area Code: 951

I'm indebted to Stan Gotleib, resident and author of *The Oaxaca/Mexico Newsletter,* for updates to this chapter. He still does orientation tours, but by appointment only. Contact him for a personal orientation tour if you are going to Oaxaca (www.realoaxaca.com). As elsewhere in the book, I explain that the lower-end houses are very basic and not in desirable neighborhoods, or may be far from downtown. In Oaxaca this sometimes means that you have to drill your own well or run electricity lines—expensive propostions.

PROS

Although Oaxaca is no longer the low-cost destination it used to be, some people would not live anywhere else. You can still find an apartment in Oaxaca for $300 to $400 if you live outside the centro. You can still rent a house for $600 to $800 without too much trouble. Invest a little time and effort and you could find an abode for about $500

If you want to get away from it all, this is almost as far away as you can get. (San Cristobal, Chiapas, is farther, but has so few permanent gringos that it's not included in this book.) If you are interested in weaving, pottery, archeology, Indian culture, or traditional Mexico as it was a century ago, then Oaxaca is for you. It has been called the craft capital of Mexico.

Oaxaca is one of Mexico's colonial cities and has one of the largest Saturday markets in the country (Toluca's market is bigger). The sidewalk cafes give the city a European charm, and the locals are quite friendly. A real treat is visiting the nearby villages. Each has its own craft specialty: rugs, pottery, linens, hand-carved wooden animals, and more.

The weather is essentially springlike all year (some say perfect), though a sweater or light jacket will come in handy. You can hang around the zócalo and watch people from all over the world walk by. You can also see various political demonstrations, as this has been a hotbed of political thought since before the Revolution. Don't take this the wrong way—it is more similar to Berkeley, California, or Austin, Texas, than a more conservative city, that's all.

Housing costs are still less than many other places in this book, but they have gone up since the last edition. A luxury home rental ranges from about $1,500 outside the centro to about $3,500 in town. Simple digs are going for about $400 in town and about $250 to $350 outside the centro.

There are cultural activities ranging from piano recitals to plays to folk dances. There are more European and Asian tourists than Americans. There is a good English-language library, the Biblioteca Circulante (Piño Suarez #519). If you stay here, you should donate your time and/or your money to them. I donated some "Mexico" Mike books years ago, but I am sure that they dumped them when they moved.

Many artists, photographers, writers, and other ne'er-do-wells have settled here. They're an amiable sort, however, and won't bother you with a lot of high-falutin' talk. There is a U.S. consular agent, Mark Arnold Leyes (Plaza Santo Domingo, kitty-corner from the church, upstairs. Phone/Fax: 01-52-951-514-3054). The Canadian consul is at located at 119 Dr. Liceaga #8, 68000 Oaxaca, Oax. (mailing address: The Consulate of Canada), at the Brena Building, across the street from Llano park on Piño Suarez. Honorary Consul: Ms. F. May. The territory includes the states of Oaxaca and Chiapas.

If you'd like to keep up on what's going on in Oaxaca, subscribe to *The Oaxaca/Mexico Newsletter* written by my old (all my friends are old now) friend Stan Gotleib with beautiful photos by Diana Ricci (www.realoaxaca.com). Subscriptions are $30 a year.

High-speed Internet connections are available for $40–$50 a month. As everywhere else, add 15 percent Mexican tax to the cost of the service.

Additional Resources

- Language Schools: There are eight good Spanish-language schools here*: Instituto Cultural Oaxaca (Fax: 01-52-951-515-3278; inscuoax@spersaoaxaca.com.mx), Amigos del Sol (Fax: 01-52-951-514-3484; amisol@oaxacanews. com), Instituto de Comunicación y Cultura (Fax: 01-52-951-516-3443; info@iccoax. com), Centro de Idiomas (Fax: 01-52-951-516-5922, ilhui@uabjo.cu. uabjo.mx), Sol y Tierra (Fax: 01-52-951-515-1225; soltierr@spersaoaxaca. com.mx), Becari Language School (Fax: 01-52-951-514-6076; becari@ becari.com), Berlitz (Phone: 01-52-951-513-3977; berlitz@berlitzoax.com.mx) and School of Spanish and Culture (contact@escuelaespanolyculture.com).

CONS

The very isolation that makes Oaxaca so different may be a minus in the eyes of many people. This is not as true as it was in the last edition, as there is now

*Used with permission from www.realoaxaca.com.

a toll road from Mexico City that cuts driving time down to five hours. But even with toll roads, it will take between two (not recommended) and three days to drive here from the Texas border. There is now a daily flight to Houston, and, of course, flights to Mexico City. The town is very conservative.

IN-BETWEENS

There has always been an expatriate community of individualists and artists in this city. Their numbers have never been great, though they now number about 400 permanent residents, with another couple of hundred during the winter. There are only about 1,000 foreigners in the entire state. If you are into Indian arts and crafts, though, you couldn't find a better place to learn about them. The archeology sites in the area are excellent.

PUERTO ESCONDIDO, OAXACA

Ambiente: Not quite the sleepy fishing village it used to be, but still pretty mellow. Tropical.

Climate: Winters are divine (70s–80s). Summers are devilishly hot (upper 80s–90s, with occasional days near 100), with rain and 90–100 percent humidity. It rains daily (though less than in Acapulco) during hurricane season (May 15 to Sept. 30). Subject to hurricanes, though less so than Acapulco.

Altitude: Sea level, with hills ringing the city

Population: 35,000 (official), 45,000 (estimate)

Housing: There is a decent variety, from bungalows and *palapas* to middle-class houses and condos. No RV park.

   Homes (buy): $18,000–$100,000, with $45,000–$75,000 being the median

   Rentals: In outlying areas, such as Villa de las Fuentes, $300–$500 monthly rentals are findable. In trendier areas, $600–$1,000 monthly rents can be found, but $2,000 and up is all too common.

   RV space: N/A

Medical Care: Barely adequate. There is a small hospital in town, but for serious conditions, go to Pochutla or Acapulco.

Area Code: 954

Many thanks to Bruce Woodworth (www.pacificcoasttravelinfo.com and www.imagemarketingservice.com) and my old friends from my Puerto days, Joe "King" Carrasco, of Austin, Texas, and John Bernheardt of Prince Rupert, British Columbia, Canada, for their help with this chapter.

PROS

   Mikey likes it.

Although the area around Puerto Escondido had been inhabited by native peoples for centuries, the town as we know it grew out of development by coffee growers who needed a port to ship their goods. I'm always amused by writers who "discover" this "sleepy fishing village" and lament that it is changing. I "discovered" it in the 1980s and I was hardly the first. The same as every beautiful place on a beach, it has had a building boom. Its "sleepy fishing village" allure is a matter of degree. It's sleepier than Acapulco, Vallarta, or even the towns between·Vallarta and Manzanillo, but it's on a caffeine rush compared to San Blas or nearby Puerto Angel. Still, it's a small town with a unique flavor that engenders relaxation and contemplation.

A History of Sorts

I lived here in the 1980s. I was on my way to Acapulco but the bus stopped here for the night. So did I. I fell in love with this (then) fairly small village with the lights from the small hotels ringing the bay. During the day the water in the bays varies from deep blue to light green. The coast runs east to west, but to keep things simple, I'll call the direction toward Acapulco north and the direction toward Huatulco south.

I lived here during one of the big land booms, when no one was sure (except perhaps the insiders who bought land in Huatulco) whether the "next big thing" was going to be Huatulco or Puerto Escondido. During that time there were investors walking around with briefcases full of money (mostly Italians) and deals were literally made on paper napkins. It was a heady time for me. I was a recovering stock market options trader who had gone bust and was able to observe the greed with a jaundiced eye. I didn't actually catch jaundice or the speculating fever (though I fought a few rounds with denque fever) and wrote a book instead. The book fared as well as most of the speculators. I made a deal on a napkin with an agent from Los Angeles, California, that was worth the paper it was printed on.

Things have changed a lot in the intervening years, the same as they have everywhere else. **While you could hardly call this a sleepy fishing village, Puerto Escondido still retains much of the old-Mexico charm and hospitality that many are searching for.** The Hotel Santa Fe (www.hotelsantafeinfo.com) is the landmark hotel at the southern end of the favored Zicatela beach area. While I don't usually mention hotels, this one has been the hub of local intrigue for years. I was nearly seduced here by an older woman who enticed me with offers of all the paperback books I could carry. Such was my short career as a gigolo.

Local Resources

There is help for Puerto visitors from Gina (ginainpuerto@yahoo.com), the Information Goddess for the Oaxaca and Puerto Tourist Bureau. Gina can be found at the western end of the Audoquin in the harbor area business and shopping district. Gina is a wonderful contact for anyone visiting Puerto.

The Puerto Language School (www.puertoschool.com), which also offers local tours and surfing lessons, offers students the opportunity to participate in community help programs as part of the language courses. There is a struggling library that would very much appreciate any English/Spanish translation books and/or almost any type of English or Spanish educational material for middle- and upper-level school-age children.

For real estate here and beach properties worldwide, see Beach Area Property www.beachareaproperty.com.

Okay, so I lapsed into travel writing.

Puerto is still small enough to have a delightful laid-back flavor. Zicatela beach is called "The Mexican Pipeline" (the waves can be as high as eighteen feet), which means it is a worldwide surfers' destination. The last time I tried surfing there I broke my nose, so it is not for beginners. Actually, it's not for anyone but very experienced surfers. Don't even think of swimming here. Stick to the milder Carrizalillo beach.

The weather is a big attraction, and milder than Acapulco. **The winter weather is heavenly.** That means temperatures in the seventies and low eighties during the day and sixties at night. The summer, while hot, is generally cooled most every day by brief but magnificent thundershowers that roll in off the Pacific Ocean and are a thrill to witness from open-air restaurants, white-sand beaches, and rocky points. If being confined to a lounge chair in the shade of a beachside *palapa* with cooling Pacific breezes on a white-sand beach is *not* heaven to you, do not visit Puerto at any time of year.

The area surrounding the town is full of palm trees and much tropical vegetation. If you go up into the hills, you'll find tiny towns tucked away that seem to be truly old Mexico. Birders will appreciate the Laguna Manialtepec bird sanctuary ten miles "north" of town. About fifty miles away is Chacahua Lagoons National Park. There are actually a couple of hot springs, so far undeveloped. The first is about sixteen miles in the same direction, then east to San Jose Monte Altapec, up in the mountains. Ask for Chucho, who rents horses, to take you there. There's another near Mazunte.

Puerto Escondido has undergone a tremendous building boom in the last several years, mostly funded by Italians, Germans, Americans, and Canadians. There was an Italian movie, *Puerto Escondido*, that won the Mediterranean academy award, which set the current boom soaring, although the boom started twenty years ago. Things have settled down since then.

A Retirement Community

There is a friendly and active year-round retirement community in the Riconada area above the Harbor. The Riconada area was the original Puerto airport land, which was subdivided in the mid-nineties and offers property that qualifies for Mexico title insurance. You can still find lots in the $20,000 range, with homes ranging from $100,000 to $500,000. Caution is advised when considering property on the Zicatela side of town, which is all *ejido* land with a questionable title that I don't believe will qualify for title insurance. Visit www.mexicorealestateinfo.com for valuable information about buying real estate in Mexico. Property is not inexpensive in Mexico, and if you find a deal that seems too good to be true, it is probably *ejido* land, which can be confiscated at the will and whim of the *ejido* (village) leaders.

Waxing Poetic

Some mornings you may wake up to see a small yacht anchored in the bay with stingrays and pelicans dancing across the wave line, something you will always remember. It is always recommended to shuffle your feet rather than high-stepping through shoreline waters due to the presence of stingrays. Nothing can ruin a vacation faster than stepping on the back of a stingray. Local lifeguards and hotels will know where to get help.

The main beaches are Carrizalillo (the main beach near town), Manzanillo (a little "north"), and Zicatela (a little "south," also called the surfers' beach). There is development of subdivisions on the last two.

Most come to Puerto Escondido for its nonresort atmosphere, white-sand beaches, fishing, or world-class surfing. There is an annual international surfing contest held every year in August.

There are many safe swimming beaches in the Puerto area, but extreme caution is advised for surfing and swimming on Playa Zicatela, the main surfing beach. There are strong riptides and the waves are among the most powerful in the world—rivaling the famed Banzai Pipeline in Hawaii. Several world-class surfers are in wheelchairs with spinal injuries from this huge and shallow surf break.

Playa Zicatela was the first public beach in all of Mexico to initiate volunteer lifeguard services and water safety programs. These programs have been aided and sponsored by the Friends of Puerto and the International Lifesaving Federation. Always swim on a guarded beach!

Playa Principle is the main beach in the harbor area and includes the "Audoquin," a pedestrian shopping, eating, and nightlife area that parallels the harbor. This is a family beach area where the panga and other fishing boats moor and depart for the daily catch. Nightlife on the Audoquin starts after 11 P.M. and lasts till early morning.

It is a wonderful walk from Playa Principle heading southeast along the white-sand, half-moon cove toward Playa Marinero and Playa Zicatela. Find beachfront restaurants with *palapas* and louge chairs along the Marinero beach—my favorite hangout for a late morning breakfast. A picturesque rocky point separates Playa's Principle and Marinero from Zicatela with a lookout area that is great for sunsets. You can stroll from the harbor business district to the southern end of Playa Zicatela in a leisurely thirty minutes—with food and liquid support services all along the way.

Continuing southeast from Zicatela is almost a mile of white-sand beach until you reach the La Punta, The Point. La Punta is a popular left point break for surfing with beachfront restaurants and *palapas* for lazy days.

Heading northwest from the harbor is an exciting cliffside walking trail at the base of massive rock formations below the Puerto Lighthouse. Farther around the point are Playa Manzanillo and Puerto Angelito—nice beaches with *palapas* and food service that are most used by the local Mexican families.

Farther up the coast, below the Riconada retirement area, is the emerald green Carrizalillo Cove with *palapa*-style food-and-beverage service at the base of 100-foot cliffs. The outer cove has a nice left point reef break for surfing and a quiet interior cove for swimming and snorkeling.

Adjoining the Riconada area to the north is Playa Bacocho, another white-sand beach bordered by massive granite rocks that meanders for several miles and is a favorite for beach walks. Enjoy Coco's Beach Club at the beginning, at the lower end of Playa Bacocho.

It is advised to avoid harbor swimming for a day or two after heavy rains due to runoff pollution from inland villages and landfills.

Housing

Housing is becoming easier to find with the building boom, and varies from simple Mexican-style houses in the Riconada area to condo-style apartments along the different beach areas. Apartments can still be found in the $250 to $600 range. There are no rentals right on the beach in the main town, and only hotels are available along the Zicatela beach area.

Since Escondido is a "fun" place, make sure that the home you choose doesn't get the music from the many nightspots that abound. I had a nice bungalow way up the hill from the beach with a great view of the bay from my hammock. Perfect, eh? I rented it during the summer, when the discos weren't operating. Come winter I was forced to dance or work (you call that a choice?) until about 3 A.M., as the music floated up the hill. There is a younger surf crowd that can party late and leave their rooms early in the lower-priced hotels and motels.

Some will want to avoid the December through April burn time when brush and field burning can cause problems for them. While the dry season offers the mildest weather, the lack of rain leaves the lush green vegetation brown—sort of a shock if you only have memory of the lush green hurricane season, which seldom brings a hurricane.

Mazunte, Zipolite, and Puerto Angel

About thirty miles south of Puerto, heading towards Huatulco, is a very popular coastal drive that leaves the main highway and meanders through the villages of Mazunte, Zipolite, and the ever-charming Puerto Angel. It is good to allow for a full-day trip when planning a drive or tour through these memorable coastal villages from Puerto or Huatulco.

Along the way, about ten miles from Puerto Escondido toward Huatulco, you will want to stop at the Iguana Wildlife Preserve and stroll through the wonderful habitat and breeding grounds for the endangered iguana. Don't forget your camara and consider leaving a small donation to help out. It is always helpful to bring change and small denomination currency for any shopping or food along the way. These are poor rural communities that will not have change for 100- and 200-peso notes.

Mazunte offers a must-see attraction—The National Mexican Turtle Center, a research facility where all varieties of sea turtles that live in the coastal waters of Mexico are on exhibit. Additionally, there are six species of freshwater turtles and two species of land turtles. A wonderful tour is available in the fifty-peso range. You'll also find a wonderful selection of organic coconut oils, creams, and cosmetics made locally.

A few miles farther south you will find Zipolite, a nudie beach; some of the greatest beachside restaurants offering cold beverages and seafood; and crafts.

At the southern end of this memorable drive lies Puerto Angel, a small harbor surrounded by sculptured granite cliffs comparable to the Big Sur coastline in California. Discover cliffside trails and enjoy the catch of the day at any number of beachside restaurants.

CONS

There is very limited high-speed Internet access, and only if you live close enough to the phone switching offices. Dial-up is frustrating from 9 A.M. to 9 P.M., with most of the traffic being usurped by the Internet cafes. Summers are ungodly hot. It could get boring living here. **You are way far away from "civilization," and an escape to Acapulco is hardly getting back to civilization.** On Christmas and Easter vacation weeks (the same as in all beach towns), the landmass seems to shift with the added weight of thousands of Mexican tourists.

Most accomodations are without phones and very popular for backpackers and European visitors. There is limited phone service and no high-speed Internet access.

HUATULCO, OAXACA

Ambiente: Resortlike, country-club flavor. Huatulco has become the resort of choice for middle- and upper-class Mexican nationals with growing visits from Canadians and Americans.

Climate: Winters are divine (70s–80s). Summers can be rather hot and dry (upper 80s and 90s, with occasional days near 100), with rain and 90–100 percent humidity. It rains daily (though less than in Acapulco) during hurricane season (May 15 to Sept. 30). Subject to hurricanes, though less so than Acapulco.

Altitude: Sea level, with hills ringing the city

Population: 35,000 (official)

Housing: There is a decent variety, from reasonable bungalows and *palapas* to expensive oceanfront villas.

Homes (buy): $180,000–$300,000 (and way up)

Condos (buy): $50,000–$300,000 (few at lower end, more at $120,000 and up)

Rentals: $400–$1,200

RV space: N/A

Medical Care: Adequate. There is a newer treatment center with adequate facilities for minor health problems and they are able to stabilize patients for transport to Oaxaca City, Mexico City, or the States. Don't move here if you have serious or chronic health problems.

Area Code: 958

PROS

Huatulco is located along the coast of Oaxaca and is made up of nine secluded bays and thirty-six pristine beaches covered with soft, golden sand on twenty-two miles of unspoiled coastline. Bahías de Huatulco (wah-tool-co) is expected by its fans to rival Cancún, Acapulco, and Puerto Vallarta in years to come.

The nine bays from east to west include Bahía Conejos, Bahía Tangolunda, Bahía Chahue, Bahía Santa Cruz, Bahía El Organo, Bahía El Maguey, Bahía Caculuta, Bahía Chachacual, and Bahía San Agustin. Currently, only two of the bays are developed: Bahía Tangolunda and Bahía Santa Cruz. Conejos, Tangolunda, Chahue, and Santa Cruz are accessible by car. The rest are enjoyed from boat trips, which are easily arranged for at the harbor.

Tangolunda, one of its largest and most spectacular bays, features deluxe hotels and all-inclusive resorts, an eighteen-hole par-seventy-two golf course, and a fishing boat harbor. La Crucecita is currently the area business center with a quaint town square complete with historic church and park area with benches and shade trees. A second business district is developing in the Chahue Bay area.

Housing

Huatulco is able to cater to all budgets. Apartments can range from $250 to $800 per month and upscale villas can range from $800 to thousands. A night out costs anywhere from $3 for something filling to $30 for an upscale meal including drinks, tip, and an ocean breeze.

Weather

Huatulco enjoys an average year-round temperature of eighty-two degrees with occasional lows of fifty-seven and highs of 100. Huatulco is formed by mountains, hills, and valleys, which are irrigated by the Coyula, San Agustin, and Copalita Rivers. As in most tropical climates, mosquitos can be a problem during the rainy season—worst at sunset and sunrise. Be sure to bring an effective repellent with deet.

History

The FONATUR, Mexico's government-funded tourist development agency, planned and funded phase one of the Huatulco resort area development with $80 million (not pesos) back in the early eighties. The Huatulco infrastructure is impressive, and the project was officially inaugurated in 1988. The building boom stalled through the nineties and is picking up again with a growing German, Italian, Canadian, and American retirement community.

This has been the promise since it was built. See my comments in the Puerto Escondido chapter about the land boom. There was a tug-of-war between the interests promoting Huatulco and Puerto Escondido as "the next big thing." Huatulco won, sort of. Similar to Loreto in the Baja, it hasn't lived up to the promoter's expectations, but there is always some travel writer from a fam trip (a familiarization trip—these are government or resort-sponsored trips for travel writers and travel agents. Ever wonder why you only read about expensive resorts in travel magazines? Because these fam trips are about the only way a travel writer can afford to travel. My hat's off to those who go on their own and do a little real reporting.) to drum up excitement in the foreign media. My guess is that it will grow slowly. There are only so many beautiful beach resorts in Mexico. They will all be "the next big thing" someday. Huatulco is touted as an "ecological resort." There's some truth to this, but a lot of ecology was destroyed in its building. Local fishermen were displaced to make room for the resort. That's not unique to Huatulco, but the official versions of how these places came to be leaves those facts out.

CONS

This town feels more like a resort than a town. There are few permanent foreign residents and few ongoing activities. It is way far away from everything. You'll feel isolated. It's quite a sterile environment, and is more likely to appeal to someone who wants the feeling of living in a country club environment. While it may someday rival Cancún, in terms of being a city with a substantial feel and community to it, that's a long way off. Since nearly everything is new construction, you'd expect that a citywide purified water system would have been installed, as in Cancún. It wasn't. You still have to depend on bottled water. If you're looking for a small, out-of-the-way town likely to give you a feel for Mexico on the Pacific Coast, I'd advise you to move up the coast to Puerto Escondido. If you're looking for a city, choose Acapulco. Prices for goods as well as property are inflated.

There is very limited high-speed Internet access, and only if you live close enough to the phone switching offices. Dial-up is frustrating from 9 A.M. to 9 P.M., with most of the traffic being usurped by the Internet cafes. Summers are ungodly hot. It could get boring living here. **You are way far away from "civilization," and an escape to Acapulco is hardly getting back to civilization.**

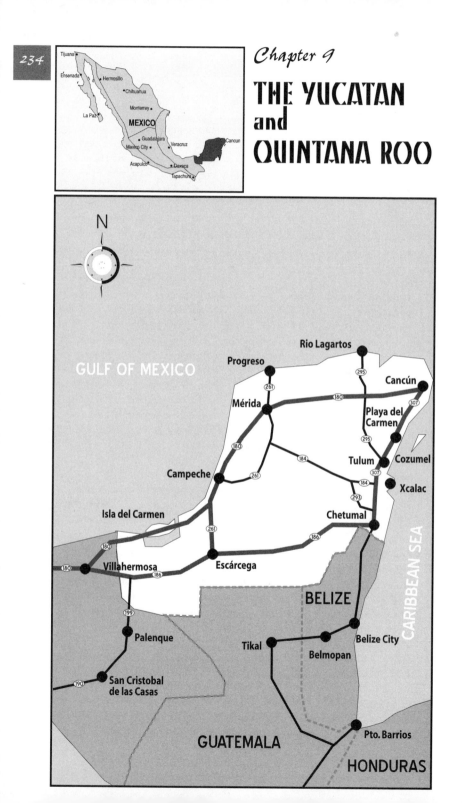

Chapter 9

THE YUCATAN and QUINTANA ROO

MÉRIDA, YUCATAN

Ambiente: Yucatan has had a long history of independence from Mexico. Consequently, the atmosphere is quite different from anywhere else. There is a grace, sophistication, and mellowness to the people that make it practically impossible to stay angry or uptight about anything.

Climate: Summer is wonderful for me, but those who know me call me "special," which is the polite Mexican way of saying I am weird. If you like "cool" days in the 90s and "hot" days that can reach 115, you'll love it here. Surprisingly, winters sometimes have cool (60s), drizzly, overcast days, though they are not the norm. Winter is usually more sunny and in the 70s. May to Aug. is warm (80s–low 90s) and it often rains. Hurricanes seem to be attracted to the area (similar to the way tornadoes in the States seem to gravitate toward trailer parks). Blessed humidity is a fact of life. Rainfall averages about twenty inches a year.

Altitude: None

Population: 842,000 (officially, but some say there are close to 1,000,000 inhabitants)

Housing: It's considerably less expensive than Cancún and most of Mexico. There are plenty of choices in all ranges.

Homes (buy): $25,000–$80,000

Condos (buy): N/A

Rentals: $200–$600

RV space (sometimes with trailer): $10,000–$35,000

Medical Care: Excellent. There are two hospitals with a 5/5 rating from *Mexico Health and Travel Safety Guide.*

Area Code: 999

A Little History

To understand why this area is so different from the rest of Mexico, a little history is in order. In 1821, the Yucatan Peninsula became an independent country. It wasn't until 1823 that they joined Mexico. They seceded from Mexico in 1840 until 1843, then again in 1845. It remained independent during the Mexican-American War. From 1846 until 1866, during the "Caste War," the native Mayans ran out nearly all Mexicans except from the walled cities of Mérida and Campeche (then part of Yucatan state—until 1853). The official government in Mérida offered the peninsula to the United States, Spain, and Great Britain in exchange for military assistance. The United States considered it, but instead invoked the Monroe Doctrine to discourage other countries from interfering.

Yucatan was reunited with Mexico 1848. In 1858, it became a territory. There were continued revolts until 1901, with some towns refusing to recognize Mexican authority until 1910. The peninsula remained isolated, with more ties to the States and Cuba by sea than to Mexico City. It was not connected to the mainland by railroad until the 1950s. Highways connected it to the mainland in the 1960s. Thus *Yucatecos* are proud of their heritage and independent. Dr. Francisco Epigmenio Luna Kan was the first person of Maya heritage to be elected governor of Yucatan, from 1976 until 1982.

PROS

Inexpensive, charming, completely different from the rest of Mexico.

If a good-sized city with a *"bella epoca"* charm appeals to you, this could be your spot. Mérida seems to operate at a different pace from the rest of Mexico. The culture is more Mayan, as are many of the inhabitants. It's hard to quantify, but they just seem to move with a graceful fluidity and treat you with a sophisticated charm and acceptance that's quite appealing. It's an international city, and you are quite likely to meet more Europeans than Americans or Canadians at the coffee shops. There are frequent free band concerts in the plaza. The food is different from most of Mexico, with a strong Mayan influence. *Puerco pilbil* (unique Mayan spices including achiote, ancho chili powder, avocado leaves, canella powder, chipotle powder, epazote, and Mexican oregano wrapped in banana leaves) is a stable. You'll eat more pork than beef here.

Even the clothing is different. The *guayabera*, a loose-fitting embroidered shirt with many pockets, is common male attire. Sadly, 100 percent cotton ones are rare and most are a polyester/cotton blend. I like the long-sleeve ones and they are scarce. Women will often wear colorful embroidered dresses in the *Yucateca* style.

Fresh seafood is plentiful, coming from Progresso, a non-Americanized beach town about forty minutes to the north. While cruise ships dock there, so far the town has not become a mini Cancún; it has a somewhat down-at-the-heels charm.

Real estate seems to be inexpensive and there are ex-haciendas outside town for sale, remnants of the days when Henequen was king. Houses are either painted in bright pastels or dilapidated. There are plenty of fixer-uppers, though from what I've seen there's a lot more fixing needed than upping. Tropical plants grow wild in your gardens.

There are Mayan ruins all over the place within short distances of the city, with cenotes (freshwater wells, often used to sacrifice virgins—something that should have promoted promiscuity, but didn't) and developed tours. It's quite possible to buy a home with a freshwater pool, or cenote, on the premises. As far as I know, virginity is not a prerequisite.

Something that is a plus to me, but perhaps not to you, is that the pools are quite warm in summer, while not approaching hot springs status, but are more similar to a warm bath.

Fishing is excellent and varied, with both fresh- and saltwater opportunities. Campeche, a few hours away, is home to stone crabs. In fact, a friend of mine in Galveston imports them for sale throughout the States.

High-speed Internet connections are available.

Medical Care

Mexico Health and Travel Safety Guide says, "Mérida's private hospitals are the finest health care facilities in the Yucatan Peninsula. Mexicans throughout southeastern Mexico make the trip to Mérida whenever they are in need of modern, comprehensive medical services. ... Our review of physicians and two private hospitals in Mérida was a simple task; they are both excellent and travelers will not have a difficult time finding adequate care. ...": Centro Médico de las Américas (Calle 54 #365 [corner of Avenida Pérez Ponce], Mérida, Yuc.; Phone: 01-52-999-926-2111, 01-52-926-2619, Emergency Phone: 01-52-999-927-3199; Fax: 01-52-999-926-4710) and Clínica de Mérida (Avenida Itzaes #242 [between Calle 25 and Calle 27], Colonia García Gineres, Mérida, Yuc. Phone: 01-52-999-920-0411, 01-52-999-920-0412; Fax: 01-52-999-925-3335).

A Unique Hotel

I don't mention a lot of hotels in this book because this is not a travel guide, but sometimes I just can't resist (guess I still have a little of that travel writer gene in my blood). One of the unique hotels that is probably one of my favorites in Mexico is here. Luz en Yucatan is in the center of the city, but a world apart (Calle 55 #499 x 60 y 58, Mérida, Yuc., 97000; Phone: 01-52-999-924-0035). Not only is it an "urban retreat," but is also offers a sensible weight-loss program that many have said is successful. You can also reserve rooms from them at www.luzenyucatan.com/.

CONS
If hurricanes scare you, stay away. Several visit Mérida as tourists every year. They are usually mild when they reach Mérida and, except for Progresso, don't seem to inflict much damage, but there will be a lot of rain and wind.

You are very far away from the rest of Mexico. Driving to the mainland will take a day. You'd better like flat land, because there's nary a hill to be seen (and they usually have a Mayan temple atop). While locals call the outlying areas jungle, it's more like scrub forest to a real jungle aficionado. The closest real jungles are in Chiapas.

If you don't like humidity, don't come. Sweating is a local sport. If heat bothers you, you will be very unhappy here, except in winter. Since it is a large city, there will be traffic, though it seems to be quite civilized.

IN-BETWEENS
You might find the Mayan culture charming. **The sense of isolation might not affect you.** You might like being near enough to Cancún and the Caribbean Coast that you can drive there, bask in the sun, and be back the same day.

CANCÚN, QUINTANA ROO

Ambiente: Hedonistic, party-til-you-drop mentality. Similar to Miami Beach.

Climate: Surprisingly, winters sometimes have cool (60s), drizzly, overcast days, though they are not the norm. Winters: low 70s to mid-70s nights, mid- to upper 80s days. Summers: low to mid-80s nights, upper 80s to mid-90s days. Hurricanes are a real possibility from July to Oct. Humidity is a fact of life, though with the sea breezes, it's not as oppressive as in Mérida.

Altitude: Sea level

Population: 397,000 (officially, though, probably closer to half a million)

Housing: Plenty of availability, several choices. While Cancún is still cheaper than Cabo San Lucas, Baja, it's up there. However, if you find an apartment or house outside the tourist zone, you can still live for less than you can in the *Bajio*. And it's cheaper to live here than anywhere else on the Mayan Riviera.

Homes (buy): $35,000–$750,000 ($150,000–$225,000 seems to be about average. Mostly two bedrooms, though. The low-end houses exist but are rare.)

Condos (buy): $50,000–$300,000 ($90,000–$125,00 is about average.)

Rentals: $300–$800 (with many condos in the $300–$500 range)

RV spaces: None in Cancún proper, one park to the north of the city, and several farther south along the coast. It's more expensive than in much of Mexico, except Baja.

Medical Care: Not as good as it should be. Adequate.

Area Code: 998

PROS

Cancún was created from a computer model by FONATUR, the Mexican government agency devoted to developing new tourist destinations. They input into a computer what American tourists wanted from a vacation, and the location—with its white sand, tropical atmosphere, and accessibility (if they built an airport)—came up. While there were a few resident fishermen living in the area and a small fishing village, the tourist zone was built from scratch and the actual town was modernized. Consequently, it was built with a purified water system and brand-new pipes.

While the town proper still seems like Mexico, the Zona Hotelera, with most of the big hotels and high-rise condos, is a sterile environment, designed to appeal to tourists who would normally not choose Mexico for a vacation. It's more like Miami Beach than Mexico, though more people speak English in Cancún. Oddly enough, prominent politicians decided to buy up the land before the development began. Go figure. Even more oddly, politicians have bought up land along the rest of the coast (called the Cancún corridor) before extensive development began there.

You can live here and not feel as if you left home.

The beaches are beautiful (if you've seen a Corona commercial, you've seen them), with powder-white sand surrounded by crystal-clear turquoise water. The discos are full of beautiful people. English is spoken almost everywhere. You can get *The New York Times, Miami Herald, The Wall Street Journal,* and *USA Today* daily. There are brokerage houses. Communications are excellent, including high-speed Internet service. There are two eighteen-hole golf courses. There are American-style condos. In fact, "American-style" sums the place up.

There is plenty of American-style food from familiar chains. Sam's and Home Mart (owned by Home Depot) stores cater to your every whim (well, most of the commercial ones anyway). There are direct flights to the United States, Canada, and Europe. The weather is nearly perfect. Both the United States and Canada have consular agents here. Scuba diving is great. Snorkeling is great. Fishing is great. The water is purified out of the tap. There are direct flights to Cuba and legitimate Cuban cigars are sold from cigar stores. I'd still avoid the ones in hotels.

Medical Care

Everybody wants to make a buck from the foreign tourists, even the sick ones. There's a widespread pattern of corruption that goes like this: You get sick at a hotel. The hotel sends a doctor or an ambulance. The hotel gets a kickback. If you go to the hospital by taxi, the taxi driver gets a kickback. You'll end up with whatever hospital or doctor is willing to pay the highest bounty. Bottom line: You could pay as much for care here as you would in the United States—and the care is not as good.

If you need serious medical care, and can live until you get to Mérida, go to a hospital there. By all means, go there if you have a surgery planned.

If you need a doctor in Cancún, go to a certified MedToGo physician first. This is yet another reason to buy *Mexico Health and Travel Safety Guide.*

If you have to be treated in Cancún, there are two choices. The better of the two is Hospitál Hospiten (3.5/5 rating by MedToGo) (Avenida Bonampak, Lot #7, Manzana 2 SM 10, Centro, Cancún, Q.R.; Phone: 01-52-998-881-3700; Fax: 01-52-998-881-3737). They have the most modern technology and all their staff physicians are board certified. They are friendly and prices for tourists are competitive. MedToGo recommends them.

AmeriMed Cancún is part of a three-hospital chain in Cabo, Puerto Vallarta, and Cancún. I've visited them and they had the best of intentions when they started. The one in Cancún just hasn't had the money to buy equipment, but it's a decent hospital (it gets a 2/5 rating from *Mexico Travel and Safety Guide*) (Avenida Tulum 260, Plaza las Americas, Centro, Cancún, Q.R.; Phone: 01-52-998-881-3400; Emergency Phone: 01-52-998-881-3434; Fax: 01-52-998-881-3466). "It should be viewed as an urgent care center and not a full-service hospital at this time," according to *Mexico Health and Safety Travel Guide.*

CONS

Gee, with all the superlatives above, what can be wrong with this place? It's a matter of what you want out of living in Mexico. Everybody seems to want something from you. **Cancún is a comparatively expensive place to live, though you get more modernized houses and condos.** City buses, for instance, cost double what they do elsewhere in the country. The economy is based on the dollar, so you can't take advantage of any fluctuations of the peso versus the dollar. The place has no real soul. You will soon wonder if you are even in Mexico, until you try to do business or have an auto accident. Then you will encounter rapaciousness that makes other locations seem tame. There are so many Ugly Americans that you will be ashamed to be from the same country.

With all the money Cancún funnels into the Mexican economy, why they couldn't have better health care is beyond me. And the practice of kickbacks for referrals, while not unique to Cancún, puts a black eye on the medical system here. If you have cardiovascular problems, I wouldn't recommend Cancún, or anywhere on the Mayan Riviera.

IN-BETWEENS

It's a great town for business (with the caveat above), a real Babbittville. Everybody seems to have a hustle of some kind going. There are some very pretty areas nearby where you can escape; my favorite is Isla Mujeres. There is also a bullring.

PLAYA DEL CARMEN, QUINTANA ROO

Ambiente: No longer a hippie haven, it is more upscale-bohemian, and still hedonistic. Lots of party animals hang out (and get hungover) here.

Climate: A good deal cooler than Cancún during the summer. Fewer winter days with cool (60s), drizzly, overcast days than Cancún, but they do happen. Winters: upper 60s to low 70s nights, mid-80s days. Summers: mid-70s to mid-80s nights, upper 80s to low 90s days. Hurricanes are a real possibility from July to Oct. Humidity is a fact of life, though with the sea breezes, not as oppressive as in Mérida.

Altitude: Sea level

Population: 65,000 (estimate. There are probably more than 1,500 foreign residents, many Europeans, mostly Italians.)

Housing: Remarkably expensive. It's more expensive than Cancún because of the lack of availability. The Playacar section has lots of modern condos.

Homes (buy): $45,000–$600,000 ($120,000–$180,000 seems to be about average, mostly two- to three-bedrooms, though. The low-end houses exist, but are rare.)

Condos (buy): $50,000–$300,000 (There are few for less than $90,000. $180,000–$220,000 is about average. Playacar has plenty of pricey condos.)

Rentals: $450–$1,200 (Low-end rentals are rare. $700 is about average.)

RV spaces: N/A

Medical Care: Barely adequate, but Cancún is nearby for emergencies

Area Code: 984

PROS

Long, long ago it seems, this was in another galaxy and was a "hippie" escape. Now, only rich hippies live here. The hippies have been forced to move farther along the coast due to high prices, and they don't get much better, except for those few areas left where you can rent a *palapa*, complete with thatched roof, no air-conditioning, and questionable plumbing. Prices are higher here than in Cancún; it's because this whole "Mayan Riviera" is an upscale tourist destination, not a city. While you can still find "relatively" inexpensive places to rent, they surely aren't going to have a beachfront or beach view unless you stand on top of your house. The lower-end houses for sale are nowhere near a beach.

The former dirt street along the main drag is now cobblestone. While this is still less developed than Cancún, it's showing the effects of development. Exclusive "all-inclusive" hotels have been built all along the coast. Groups of European tourists flock to them. The ferries to Cozumel are packed during the tourist season. **There is a decent-sized community of expatriates and you will soon make their acquaintance.**

While not "undiscovered," there is still plenty of charm to this small town.

The beaches are just what you'd expect from the Corona beer commercials on TV. White, white sand, turquoise waters. **The atmosphere is still laid-back.** There is enough development so that you won't feel as if you are on a primitive isle, but, at the same time, you won't feel overwhelmed as you would if you were in Cancún. **The snorkeling and scuba diving are excellent.** There is such a variety of tourists, including many Europeans, that you will always have someone to talk to. If you are an upscale bohemian, you will still fit in. If you are single, you won't have to stay that way for long. **There is a topless beach.**

CONS

The transient nature of the place will get to you after a while. The fall storms can be a really unpleasant experience. Because it is a small town and there are a lot of foreigners, everything costs more than it should. If Sam's doesn't have what you need, you'll have to go to Cancún. **Property values have escalated since the last edition of this book and will probably continue to do so.**

Some reporters have called this one of the fastest-growing communities in Mexico. With this rapid growth in population, the character for which you moved will disappear in time.

IN-BETWEENS

There is now a Sam's, so the shopping trek to Cancún is no longer necessary.

It's still sort of laid-back but not isolated. It's not "another Cancún" yet, but the time is probably coming when it will be. **It's not for everyone.**

COZUMEL, QUINTANA ROO

Ambiente: Caribbean-style, laid back, very friendly

Climate: Winters: upper 60s to low 70s nights, mid-80s days. Summers: mid-70s to low 80s nights, upper 80s to low 90s days. Hurricanes are a real possibility from July to Oct.

Altitude: Sea level

Population: 132,000 (official). San Miguel: 90,000.

Housing: Special note on housing: If you arrive during the low season (May to Nov.), you're more likely to find less-expensive accommodations, but expect the rent to go up in Dec. The same applies to purchasing. Sellers are likely to be inundated with lookey-loos during the season, but more likely to reduce the asking price when there is less traffic.

Homes (buy): $150,000–$400,000 ($165,000–$195,000 is about the average.)

Condos (buy): $200,000–$400,000

Rentals: $500–$2,000 ($700 seems to be about average. The farther you are from downtown, the less you'll pay. Outside San Miguel, prices drop.)

RV space: N/A

Medical Care: Adequate. For serious conditions, go to Mérida. Do not go to Cancún unless you have to.

Area Code: 987

PROS

Cozumel is the name of the island. Although there are small communities around the island, San Miguel is the main town.

What a difference twelve miles makes! That's how far this largest inhabited island in Mexico is from the mainland. This is a completely different world from Cancún, or even Playa. **The pace is so much slower, the people so friendly, that those who've settled here swear it's the best place in the world.** One word often used to describe *Cozumeleños* is "sweet." I usually don't go along with such generalizations but, in this case, I concur. They have got to be the nicest people in a country noted for nice people.

For anyone thinking of moving here, besides my usual caveat of living in any place for several months before buying property, I recommend you visit the Web site www.cozumelmycozumel.com and participate in the discussion board before you leave. Of all the bulletin boards I've seen about Mexico, I found this one to be especially valuable for people other than just tourists. Be sure to read my "Cons" section below as well. **This is a special place, but it is not for everyone.** The purpose of this book is to help you to find the communities where you'll fit in and save you some time.

The island has more than just beaches and diving. It claims to be 96 percent jungle (though, as with my caveat about the Yucatan jungle, it's not the same as the Amazon, or even Chiapas). Still it's pretty interesting scenery. Wildlife includes a lot of "Cs"—cenotes, crocodiles, and iguanas. (Okay, it's only a couple of "Cs," I was never very good at math.)

You can live comfortably here without a car. Bicycles, motor scooters, and taxis are the main way of getting around. If you desire a Caribbean-style life at less than it costs to live in non-Mexican Caribbean islands, it's a comparative bargain. **One of "Mexico" Mike's highest accolades is that it is quiet—as long as you are far, far away from where the cruise ships dock or the nightlife.** High-speed Internet service is available, subject to the caveat below.

If you want to get a taste of elegant living here at a very nice upscale villa, try Casa Cascada (www.cozumelmycozumel.com/Pages/CasaCascada.htm#). For from about $600 to $1,000 a week (depending on the season), a family or group of up to eight people can get a villa with private pool, kitchen, maid service, and a waterfall outside your room. The American owners, Carey and A. J., are a wealth of information about everything Cozumel. If their villa is the wrong size for you, contact them anyway and they'll help you find something nice.

CONS

It's an island. Everything must be brought in by boat or plane, so bulky items will be unreasonably expensive. In the past, islanders would make the ferry/bus/taxi trip to Cancún several times a year to cart back items such as good-quality bath towels, attractive light fixtures, and cheap ibuprofen and lawn furniture. There's now a Sam's Club in Playa del Carmen, so the previous all-day adventure has become an easy pop over on the ferry and a five-minute cab ride to Sam's.

People really do get "island fever." The cure is usually just getting away for a while, so it's not serious. But you're isolated from the rest of Mexico. While there's lots to do here and places to explore, you'll have been to them sooner or later. Live here for several months before you make the plunge, so to speak. The community of approximately 1,000 full-time foreigners (which swells to about 1,500 in the high season) is pretty large for such a small area, but you'll know them all before long.

Phone connections are still less than perfect. Ah, heck, locals say it is "slower than molasses." The DSL service by Telmex/Prodigy is more of an "almost always on" service than "always on." Fortunately, the Telmex office on the south end of town on Ave. 65 has heard of customer service and can often help you with problems if you go there in person. There used to be a tradition here that you had to "tip" the repairman to fix your phone system. If he didn't think he was going to get a tip, he wouldn't come. The company is trying to eliminate that.

This is not somewhere to choose if you are on a tight budget. Not only is housing more expensive than in mainland Mexico (it ain't cheap anywhere on the Mayan Riviera), but basics such as food also cost more because everything (well, except for fish, which don't have to be transported by boats) is "imported" from the mainland. **Electricity is more expensive than on the mainland; you'll pay about four times as much for electricity as in the States.** Figure a minimum of $250 a month just to air-condition a large, well-sealed, one-bedroom casa—and that's only using the AC at night! Locals either build to take advantage of the cross-island breezes, do without AC, or just run it at night in the bedroom. Gas and water prices are low, which is why an electric stove can't be found on the island.

While the people, both locals and expats alike, are friendly, if you aren't a diver, you may feel somewhat left out. I'm a diver of sorts (certified, but don't dive much) and became one just so I could answer the question "Do you dive?" affirmatively. It's the same reason I used Nikon cameras when I was a photographer—just so I wouldn't feel as if I were a leper around my journalist friends. If you don't learn to dive, at least pick up some of the lingo.

IN-BETWEENS

There's a constant influx of tourists, so you could expand your social horizons from other expats if you are into temporary liaisons. **If you are a nature lover, you'll be happy here, but if you prefer a place with more variety of scenery, you'll find it limiting.** But with perfect beaches and a perfect ocean, that's plenty for plenty of people. If you're a smoker, you'll run into some U.S.–style intolerance when it comes to renting an apartment or villa (mostly from gringo owners). (The paradox is that many of those who kicked the habit back home start smoking again because the prices are so low. Go figure!) You can smoke in restaurants and on the street without getting doused by a nonsmoking Nazi, however.

XCALAC (ALSO SPELLED XCALAK), QUINTANA ROO

Ambiente: Very laid-back. If scuba diving is your forte, you will be in heaven. If you are a fisherman, especially a fly fisherman, you won't want to leave.

Climate: Warmer than Cancún, less likely to have overcast days in winter. Days: mid-80s. Nights: low to mid-70s. May to Aug. is warmer (days: upper 80s, nights: mid-70s to low 80s). It often rains, and hurricanes may blow you away from July to Oct. Humidity is a fact of life, though with the sea breezes, it's not as oppressive as in Mérida.

Altitude: Sea level

Population: Approximately 1,000

Housing: Improved from the last edition. There are still primitive *palapas*, but there are some houses or condos for rent. Wind generators still supply some power, but there is now dependable (pretty much) electricity.

Homes (buy): Very few and very pricey. Mostly lot sales to build a house.

Condos (buy): $95,000–$300,000

Rentals: $400–$900 ($550 is about average—limited availability)

RV spaces: N/A

Medical Care: Very simple. You'll have to go to Chetumal for anything serious.

Area Code: 983

PROS

Essentially, you can still get away from it all here—though it has been modernized tremendously in the past few years. There is now a paved road from Majahual (the turnoff from the Cancún-Chetumal road) to get here. There is now electricity—pretty much. There are now more tourist developments. There are hotels. **This former little fishing village, stuck as an afterthought onto the peninsula that juts down toward Belize at the tip of Mexico, is gorgeous.** The beaches are not quite as nice as in Cancún (nice sand, but rocky in spots), but the coral reefs are magnificent. **The scuba diving is world-class here, some say better than Cozumel.** It is here that I learned to dive.

For complete information on the area, contact Andy and Ruth Sanders, owners of Sandwood Villas (Phone from within the States: 011-52-983-831-0034, or in the States: Al Sanders at 952-898-1667; scubadad12007@yahoo.com, or asanders@atnmail.com; www.sandwood.com). They can steer you in the right direction about buying property and living here. While you're here, their villas/condos are a wonderful place to stay. **The Chinchorro Banks are just offshore and they are teeming with fish. Fishing is magnificent, for tarpon, permit, and many more game fish, both in the bays and out in the blue water.** Fly-fishing is catching on. You can really enjoy the nature and quiet at night. Thank God it is still quiet at night, though there is a rudimentary nightlife.

There's still not a lot to the town, but it is developing. Fortunately, the nature of the foreigners who live here makes them people who coexist with the local community. If I were to retire, this would be one of my first picks. You could write or paint great things here. But be aware that it is changing. It has been "discovered," and large tourist hotels are already there and more are coming. Will one of my very favorite places become another Cancún? I don't think so. Until there are frequent direct flights from the States to Chetumal (unlikely), only those who are willing to work at getting away will end up here (he said hopefully).

CONS

This place is really isolated. **Medical care is inadequate.** If you get really sick, you will have to go to Chetumal or Cancún for treatment. Communications are spotty. **The very isolation that attracted you may wear thin after a while, although it is becoming less isolated every day.**

You'll need air-conditioning. Your electric bills will be higher. There is no high-speed Internet service, and you'll find dial-up to be "dial and pray."

There are few permanent expatriate residents. You won't have much of a social life, and what there is centers on the dive shops and bars.

IN-BETWEENS

Change has come. This is not overwhelming yet, but who knows what the future holds? I still consider this an outpost of serenity, but if that changes it is not my fault because I included it in this book. Progress is inevitable, and no place in a perfect setting can remain isolated forever. The international interests and Cancún businessmen bought large tracts of land for developments long before you read this.

I can only compare the land boom that's still going on to the one in Puerto Escondido in the eighties when I lived there. Puerto survived. So will Xcalac. Even with the new highway from Majahual, it's still a four-hour drive from Cancún.

I don't mean to be a Gloomy Gus. **These changes will make life better for those who actually live here and will enable more people similar to you and me to appreciate the area.** It will not become "another Cancún," but it will become something that it isn't today. There are people who moan about several other places in this book that have been "ruined" by development. I am not so arrogant that I want a beautiful area all to myself. I can only pray that the developers pursue their goal with consideration. There will always be unspoiled places—they will just be harder to find.

Chapter 10
THE GULF COAST

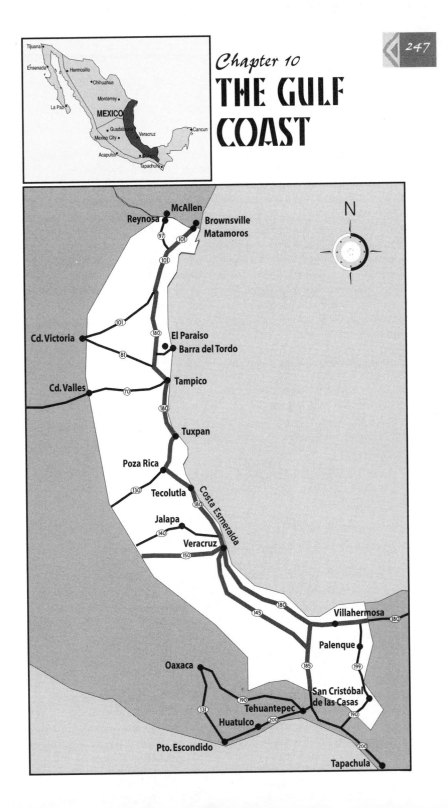

This is an area that few foreigners think about for moving to Mexico. It will attract the more adventurous types, avid fishermen, and those who don't want to have a lot of gringo neighbors. There is one desirable location a day's drive from the Texas border, with miles and miles of unspoiled beaches. Farther south, the beaches are tropical with coconut palms. Veracruz is the only big city on the coast. A little farther inland, Jalapa (also spelled Xalapa) is a conservative colonial city. I didn't include Tampico in the last edition and nobody noticed. If there are more than a dozen foreigners living there, I'd be surprised.

The roads are often bad and the weather can be less than perfect, with hurricanes in the summer and occasional cold fronts (where the temperature might drop to forty degrees) for a few days. It is close to the U.S. border. There are no really good medical facilities outside Veracruz or Jalapa.

The atmosphere is laid-back. The people are really friendly. The seafood is excellent. Because a number of French soldiers deserted after the fall of Maximilian, there is a slight French influence in the area north of Veracruz and south of Tampico.

EL PARAISO, TAMPICO

Ambiente: Isolated, for nature lovers

Climate: Winters: 70s to mid-80s days, 60s nights. Summers: Upper 80s days (occasionally low 90s), mid-70s nights (occasional nights in 50s or even 40s). Not as subject to hurricanes as towns farther south, but the possibility does exist.

Altitude: 45 feet

Population: Perhaps 500 in Barra del Tordo (closest fishing village), maybe 3,000 in Aldama (nearest town on the highway, twenty miles from El Paraiso)

Housing: Limited

Medical Care: Nonexistent

Area Code: Aldama: 835, Tampico: 833

This is potentially an area that will have development rivaling that of the northern Baja. It is close to the border, on the Gulf of Mexico, and still pristine. However, as with all plans for development in Mexico, it may take some time to get going. I am in personal contact of the owner of this development and will be glad to keep you up to date. Contact me directly at mexicomikenelson @mexicomike.com before you get your heart set on moving here.

PROS

This is one of my favorite places in Mexico. Only five hours from either McAllen or Brownsville, Texas, it could be a great alternative to the Rio Grande Valley of Texas, where thousands of Winter Texans (snowbirds) flock every year. Right now, it is not set up for a retirement community, but the owner, Francisco Haces, has big plans and has moved forward a great deal since the last edition of this book. He intends to build an exclusive subdivision for retirees in a remote, ecological paradise.

Since the last edition, a new road has been built to the resort and financing talks are underway. I would be very surprised if this doesn't take off in the next year or two.

The plan is to have small houses and to offer complete pampering—from catered meals with a dietary consultant on the premises, to an ecological golf course, to birding trips, and scads of activities. I thought that the words "ecological" and "golf course" went together about as well as "army" and "intelligence," but Francisco explained that there is sufficient rainfall and morning dew there to allow him to build a course without having to waste water keeping it up. Okay. If he is able to pull it off, this will be a great place to winter. I have high hopes for his venture, but one never knows. It is at least a year, and maybe two, from fruition.

To check on the progress of this venture, e-mail me. For pictures of the area, go to www.mexicomike.com and click on the "Cool Places" button. From there, you can also make reservations to visit El Paraiso. At the moment, it's a unique resort that has been in operation for several years. The deepest cenote in the world is nearby, birding is stupendous, and it is just a wonderful laidback area to forget your cares. Fishing is great for bass, snook, and tarpon in the river and trout, redfish, snapper, skipjack, pompano, and flounder in the Gulf. **The beach is unspoiled, and the atmosphere is tranquil.**

CONS

It is really isolated. **Once you are there, you are there.** Right now, it is ideal for those who want to get away from it all. Once Francisco gets his retirement community going, there will be activities and social life, but it will be a small community.

IN-BETWEENS

You will either love it or hate it.

A Story about El Paraiso (the resort): "Paradise" is overused in travel writing, yet people identify with it, so I'll join the rank of hacks and use it. Define it as you wish. For some, paradise would be a packed disco on a Cancún Saturday night and a pocketful of money and gold cards. For those people, El Paraiso Resort in nearby Tamaulipas will not do.

If your idea of paradise is a quiet, comfortable, romantic place, set in a unique river landscape with respect for the ecology, miles of absolutely deserted beaches, and thousands of birds (including wild parrots that fly over your room twice a day), then this might be your sort of retreat.

El Paraiso Resort is near Barra del Tordo, Tamaulipas, which is only five hours south of the Texas/Mexico border at McAllen or Brownsville. **It can be a romantic getaway, a naturalist's dream vacation, the spot for your next spiritual retreat, or a good location for your company's board meeting or small convention.** If you are a fisherman, it is very close to heaven.

El Paraiso is an ecological cornucopia. Francisco Haces realized that a few years ago and started billing his lodge as an ecotourism place. To be sure, you can still fish in the river in front of the lodge, or in the Gulf of Mexico only minutes away, but catch-and-release is encouraged. I have gotten to know Francisco as a friend over the years and he (like a lot of us) has gone through a transformation in the past few years.

This is a quiet, romantic getaway spot. Imagine being ferried to your weekend hideaway in a motorboat. Once you are there, the atmosphere, particularly at night, is that of being in a remote tropical paradise. The *cabañas* and grounds are illuminated with a soft yellow light.

The lodge is set high on a bluff overlooking the river. On the way to your room, you'll pass a sparkling swimming pool and several neatly furnished individual *cabañas* with ornamental thatched roofs, air-conditioning, and tiled bathrooms. There's a family room where meals are served and guests can gather to chat. To me, the advantage of a place such as this over a high-rise resort is that you can socialize. Kiko will be around to greet you and make sure that your stay is a pleasant one.

Naturalists will love the fact that they can see dozens of sea- and shore-birds, including osprey, hawks, egrets, eagles, cranes, and parrots. In the winter, ducks abound. Fish, including tarpon, snook, and bass, jump in the river and its estuaries.

During the day, you can take advantage of boat rides down lagoons to catch glimpses of dozens of species of birds or to explore the estuaries. Farther down the river is the Gulf of Mexico, with miles and miles of truly deserted white-sand beaches. Imagine you and your sweetie frolicking on fine white sand with miles of pounding surf and driftwood your only companions. The endangered Kemp's ridley sea turtles use the area to nest, up the coast a ways.

The deepest cenote in the world.

Nearby, back toward the highway, is the deepest cenote (spring-fed pool or well) in the earth (1,070 feet deep). It is the deepest on Earth—yes, deeper than the ones in the Yucatan (the deepest of which are about fifty feet). Two divers from the University of Texas discovered its bottom, but one died of the bends on the way up. The survivor returned recently to finish his exploration. The water is as clear and turquoise as any cenote in the Yucatan. There is also a sulfur hot spring and a cave in the neighborhood. To get there from McAllen or Brownsville, drive down Hwy. 97 or 101 to Hwy. 180 and keep going south toward Tampico. At Aldama, take a left toward the Gulf of Mexico and drive forty-one kilometers. The scenery changes dramatically from the flatland you've just traversed to gentle rolling hills. Ignore the Coca Cola sign at kilometer 37. At kilometer 41, you'll see a Coca Cola sign that reads "El Paraiso." Turn left again and go through a pasture. (Yes, you can drive it in the family sedan, unless it has rained recently. Watch that cow!) The parking lot is a nice cleared field shaded by 100-year-old trees. There's twenty-four-hour security. You can also drive directly here now, but the instructions are a bit convoluted, so call or e-mail me.

You can also fly to Tampico. Kiko can arrange to meet you at the airport and take you to El Paraíso. Rates are reasonable and include three excellent meals daily. You really have to make a reservation; visit www.mexicomike.com, click on "Cool Places," and e-mail me. There are special rates for groups.

TECOLUTLA, VERACRUZ

Ambiente: Mexico of yesteryear. Small fishing village, few foreigners.

Climate: Winters: upper 70s days, mid-60s nights (occasional nights in the 50s or even 40s). Summers: 85–90 days, 70–75 nights. During the rainy (and hurricane) season (May to Sept.), there are severe storms. Subject to hurricanes.

Altitude: Sea level

Population: 2,000

Housing: Limited

Homes (buy): $15,000–$120,000, with some nice ones in the $40,000–$50,000 range. The low-end ones are rare and generally are simple Mexican homes. The higher-end ones are nearer the beach.

Condos (buy): N/A

Rentals: $150–$350 (Hard to find)

RV space (sometimes with trailer): There are a few RV parks, but no lots for sale.

Medical Care: Barely adequate

Area Code: 766

PROS

Tecolutla is the largest town in this collection of small communities along the Gulf of Mexico between Tecolutla and Cardel, just north of Veracruz. Tecolutla is on the beach and has almost–white sand (there's a tinge of volcanic gray to it) beaches with palm trees almost to the water's edge. The seafood is excellent and the fishing very good. **There is a French influence, as it was here that many of the deserters from the French army hid out after their rout at Puebla.** Although the food is not really French, it has a basis in French cuisine so that it is unique in Mexico. You won't meet any French speakers here, but there is French blood in the veins of many of the residents. Some of them have blue eyes!

Housing is inexpensive, if hard to come by. There are some developments along the beach between Casitas and Nautla, with condos and homes, but Tecolutla itself has only modest homes with a few rentals. For those drawn to these laid-back communities, it will be worth the effort to find an abode here. The people are friendly, the weather is fine during the winter (except for those few times when a norther—Texan talk for a cold front—blows in and the temperature drops to the forties), and everything is reasonably priced.

There are RV parks, but they do not offer a lot of services. If you are looking for a place to get away from it all, this is it.

CONS

This is really off the beaten track. There will be little English spoken. The very smallness of the communities may get to you after a while. There are few foreigners, except a few RVers during the winter. Medical care is barely adequate, though there is a good doctor in Casitas, a friend of mine, who has a traveling clinic and goes into the smaller communities to help those less fortunate than himself. If you feel generous (or sick), look up Dr. Silvero Herrera in Casitas. **For serious emergencies, you'll have to go to Veracruz or back to the States.**

IN-BETWEENS

The scenery is tropical. You could settle here and write or paint to your heart's content. If you are self-sufficient, or if your budget is slim, this could be your place. **If isolation doesn't appeal to you, then you had better look elsewhere.**

VERACRUZ, VERACRUZ

Ambiente: Sultry, sophisticated. It is very similar to New Orleans with music, dancing, parades, and Mardi Gras (*Carnaval*). Few foreigners and not much English spoken.

Climate: Winters: upper 70s days, mid-60s nights (occasional nights in the 50s). Summers: 80–90 days, 70–75 nights. During the rainy (and hurricane) season (May to Sept.), there are severe storms. Seldom gets hit by hurricanes.

Altitude: Sea level

Population: 593,000 (official of the metro area, though estimates are about 700,000. The city is 412,000.)

Housing: Not as inexpensive as it should be, thanks to weekend home owners from Mexico City.

Homes (buy): $40,000–$750,000

Condos (buy): $30,000–$150,000

Rentals: $400–$1,500 ($600 here will get you a decent apartment.)

RV space: N/A

Medical Care: Remarkably good. Plenty of doctors and specialists.

Area Code: 229

PROS

On old maps and in old texts you'll see this spelled as two words, "Vera Cruz." Today, that would be incorrect and the combination of the two words is correct.

  This is a lively place. There is always music in the square, from marimba bands to navy band concerts. The *danzon* is a big weekly street dance. **The**

seafood is the best in Mexico. The weather is generally warm in the winter, except for those few times when a *norteño* makes it this far south and drops the temperatures to the upper forties. These spells last only a day or two and then warm weather returns.

Housing is comparatively reasonable and varies from condominiums to apartments to houses. Because this is Mexico's most important port, it has the flavor of a world-class seaport. **The Carnaval is the best in Mexico, and some prefer it to the one in New Orleans.**

There is a strong Lebanese community, with social clubs and restaurants. Medical care is very good, and Mexico City is only a few hours away. *Mexico Health and Safety Travel Guide* lists one hospital with a 4.5/5 rating: the Hospital de la Sociedad Española de Beneficencia de Veracruz (16 de Septiembre #955, between Escobedo and Abasola; Phone: 01-52-229-932-0021, Emergency Phone: 01-52-229-931-4000; Fax: 01-52-229-932-1100). There is an American consular agent.

CONS
There is no organized foreign community and retirees won't find many *paisanos* to socialize with. **The weather is humid all the time. The beach is not very pretty, being volcanic gray sand.** There is one RV park, but it is no more than a place to park (on the beach, though) with some limited electricity and no dump station. **It is a noisy city.** In fact, its very character exudes noisiness, unless you are in one of the elegant suburbs. **The traffic is bad.**

IN-BETWEENS
This is a place for people who like a lot of excitement. **The atmosphere is sultry and decadent.** For someone who wants to spend some lively time in an exciting Mexican cosmopolitan community, it could be just the ticket. For someone who wants to retire, it might be a little too intense. **If you like New Orleans, you'll like Veracruz, as the atmosphere is very similar.**

JALAPA (ALSO SPELLED XALAPA), VERACRUZ

Ambiente: Sophisticated, conservative, very much "old" Mexico. Few foreigners and not much English spoken.

Climate: Winters: low 50s days, mid-60s nights (occasional nights in the 40s). Summers: mid-60s to upper 70s days, low 60s–70s nights.

Altitude: 3,569 feet

Population: 373,000 (official. Estimates are about 600,000 for the city and 1,000,000 for the metro area.)

Housing: Reasonable

Homes (buy): $30,000–$500,000, with $120,000–$160,000 being about average. There is buying pressure from rich residents from Mexico City moving to the area. The closer you are to downtown, the more expensive the house.

Condos (buy): N/A (There are several new and large condo projects being built, so this will change.)

Rentals: $200–$1,000 ($450 here will get you a decent apartment.) Apartments closer to downtown are more expensive.

RV space: N/A

Medical Care: Remarkably good. Plenty of doctors and specialists, though *Mexico Health and Safety Travel Guide* lists no facilities and disagrees with me. Locals say that CEM (Centro de Especialidades Medicas) and other hospitals/clinics provide good to excellent attention.

Area Code: 228

PROS

First, let me clarify the "X" versus the "J" controversy for spelling the city. In the original Nahuatl, or the language spoken by the Aztecs, it has an "X." The Spaniards had different ways of pronouncing "X," so in this case, the "X" became a "Hah," resulting in the town being called "Hah lap ah." "H" exists in Spanish, but seems to be usually silent. For example "Hay sus" is spelled "Jesus." So the "X," pronounced as an "H," became a "J." Are you with me so far? So some scribes wrote the name of the town with a "J." When the Spaniards got to the Mayan areas, they pretty much just used a "shhh" sound for "X," so Xcalac is pronounced "Eshhh ca lak." "Xcaret" is pronounced "Shh car et." In official Mexican documents, you'll see the "X" used, but around town it is a toss-up. The phone directory lists it with a "J."

Jalapa has always been a cultural center. Sometimes you'll hear it referred to as the "Athens of Veracruz." Locals are called *Jalapeños.* There are three universities, several art galleries, and an anthropology museum that some say is even better than the one in Mexico City. Here's a little story about the museum. Originally, it was larger than the one in Mexico City. When the Mexico City powers-that-be found out, they enlarged theirs. Size does matter, at least to archeologists. There are also science museums and a symphony that is considered world-class.

To learn more about the area, there is no better source than www.xalapa. net. If you're thinking of moving here or taking an extended vacation, Roy B. Dudley, a thirty-two-year resident of Jalapa, "*El Gringo Jalapeño,*" can help you tremendously. Besides being a crackerjack photographer, he offers orientation seminars for living in the area, details of which can be found at www.xalapa. net/roy. If you'd like to get married in Jalapa, with the wedding in a beautiful colonial church and the reception in a romantic ex-hacienda, he can also set the whole thing up and take the pictures to boot. He also has some very nice, reasonably priced apartments for rent. His e-mail is mail.xal.megared.net.mx.

Since it's surrounded by coffee-growing country, you'll find lots of coffee shops to while away your time. **Because of the cultured and educated popula-tion, you'll find interesting people to talk to.**

The weather is much cooler than Veracruz on the coast, and most people find in invigorating. The city is large but traffic isn't as bad as it should be, and it still has an old-world feel to it. In my opinion, even downtown is quieter than Veracruz.

CONS

There isn't much of an expatriate community so unless you speak Spanish, you could feel isolated here. **While it's relatively inexpensive, it's not a cheap city.** There are so many things to do here that I can't really think of many cons. It's either your kind of place or not. Stay here for a few weeks before you make up your mind.

IN-BETWEENS

If intellectual pursuits attract you, you'll feel right at home. Particularly if you speak Spanish, you'll soon find yourself with a crowd of like-minded people. If you're looking for a community of people who discuss art and ideas, you will love it here. If you're looking for a community of retirees who sit around and drink and talk about old times, you'd best keep looking.

Chapter 11

GENERAL INFORMATION
AA AND OTHER TWELVE-STEP PROGRAMS

Staying Sober in Mexico — Pitfalls and Solutions

It's ludicrous to include a chapter such as this and pretend not to be a recovering drunk. If breaking my anonymity keeps one of my brothers or sisters sober, it's a good thing. When I first moved to Mexico with a little more than a year of sobriety, I would have loved to have seen something similar to this. We all owe a debt of gratitude to the editors at the publishing house printing this book. When I moved from self-publishing it to having this company do it, keeping this chapter was one of my conditions. Come to think of it, it was my only condition. That's how strongly I feel about it. Buy more of their books!

You'll find AA throughout Mexico, even in small towns. Spanish for "meeting" is *reunión* or *sesión*. NA has a presence in the larger towns. Alanon is almost everywhere. OA, SALA, and other programs are less likely to be found outside major cities or towns with lots of gringos. AA is very visible.

Anonymity—The Mexican Way

Look for the AA symbol inside a triangle and a circle, usually on a blue background, jutting out from buildings. Meetings are usually at 8 or 8:30 P.M., in Spanish. **Even if you don't speak Spanish, you'll be welcomed as an honored guest and often asked to speak.** This is true all over the world. I have been to meetings in Cuba (try finding a meeting there!), Europe, and England (where they speak a foreign language, vaguely similar to English) and have always been welcome. Come to think of it, these are the only places where I can count on being welcome. Go ahead. It will do you good. Meetings last an hour and a half and there are usually refreshments, brought to you by a member while you remain seated. The coffee is likely to be sugared. Birthdays are celebrated as if you are in the States, except you might get tamales instead of cake, or both. Have a ball.

My first ex, no wait, my second ex-wife didn't speak a lick of Spanish, yet she got to really enjoy the Spanish meetings. Her first meeting was held over a movie theater in Taxco. We expounded (what else do drunks do?) over the sounds of, I think, *Dirty Harry* in Spanish. "And I am so grateful for … (*"Make my day, punk … Blam! Blam!"*)." It was a hoot.

One time I was in a tiny town on the West Coast and needed a mechanic. It was Sunday morning. I asked why he was the only one open. He said, "Because I'm the only one sober. I'm *un AA* (pronounced *doublay ah*)." My truck and I stayed a week in that town and went to all the meetings. I made a lot of friends.

Don't be afraid to mention that you're a friend of Bill W. to another gringo. It saved my life twice. Once I was on the beach in Puerto Escondido and mentioned it to a woman about the time I was really shaky. She brightened up and said, "Oh, I'm traveling with a sober companion. Want to have a meeting?" A similar situation happened while waiting in line for the ferry to Cabo. What have you got to lose? Better yet, what have you got to gain?

Mexicans are more likely to identify themselves as *alcohólicos, AAs (doublay ahs)*. Asking if they are *"un amigo de Guilermo W."* seldom works. Just say you're a *doublay ah* and see what happens. If he's not, he won't understand anyway.

English-Speaking Meetings

You'll find English-speaking meetings in most towns with a large gringo presence. Take your International Directory and check my Web site for possible updates. In the last edition I included meetings, times, and locations. They're more likely to change than we are, so I'm only putting them on the site now. But please, contribute changes. The address is www.mexicomike.com/aa/aa.htm, or just click "Living/Travel" from the menu at left, then "AA Meetings."

I have to be rigorously honest and admit that my directory gets out-of-date too. Just as everywhere else in the world, locations change, so if a meeting is no longer where I said it was, you have two courses of action (aside from giving up and giving in). Believe me, looking for a meeting is often a better choice than going back to your hotel where the "Chug-tequila-till-you-barf" contest is going on. The first option is to check the local English-language newspaper if there is one. The second option is to find a Spanish meeting and ask.

Moving Choices

Some of us will base our decision on which town to move to on the availability of meetings. Perhaps this list will grow, but currently your best choices (in no particular order) are: San Miguel de Allende, Lake Chapala, Guadalajara (fewer), Puerto Vallarta, Mazatlán, Oaxaca, Mexico City, Kino Bay (winter), San Carlos, Puerto Peñasco, most of the Baja, Cancún, Cozumel, Playa del Carmen, some other towns on the Mayan Riviera, Puerto Escondido (winter), Acapulco, and Ixtapa/Zihuatanejo. Hopefully, there will be others I don't know about.

Web Sources

Mexico City AA has a Web site, www.aamexico.org. If you click on their "Additional Recovery Sources," you might find meetings around the country as it grows. Cancún sort of has a Web site, though it wasn't up yet when I wrote this, www.aa-cancun.com. Ixtapa/Zihuatenejo: www.zihua-ixtapa.com/zihua/aa.html. There's a complete listing of Spanish meetings at www.aa.org.mx. And, of course, my site has an occasionally updated list with contact numbers for the whole country, www.mexicomike.com/aa/aa.htm. Oaxaca may have a schedule in the classifieds, www.oaxacatimes.com/html/classifieds.html.

Go to Any Lengths

One night I was in San Miguel de Allende and the English-language meeting (published in the English-language newspaper) had moved. I was ready to get drunk with my boozing traveling companion, whom I'd left at the hotel bar. It was a close call. I wandered the late-night streets of town, bemoaning my fate. "Poor me, poor me, pour me a tequila." For some reason, just before I gave up and went to the bar, I looked up and I saw the familiar triangle in a circle. I was in front of a Mexican AA club. The meeting was over, but the guys there could see that I was in trouble. Six of us piled into a Volkswagen and went roaring down the midnight streets into a *barrio* that I'm sure no tourist had ever been to. That was around twenty years ago.

There I was, in a car of strangers who spoke no English (my Spanish was poor then), going to God knew where. A bar full of happy (?) Americans seemed a lot more inviting. Oh, well. They took me to a midnight meeting. Although I didn't understand a word they said, I felt the companionship and caring that is universal. Those guys saved my life. So if a meeting has moved, don't use that as an excuse to get drunk. Get off the pity pot and find a Mexican meeting. Then let me know about any changes.

Meetings Are Different

For Alanon and NA, etc., an AA meeting place will be able to direct you to one, maybe. **NA is not as "popular." You'll be welcome at an AA meeting.** There are two different types of AA in Mexico. One is *"Grupo de Viente Cuatro Horas"* (twenty-four-hour group). These are more similar to institutional settings and the message here is hard core, "put-the-plug-in-the-jug"-type. If you see *"24 Horas"* on the sign, you'll know. I don't like them as well as "regular" meetings, but hey, a meeting in need is a meeting indeed.

The other is more similar to what you are used to. Be prepared for one-and-one-half-hour-long meetings, with long orations and lots of slang. They are very emotional. You'll be asked to say something. Do your best and take care of yourself. It doesn't matter if anybody understands you and you have to speak in English. The language of the heart is universal. **If the above fails and you can't find a meeting, try putting up signs in your hotel and tell others about a meeting in your room. Then stay there.** Read the Big Book (of course you brought it, right?).

The Myth of Refusing a Drink

While we're on the subject of drinking (duh! This is a chapter on AA meetings), forget the myth that it is a shooting offense to refuse a drink offered by a Mexican. You can refuse to do anything you want if you do it politely. I've never been shot in sobriety. Many times Mexicans are only offering to share something with you because they are being polite. They would never expect you to do something that would cause you harm. **If you simply say, *"No gracias, no bebo cerveza (tequila, ron,* etc., or simply *alcohól), pero quisiera un refresco,"* you'll probably get a soft drink and no one will be offended—except a drunk and you don't need to be around him anyway.** I have left business parties when the drunks got pushy; I never lost any business. Speaking of business parties, tip the waiter to keep you supplied with *agua mineral o refrescos.* Waiters will constantly be around to give you booze, but get lost when trying to find a Coke.

If someone insists that you have a drink, be as polite as possible, and just as insistent. Plead illness, medication, or whatever you are comfortable with. Saying *"soy alérgico a alcohól"* sometimes does the trick, but saying you are an alcoholic *(alcohólico)* may elicit a blank stare. *If all else fails, get up and walk away.* Offending a drunk does not rank as a punishable offense in any country, and you have to remember what's really important.

Slippery Slopes

Be especially careful ordering tonic water, or *agua quina*, in bars or restaurants. You'll often end up with gin and tonic because the waiter thought you didn't speak Spanish well enough to know what you wanted. It's happened to me. Stick with *agua mineral,* or Coke or 7-Up, or a local soft drink. There are some great local ones. Toni-Col on the West Coast, especially near Mazatlán, is one of the best. It does have caffeine, so if you are trying to avoid that, you'd best avoid Toni-Col, but darn, it is good. It's similar to vanilla Coke. Of course, I have heard of drinkers who ordered J&B and soda and got Jim Beam and Coke.

When asking if a dish has alcohol in it, be sure to ask if it has wine too. **For some reason, wine is not considered alcohol by waiters.** Often they will say "Oh, no, there is no alcohol, only a little wine." I subscribe to the school that it does not cook out. Even if you don't believe that to be true at home, believe it in Mexico. Trust me.

Ah, vanilla! One of the great bargains in Mexico is the quart bottles of vanilla. Be sure to check the label for the alcohol content. Some are 80 percent alcohol with a smidgen of vanilla. I've settled on the brand *La Vencedora*, which has 8 percent alcohol and the rest is pure vanilla.

It's rare, but I have had Amaretto poured over flan, the great dessert. My dog sniffs everything before he eats or drinks it; I follow his lead. Always use the sniff test before eating anything with a sauce on it. If you accidentally imbibe something with booze, spit it out and don't worry about it. It happens to the best of us. Just don't take a second swig or taste, and forget about it. I obsessed about a situation such as that once, when given some gin in my tonic water. I called another AA. She told me to shut up and forget it. Damn, she was good.

The only events I avoid are party boats that cruise around the bays of everywhere with a bay. I hate being a captive with a bunch of drunks. Maybe you can handle it. It's up to you, but bring something to drink because they never stock enough nonalcoholic beverages.

Fancy Coffee is Boozy Coffee

Coffees with fancy names such as "Sexy, Spanish, German, or Lithuanian" (just kidding about the last one) are suspect. If it costs more than plain coffee (*Americano* or *negro* or *cafe con leche*), then it's a booze drink.

That 10,000-Pound Phone

Oh, you did bring several phone numbers of sober buddies right? And you did get the phone numbers of everyone at the meetings you attended in Mexico, right? Of course you did. Now, if you were a clutterer (my other group is Clutterless Recovery Groups, www.clutterless.org), you probably lost them, so keep a notebook with you at all times, and don't just scribble things on pieces of paper. If nothing else, you can always send me an e-mail (mexico mikenelson23@mexicomike.com). I don't promise I'll answer promptly, but it'll make you feel good to "talk" to another alkie. Talk it out, don't drink it out.

If you have an AA medallion or ring and wear it, you'll be surprised at the people you'll meet. If we ever meet in person, I'll tell you a story that was related to me about how that saved on AA's life. You never know.

That's all the sobriety wisdom I have, and I hope it helps at least one person. **The main thing to remember is that you are not alone even in Mexico and that you can still have a great trip as a traveler and a great life if you move to Mexico and not lose your program.**

Here's wishing all my *hermanos y hermanos* twenty-four hours *de sobriedad.*

—"Mexico" Mike

U.S. AND CANADIAN CONSULATES

U.S. CONSULATES

Note: When calling from outside Mexico, all of the following phone numbers have 011-52 as prefixes.

- Consulate Mexico, D.F.: Embassy of the United States, Paseo de la Reforma 305, Colonia Cuauhtemoc, Mexico, D.F. 06500; Phone: 555-080-2000; Fax: 555-525-5040; E-mail: ccs@usembassy.net.mx; Web site: www.usembassy-mexico.gov/.
- Consulate Nuevo Laredo: Allende 3330, Col. Jardín, Nuevo Laredo, Tamps. 88260; Phone: 867-714-0512; Fax: 867-714-7984. Office Hours: 8 A.M.–12:30 P.M., 1:30–5 P.M. Principal Officer: Michael L. Yoder.
- Consular agent in Acapulco (an extension of the embassy in Mexico City): Hotel Acapulco Continental, Costera M. Alemán 121, Office 14, Acapulco, Gro. 39670; Office: 744-469-0556; Phone/Fax: 744-484-0300; E-mail: consular@prodigy.net.mx. Consular agent: Alexander Richards.
- Consular agent in Cabo San Lucas (an extension of the consulate in Tijuana): Blvd. Marina Local C-4, Plaza Nautica, Centro, Cabo San Lucas, B.C.S. 23410; Phone: 624-143-3566; Fax: 624-143-6750; E-mail: usconsulcabo@hotmail.com. Consular agent: Michael J. Houston.
- Consular agent in Cancún (an extension of the consulate in Mérida): Segundo Nivel No. 320-323, Plaza Caracol Dos, Blvd. Kukulkan, Zona Hotelera (Hotel Zone), Cancún, Q.R. 77500; Phone: 998-883-0272; Fax: 998-883-1373; Mailing Address: Apdo. Postal 862, Cancún, Q.R.; E-mail: uscons@prodigy.net.mx, Lynnette@usconscancun.com. Consular agent: Lynnette Belt.
- Consular agent in Cozumel (an extension of the consulate in Mérida): Offices 8 and 9 (second floor, taking the stairs to the right), "Villa Mar" Mall (located inside Juarez Park, which is another name for the Main Square, or "Plaza Principal"), between Melgar and 5th. Ave., Cozumel, Q.R. 77600; Mailing Address: Av. 35 Norte No. 650 (between 12 bis and 14 Norte), Cozumel, Q.R. 77622; Phone: 987-872-4574 or 872-4485; Fax: 987-872-2339; E-mail: usgov@cozumel.net, usca@cozumel.net. Consular agent: Anne R. Harris.
- Consular agent in Ixtapa (an extension of the embassy in Mexico City): Hotel Fontan Blvd. Ixtapa s/n, 40880 Ixtapa, Gro.; Mailing Address: Apdo. Postal 169, Zihuatanejo, Gro. 40880; Phone: 755-553-2100; Fax: 755-553-2772; E-mail: liz@lizwilliams.org, lizwilliams@diplomats.com. Consular agent: Elizabeth Williams.
- Consular agent in Mazatlán (an extension of the consulate in Hermosillo): Hotel Playa Mazatlán, Playa Gaviotas No. 202, Zona Dorada, Mazatlán, Sin. 82110; Phone/Fax: 669-916-5889; E-mail: mazagent@mzt.megared.net.mx. Consular agent: Patti Fletcher.
- Consular agent in Oaxaca (an extension of the embassy in Mexico City):

Macedonio Alcala No. 407, Office 20, Oax., Oax. 68000; Phone: 951-514-3054 or 516-2853; Fax: 951- 516-2701; E-mail: conagent@prodigy. net.mx. Consular agent: Mark A. Leyes.

■ Consular agent in Piedras Negras (an extension of the consulate in Nuevo Laredo), Prol. General Cepeda No. 1900, Fraccionamiento Privada Blanca, Piedras Negras, Coah., 26700; Phone: 878-795-1986, 795-1987, 795-1988; U.S. Phone: 830-773-9231; E-mail: usconsularagencypn @hotmail.com. Consular agent: Dina L. O'Brien.

■ Consular agent in Reynosa, Tamps. (an extension of the consulate in Matamoros): Calle Monterrey No. 390 (corner with Sinaloa), Col. Rodríguez, Reynosa, Tamps., 88630; Phone: 899-923-9331, 923-8878, or 923-9245; E-mail: usconsularagent@hotmail.com. Consular agent: Roberto Rodríguez.

■ Consular agent in San Luis Potosí (an extension of the consulate in Monterrey): Edificio "Las Terrazas," Ave. Venustiano Carranza 2076-41, Col. Polanco, San Luis Potosi, S.L.P., 78220; Phone: 444-811-7802 or 444-811-7803; Fax: 444-811-7803; E-mail: usconsulslp@yahoo.com. Consular agent: Carolyn H. Lazaro.

■ Consular agent in San Miguel de Allende (an extension of the embassy in Mexico City): Dr. Hernandez Macías No. 72, San Miguel de Allende, Gto.; Mailing Address: Apdo. Postal 328, San Miguel de Allende, Gto.; Phone: 415-152-2357; Fax: 415-152-1588; E-mail: coromar@ unisono.net.mx. Consular agent: Philip J. Maher, Rtd. Col.

CANADIAN CONSULATES

■ Consular agent in Mazatlán: United Mexican States, Mailing Address: Consulate of Canada, P.O. Box 614, Mazatlán, Sin., 82110; Street Address: Consulate of Canada, Hotel Playa Mazatlán, Ave. Playa Gaviotas 202, Local 9, Zona Dorado, Mazatlán, Sin., 82110; Phone: 669-913-7320; Fax: 669-914-6655; E-mail: mazatlan@canada.org.mx. Territory includes the state of Sinaloa. Consular agent: Honorary Consul Ms. D. Jassan.

■ Consular agent in Guadalajara: United Mexican States, Consulate of Canada, Hotel Fiesta Americana, Local 31, Aurelio Aceves No. 225, Vallarta Poniente, Guadalajara, Jal., 44100; Phone: 33-615-6215/6270/6266 or 33-616-5642; Commercial Main: 33-616-5642; Fax: 33-615-8665; Web site: www.canada. org.mx; E-mail: gjara@dfait-maeci.gc.ca. Territory includes the state of Jalisco except coastal area and Puerto Vallarta. Consul and Trade Commissioner: Ms. J. Lemay.

■ Consulate in Puerto Vallarta: United Mexican States, Consulate of Canada, Edificio Obelisco Local 108, Avenida Francisco Medina Ascencio No. 1951, Zona Hotelera Las Glorias, Puerto Vallarta, Jal., 48300; Phone: 322-293-0098, 322-293-0099; Fax: 322-293-2894; E-mail: vallarta@canada.org.mx. Territory includes Puerto Vallarta, Jalisco Coast, the states of Colima, and Nayarit. Consular agent: Honorary Consul Ms. L. Benoit.

■ Consulate in Mexico, D.F.: United Mexican States, The Canadian Embassy,

Calle Schiller no. 529, Colonia Bosque de Chapultepec, Polanco, Mexico, D.F., 11580; Mailing Address: The Canadian Embassy, Apartado Postal 105-05, Mexico, D.F., 11580; Phone: 55-57-24-79-00; Commercial: 55-57-24-79-82; Consular: 55 57-24-79-43; Immigration: 55 57-24-79-83; Political: 55-57-24-79-85; Public Affairs: 55-57-24-79-81; Emergency (twenty-four hours, consular only, no visa or trade info.): 800-706-29-00; Fax (Administration): 55-57-24-79-80; Web site: www.canada.org.mx; E-mail: embassy@canada.org.mx.

- Consulate in Monterrey: United Mexican States, Consulate of Canada, Edificio Kalos, Piso C-1, Local 108-A, Zaragoza 1300 Sur y Constitution, Monterrey, N.L., 64000; Mailing Address: Consulate of Canada, 1300 de la Calle Zaragoza, Monterrey, N.L., 64000; Phone: 818-344-2753/2906/2961/3200/9045 or 818-345-9105/9165; Commercial Main: 818-344-2753; Fax: 818-344-3048; E-mail: mntry@dfait-maeci.gc.ca or Monterrey@canada.org.mx. Territory includes the states of Coahuila, Neuvo Leon, and Tamaulipas Consul. Trade Commissioner: Mr. R. Langlois.

- Consulate in Oaxaca: United Mexican States, Consulate of Canada, Pino Suarez No. 700, Interior 11B, Plaza Brena, Colonia Centro, Oaxaca, Oax., 68000; Mailing Address: Consulate of Canada, Apartado Postal 29, Sucursal C. Colonia Reforma, Oaxaca, Oax., 68050; Phone: 951-513-3777; Fax: 951-515-2147; E-mail: oaxaca@canada.org.mx. Territory includes the states of Oaxaca and Chiapas. Consular agent: Honorary Consul Ms. F. May.

- Consulate in Cancún: United Mexican States, Consulate of Canada, Plaza Caracol II, 3er piso, Local 330, Boulevard Kukulcan Km 8.5 Zona Hotelera, Cancún, Q.R., 77500; Phone: 998-883-3360/883-3361; Commercial Main: 011-52-98-84-3716; Fax: 998-883-3232; E-mail: cancun@canada.org.mx. Territory includes the states of Campeche, Yucatan, and Quintana Roo. Consular agent: Honorary Consul Mr. D. Lavoie.

- Consulate in Acapulco: United Mexican States, Consulate of Canada, Centro Comercial Marbella, Local 23, esq. Prolongacion Farallon S/N, esq. Miguel Aleman, Acapulco, Gro., 39690; Mailing Address: Consulate of Canada, Centro Comercial Marbella, Local 23, esq. Prolongacion Farallon S/Nesq. Miguel Aleman, Acapulco, Gro., 39690; Phone: 744-484-1305 or 481-1349; Fax: 744-484-1306; E-mail: acapulco@canada.org.mx. Territory includes the states of Guerrero and Michoacan. Consular agent: Honorary Consul Ms. D. Vandal.

- Consulate in Tijuana: United Mexican States, Consulate of Canada, German Gedovius 10411-101, Condominio del Parque, Zona Rio, Tijuana, B.C.N., 22320; Phone: 664-684-0461; Fax: 664-684-0301; E-mail: tijuana@canada.org.mx. Territory includes the states of Baja California and Sonora. Consular agent: Honorary Consul Mr. R. Encinas.

- Consulate in San José del Cabo: United Mexican States, Consulate of Canada, Plaza José Green, Local 9, Boulevard Mijares s/n, Colonia Centro, San José del Cabo, B.C.S.; Mailing Address: Consulate of Canada, P.O. Box 23400, San José del Cabo, B.C.S.; Phone: 624-142-4333; Fax: 624-142-4262. Consular agent: Honorary Consul Ms. Dillman.

RECOMMENDED READING

BOOKS BY "MEXICO" MIKE

All of Mike's books can be ordered from www.mexicomike.com, by calling 888-234-3452, or by sending a check or money order (in U.S. funds), payable to Mike Nelson, 508 N. 10th St., Ste. C-10, McAllen, TX 78501-9423. Please add $5.50 for shipping and handling.

"Mexico" Mike's Bastante Español, Modismos Y Slang (with enough slang to make you sound cool) (published 2005). It's available online at www.mexico mike.com as an e-book. Just click "Books." A printed edition is also available. I'm not a linguist, cunning or otherwise. I've taken the most common mistakes (mostly learned the hard way) and given you easy ways to avoid them. There's a lot of humor in this little book. For instance, don't confuse *sopa*, soup, with *jabón*, soap, just because they sound similar in English. I did and it was hilarious. $12.95, e-book. $17.95, printed.

Instead of boring you with a lot of grammar rules and phrases such as "The red vase is on the table," or "Your mother makes good tortillas," I'll give you the common questions you'll get, such as "Where are you going?" from the drug police. I've found that confusing "Where are you going?", *¿A donde va?*, with "Where are you coming from?", "*¿De donde viene?*", seems to upset them. If you're heading south and you say you're going north, they either think you are crazy, lost, or lying. Cops being cops, they usually opt for the latter. The best answer to *"¿De donde viene?"* is *Estados Unidos* (or *Canadá*). If they tack an *"anoche"* on the end, it means, "Where were you last night?" Try not to smile lustily and look at your traveling companion.

Knowing what others are saying is more important to foreigners than what they're going to say. Naturally, I'll cover every driving situation you'll run into (or hopefully won't run into). I will keep you out of trouble. For instance, instead of asking a butcher if he has *huevos*, you'd better ask him for *blanquillas*, if you don't want to offend his manhood. I found this out the hard way since all my Spanish books had only *huevos* for eggs. *Chichis* is an impolite way to refer to a woman's breasts (among others). Use *senos*, which is rather clinical, or, more commonly, *pechos* instead. The polite way to say "penis" is *pene*. Naturally, I include the not-so-polite words for everything.

More Than a Dozen of Mexico's Hidden Jewels (revised 2005) is a collection of stories for the armchair adventurer about places that are truly unique. Journey to Xilitla, where an eccentric Englishman who was a friend of Dali, Picasso, and Bogart built a surrealistic sculpture garden in an orchid jungle. Visit the Zone of Silence, where UFOs are reputed to land. Relax at El Paraiso, an ecological resort near the Texas border with unspoiled beaches where the endangered Kemp's ridley sea turtles lay their eggs and flocks of parrots commute over your *cabaña*. Discover the little-known but exotic Gulf Coast and its Emerald Coast. Find an old-growth forest an hour from Mexico City. Many have used this book as a planning guide for their trips. $9.95.

Spas and Hot Springs of Mexico, Second Edition (published 1998). The book is old, but the hot springs information is still accurate. The spas all still exist, but updated prices and reviews are at www.spagetaway.com. The travel essay stories are timeless. If you love to explore hot springs, Mexico has more than 1,000. The major ones are covered (including driving directions, chemical water composition). Besides reviews of still existing spas (most of which are still very good), it has adventure travel stories and love stories. When it comes to hot springs, there is nothing else to compare it to. *Mexico File* said *Spas and Hot Springs of Mexico* is "the Michelin and Zagat of the upscale, spiritual." *New Orleans Times-Picayune* said, "Nelson gives a synopsis of the spirit of the place." $12.95.

OTHER GOOD BOOKS

Mexico Health and Safety Travel Guide by Robert H. Page, M.D., and Curtis R. Page, M.D., (MedToGo LLC, P.O. Box 25847, Tempe, AZ 85258-5487; Phone: 866-MedToGo; www.medtogo.com). Authoritative, updated, and comprehensive guide to medical care while traveling or living in Mexico. Not only do they have practical safety and emergency medical care information but they discuss a variety of medical issues of concern to anyone going to Mexico. The bulk of the 465-page book is comprehensive, no-holds-barred reviews of Mexican hospitals and doctors in the towns and cities gringos will want to know about. I talked with the authors and was very impressed. They personally visited each and every hospital and clinic they reviewed and met the doctors they recommend. An absolute must! $19.95.

Traveler's Guide to Mexican Camping by Mike and Terri Church (Rolling Home Press, www.rollinghomes.com/default.htm). They also have a Baja RVing book, an Alaska RVing book, and a Europe RVing book. The bottom line is that if you are an RVer and are going to Mexico, you absolutely must have this. All of these have been in print for years and are updated about every year or so. Available in bookstores or online. $19.95.

Breaking Out of Beginner's Spanish by Joseph J. Keenan is the best Spanish-language book I have ever seen. It is not for rank beginners, but is dandy for those who have some grounding in the language. It will help you to avoid some of the common errors that brand you as a gringo who learned your language in school. Published by the University of Texas Press (P.O. Box 7819, Austin, TX 78713-7819). Available at bookstores. $14.95.

How to Buy Real Estate in Mexico by Dennis John Peyton is the definitive resource on buying property in Mexico. Dennis is a lawyer licensed to practice both in Mexico and in the United States. Consequently, the advice he gives is accurate, if somewhat lawyerly. If you really want to know what you are doing, get this book. Although there are some differences of opinion between *The Gringo's Investment Guide* and Peyton's book, you should read them both before signing on the dotted line. (Law-Mexico Publishing, 2220 Otay Lakes Rd., Ste. 502, East Lake, CA 91915; Phone: 800-LAW-MEXICO). $24.95.

The People's Guide to Mexico by Carl Franz and Lorena Havens. Now in its thirtieth year, this is a classic. No travel guide, it is a cultural guide. This is the one book that tells you what living in Mexico is like from the ground up. It is aimed at those who want to understand the culture of Mexico and the Mexican people. Although much of the information is geared to those on a tight budget or those who live a bohemian lifestyle, it contains invaluable information applicable to everyone. Published by Avalon Travel Publishing. Available at bookstores.

Travellers Guide to Mexico (published in Mexico) is the best source for tourist and business information about Mexico City and the country. It is chock-full of color photographs and interesting articles. You will find it in all the top-notch hotels and at bookstores. Buy a copy if you want to know more about the culture, doing business in Mexico, or if you intend to do any upscale traveling to the main tourist spots. Published by Prometur S.A. de C.V. (Gral. Juan Cano 68, San Miguel Chapultepec, 11850 Mexico, D.F.)

Guidebooks for Mexico I recommend are *Lonely Planet* and *Moon Handbook.*

BIBLIOGRAPHY

GENERAL COUNTRYWIDE WEB SITES

- www.mexicomike.com—The author's site with frequently updated information and more than 100 pages to help you understand Mexico. He also publishes an online newsletter.
- www.imagemarketingservice.com—Image Marketing Service develops travel and real estate guides for Mexico and California.
- www.mexperience.com—Excellent site devoted to general information about all of Mexico. Great newsletter.
- www.megared.net.mx—Lists cable Internet connections in selected cities.
- www.profeco.gob.mx—PROFECO, Procuraduría Federal del Consumidor, or the Mexican Consumer Protection Agency. This is where to complain about just about anything or get prices on food, medicines, or just about anything. It's in Spanish, so go to the left-side menu, click, *"Consumo imformato,"* then *"Quién is quién en ... "* Then click *"los precios"* (for prices) from the side menu, then *"Precios Mínimos y Máximos,"* then *"Seleccione Ciudad."* Then pick a city. You'll get a drop-down menu of major consumer items. If you want to make a complaint against a business, gas station, cop, government official etc., choose *"Presenta tus quejas o denuncias."*
- www.translate.google.com/translate?hl=en&sl=es&u=http://www.soler.com.ar/ general/inftec/2000/otros/fideic/fidei.htm&prev=/search%3Fq%3D fideicomiso%26hl%3Den%26lr%3D%26ie%3DUTF-8—A very complete explanation of what the bank trust *(fideicomiso)* is all about.

CANADIAN SPECIFIC

- www.canadiansresidentabroad.com—Online magazine directed to Canadians living abroad. 100 York Blvd., Suite 600, Richmond Hill, Ontario, L4B 1J8, Canada; Phone: 905-709-7911; Fax: 905-709-7022.
- www.escapeartist.com/Offshore_Finance_Canada/Moving_Abroad.html—

Good article on the tax ramifications of living abroad.

▪ www.cra-arc.gc.ca/menu-e.html—Canada Customs and Revenue Agency (CCRA, formerly Revenue Canada).

MEXICAN CONSULAR OFFICES IN THE UNITED STATES

▪ www.nafinsa.com/consulatedir.htm—Directory of all Mexican consulates and embassies in the United States.

MEXICAN CONSULAR OFFICES IN CANADA

▪ www.embamexcan.com/DIRECTORIES/DirectoriesSubMconsulates.shtml— Click on your city on the map to get address and phone numbers.

CITY- AND AREA-SPECIFIC SITES

▪ www.cozumelmycozumel.com—All about Cozumel, living and tourist stuff. Lively discussion board.

▪ www.realoaxaca.com—Interesting hard news and living tidbits about Oaxaca published by two expats, Stan Gotlieb and Diana Ricci. They publish an interesting online newsletter. Subscriptions are $30 a year.

▪ www.pacificcoasttravelinfo.com—Pacific Coast Travel Info. is your one-stop travel guide for Mexico and California.

▪ www.xalapa.net—Jalapa (Xalapa), Veracruz site.

AA MEETINGS

▪ www.aamexico.org/—Mexico City with links to other cities. English.

▪ www.zihua-ixtapa.com/zihua/aa.html—Ixtapa/Zihuatanejo. English.

▪ www.aa-cancun.com—Cancún. English.

▪ www.aa.org.mx—All Mexico. Spanish.

▪ www.oaxacatimes.com/html/classifieds.html—Oaxaca sometimes has a schedule in the classifieds. English.

GETTING RID OF STUFF SO YOU CAN MOVE

▪ www.clutterless.org—Clutterless Recovery Groups, Inc., a support program for clutterers.

RELOCATION SERVICES

There are many of these, but the only one I can recommend without hesitation is Cetra Relocations, based in Mexico City, but they can help you move anywhere in the Republic. I consider the general manager, Jesus Garcia, a friend and a straight shooter. He is extremely knowledgeable about all of Mexico, honest, friendly, and goes way beyond the call of duty to help make your move to Mexico a good experience (from outside Mexico Phone: 011-52-555-261-4390; Fax: 011-52-555-261-4310; www.cetra.com.mx; E-mail: jesus.garcia@cetra.com.mx).

REAL ESTATE

- www.translate.google.com/translate?hl=en&sl=es&u=http://www.soler.com. ar/general/inftec/2000/otros/fideic/fidei.htm&prev=/search%3Fq%3D fideicomiso%26hl%3Den%26lr%3D%26ie%3DUTF-8—Translated page of a complete explanation of what a *fideicomiso* entails.

Jalapa, Veracruz
E-mail Roy Dudley: mail.xal.megared.net.mx. Apartments for rent.

Cozumel, Quintana Roo

- www.spagetaway.com/yucatan/luz/luz_main.htm—For long-term stays at Luz de Yucatan, Mérida, and Yucatan. Also spas nationwide.
- www.cozumelmycozumel.com/Pages/CasaCascada.htm#—For long-term stays in Cozumel. Casa Cascada. E-mail Cary Anne Sutton: careycsutton@ hotmail.com.

DRIVING

- www.sct.gob.mx/—Toll road rates.
- www.mexicomike.com—Much of this site is devoted to driving and RVing.
- www.nelsontravelinsurance.com—Pretty neat section devoted to driving tips and tricks in the Club Viajero section (members only). Mileage distance and time calculator, itineraries for all major routes in Mexico.

BUSINESS RESOURCES

All Country

- www.investinmexico.com.mx/pied/cds/pied_bancomext/homepied— Investing in Mexico.
- www.economia.gob.mx—Official government economy site.
- www.dfait-maeci.gc.ca/mexico-city/menu-en.asp—Canadian embassy site.
- www.nafta-sec-alena.org/DefaultSite/index.html—NAFTA information.
- www.embamexcan.com—Mexican embassy in Canada.

Guadalajara

- U.S.: amcham.com.mx—American Chamber of Commerce. Av. Moctezuma 442, Col. Jardines del Sol, 45050 Zapopan, Jal.; Phone: 01-52-33-634-6606; Fax: 01-52-33-634-7374; E-mail: direccion_dgl@amcham.com.mex.
- Canadian: www.mexconnect.com/MEX/cancham/gdl.html—Canadian Chamber of Commerce. Circunvalación Agustín Yañez 2567 E, Guadalajara, Jal. 84150; Phone: 01-52-33-630-5005; Fax: 01-52-33-630-5055; E-mail: cancham@prodigy.net.mx.

Mexico City

- U.S.: amcham.com.mx—American Chamber of Commerce. Lucerna 78 Col. Juárez, 06600 Mexico, D.F.; Phone: 01-52-555-141-3800; Fax: 01-52-555-703-3908/2911; E-mail: membresia@amcham.com.mx.
- Canadian: www.cancham.com.mx/—Canadian Chamber of Commerce. Camara de Comerciao del Canada, Manuel Avila Camacho 1, Cpl. Polanco, Chapultepec, 11560, Cd. de Mexico, D.F.; Phone: 01-52-555-580-2873.
- Camara de Comerciao del Canada en Mexico, A Cantu 11 P-7, Col. Anzures,

11570, Cd. de Mexico, D.F.: Phone: 01-52-555-545-3997.

Monterrey

- Canadian: www.cancham.org.mx, info@cancham.org.mx. Canadian Chamber of Commerce. Zaragoza 1300 Sur, Edif. Kalos, Piso A2 Ofic. 201, 64000, Monterrey, N.L.; Phone: 01-52-818-343-1899; Phone/Fax: 01-52-818-343-1897.
- U.S.: amcham.com.mx—American Chamber of Commerce. Río Manzanares 434 Oriente Col. Del Valle 66220 Garza García, N.L.; Phone: 01-52-818-114-2000; Fax: 01-52-818-114-2100; E-mail: socios_mty@amcham.com.mx.

Working in Mexico

- www.teach-english-mexico.com—Teaching jobs. InterNetworks of Palm Springs, CA. Phone: 800-426-0161. Mark Farley, founder and owner, BBB member.
- www.mexicoconsulting.net—Mexico Consulting Group, John Schick. Phone: 415-788-4444. Advice on starting or buying a business anywhere in Mexico. Generally works with multimillion-dollar projects, but will work with smaller, serious investors. Clients range from Fortune 500 companies to individuals buying or starting small businesses.
- www.mexicomike.com—Click "Working" for info. "Mexico" Mike is also available for consultations on setting up a business. Phone: 888-234-3452; E-mail: mexicomikenelson23@mexicomike.com.
- www.mexicomikeconsulting.com – This site is specifically for those wishing to work in Mexico.

MEDICAL INSURANCE

- www.medtogo.com/preparation/pg-health_care_system.asp—For detailed information about the National Hospital Insurance System, IMSS, health care system.
- www.medtogo.com/preparation/pg-health_insurance.asp—For a variety of insurers that offer travel or expatriate medical insurance policies.
- www.internationalpro.com—Medical insurance coverage for Americans and Canadians.
- www.medipac.com—Medical insurance coverage specifically for Canadians.

MEDICAL ISSUES

- www.profeco.gob.mx/html/precios/queretaro/medics.htm—This happens to be for the city of Querétaro, but it's a pretty good source.
- www.istm.com—For physicians specializing in tropical medicine.
- www.cdc.gov—For potential epidemics abroad.

LANGUAGE SCHOOLS

- www.goethe-verlag.com/tests/ZMEXICO.HTM—For a listing of several throughout Mexico.
- www.spanishamigos.com/mexicoguanajuato.html—Another listing of several schools throughout Mexico.

Guanajuato
- www.ugto.mx/english/index.htm—University of Guanajuato.
- www.spanish-immersion.com—Instituto Miguel de Cervantes.
- www.academiafalcon.com—Academia Falcon.

San Miguel de Allende
- www.instituto-allende.edu.mx—Instituto Allende.
- www.warrenhardy.com—Warren Hardy School.
- www.mexicospanish.com—Habla Hispana.
- www.geocities.com/centrobilingue—Centro Bilinqüe.

ENGLISH-LANGUAGE SCHOOLS FOR KIDS
Mexico City
- The American School, Bondojito No. 215 Colonia Las Americas Mexico, D.F. 01120; Phone: 01-52-555-227-4900; Fax: 01-52-555-273-4357; www.asf.edu.mx/enghtm/sections/mission/index.html.
- The Westhill Institute, Domingo Garcia Ramos 56, Prados de la Montana I, Santa Fe Cuajimalpa, Mexico City, D.F., 05610; Phone: 01-52-555-292-4222; Fax: 01-52-555-292-4223; westhill.edu.mx.
- Greengates (British), Av. Circunvalación Poiente 102, Balcones de San Mateo, Edo. de Mexico 53200; Phone: 01-52-555-373-0088; Fax: 01-52-555-373-0765; E-mail: sarav@greengates.edu.mx; www.greengates.edu.mx.

Monterrey
- The American School Foundation of Monterrey, Rio Missouri 555 Ote., Colonia del Valle, Garza Garcia, N.L., 66220. Mailing Address: APDO 1762, 64000, Monterrey, N.L.; Phone: 01-52-818-153-4400; Fax: 01-52-818-378-2535; www.asfm.edu.mx.
- Pan American School, Monterrey Campus, Hidalgo 656 Pte., Monterrey, N.L., 66400. Mailing Address: APDO 474, 64000, Monterrey, N.L.; Phone: 01-52-818-342-0778; Fax: 01-52-818-340-2749.

Puerto Vallarta
- American School of Puerto Vallarta, Albatros 129, Marina Vallarta. Puerto Vallarta, Jal., 48354. Mailing Address: APDO 2-280, Marina Vallarta, 48354 Puerto Vallarta, Jal.; Phone: 01-52-322-221-1525; Fax: 01-52-322-221-2373; www.aspv.edu.mx.

Guadalajara
- The American School Foundation of Guadalajara, Colomos, APDO 6-280, Col. Providencia, CP 44640 Guadalajara, Jal.; Phone: 01-52-33-648-0299; Fax: 01-52-33-817-3356; E-mail: asfg@asfg.mx; www.asfg.mx.

Tampico
- The American School of Tampico, Calle Hidalgo s/n, Colonia Tancol, Tampico, Tamp. 89320. Mailing Address: APDO 407, 89000 Tampico, Tamp.; E-mail: ast2000@prodigy.net.mx; www.ats.edu.mx.

NEWCOMER'S CLUBS

- Mexico City—Hours: Mon., Wed., Fri. 9 A.M.–12:30 P.M.; Phone/Fax: 01-52-555-520-6912; E-mail: Newcomers@newcomers.org.mx; www.newcomers.org.mx.
- Cuernavaca—www.clickoncuernavaca.com/newcomers/Newcomers.htm. Admon de Correos, APDO 376-3, Cuernavaca, Mor. 62250; Phone: 01-52-777-315-2272; E-mail: Justandiemx@aol.com.
- Monterrey—www.newcomersofmty.8m.com. E-mail: newcomersgroup@ yahoo.com. Monthly meetings (subject to change): Applebee's, Ave. Vasconcelos #158 Ote. L-1 Col. Jardines del Campestre. Second Tuesday of the month, 9:30 A.M. (unless it is on or near a holiday).

TRAVEL

- www.spagetaway.com—Travel wholesaler representing spas in Mexico and Belize. Phone: 800-321-4622.

MAPS

- www.gonetomorrow.com—Treaty Oaks Maps, Guia Roji.

ENGLISH-LANGUAGE NEWSPAPERS

- www.guadalajarareporter.com—*The Guadalajara Reporter.*
- www.gringogazette.com/—*The Gringo Gazette*, Cabo San Lucas, Baja California Sur.
- chiapas.mediosindependientes.org—Independent Media Center, Chiapas. Bilingual newspaper covering Chiapas and Oaxaca.
- www.oaxacatimes.com—*Oaxaca Times.*
- www.rptimes.com—*Rocky Point Times*, Puerto Penñasco, Sonora.
- www.pacificpearl.com—*Pacific Pearl*, Mazatlán.
- www.thenewsmexico.com/ — *The News*—Mexico City–based national paper.

TELEPHONES

- www.cft.gob.mx/campana/regiones.html#—Updated area codes for all Mexico.
- www.seccionamarilla.com.mx—Yellow pages for all of Mexico.

CELL PHONES

- www.cellularabroad.com/mexicocellService.html—For phone rentals and temporary traveling phones.
- www.gorillamobile.com—For calling Mexico from your U.S. cell phone.
- www.iusacell.com.mx—Iusacell.
- www.telcel.com—Telcel.
- www.pegasopcs.com.mx—Telefonica Moviles.
- www.unefon.com.mx—Unefon.
- www.cellular-news.com/coverage/mexico.shtml—For a complete listing of cell phone providers and links to their pages.